Blogging
FOR
DUMMIES®

by Brad Hill

WILEY

Wiley Publishing, Inc.

Blogging For Dummies®

Published by
Wiley Publishing, Inc.
111 River Street
Hoboken, NJ 07030-5774

www.wiley.com

Copyright © 2006 by Wiley Publishing, Inc., Indianapolis, Indiana

Published by Wiley Publishing, Inc., Indianapolis, Indiana

Published simultaneously in Canada

For general information on our other products and services, please contact our Customer Care Department within the U.S. at 800-762-2974, outside the U.S. at 317-572-3993, or fax 317-572-4002.

For technical support, please visit www.wiley.com/techsupport.

Wiley also publishes its books in a variety of electronic formats. Some content that appears in print may not be available in electronic books.

Library of Congress Control Number: 2005936646

ISBN-13: 978-0-471-77084-8

ISBN-10: 0-471-77084-1

Manufactured in the United States of America

10 9 8 7 6 5 4 3 2 1

1B/RT/QR/QW/IN

WILEY

About the Author

Brad Hill has worked in the online field since 1992 and has written twenty books. As a best-selling author, columnist, and blogger, Hill reaches a global audience of consumers who rely on his writings to help determine their online service choices.

Brad's books include a *Publishers Weekly* bestseller and a Book-of-the-Month catalog selection. Brad's titles in the *Dummies* series include *Google For Dummies* and *Building Your Business with Google For Dummies.* He is a lead blogger for Weblogs Inc., where he covers Google, Yahoo!, digital music, and RSS. Brad operates independent blogs about dogs (www.fourfooted.com), classical music (www.undeadmusic.com), and his own bad self. He and his wife maintain a photoblog about their adventures at home and on the road. Brad's main site, from which you can connect with all his blog projects, is www.bradhill.com.

Brad is often consulted in the media's coverage of the Internet. He appears frequently on television, radio, and Webcasts, and has been quoted in *Business Week,* the *New York Times,* and innumerable other publications. Brad has not won the Nobel Prize, and probably never will. He is not bitter about being slighted.

Author's Acknowledgments

Every book is a partnership of author and editor. Susan Pink is the editor of this book and a collaborator in others projects as well. She had to read every page of this thing, and deserves commiseration. I depend on her careful reading, incisive comments, and dog stories. Susan has an uncanny gift for remaining calm during the most intense deadline crises. I have tried to break her unearthly serenity, to no result.

Colin Banfield had an unusually difficult job as technical editor of this book, with its coverage of many blog services and programs. His insights were invaluable.

Many thanks to Melody Layne at Wiley Publishing for launching this project and to Steve Hayes for cultivating its first seeds.

Continued thanks to Mary Corder.

Many thanks to all the copy editors and production experts who pored over every page of the manuscript — except for page 239, which somehow got printed in the original Portuguese.

Publisher's Acknowledgments

We're proud of this book; please send us your comments through our online registration form located at www.dummies.com/register/.

Some of the people who helped bring this book to market include the following:

Acquisitions, Editorial, and Media Development

Project Editor: Susan Pink

Acquisitions Editor: Melody Layne

Technical Editor: Colin Banfield

Editorial Manager: Jodi Jensen

Media Development Manager: Laura VanWinkle

Editorial Assistant: Amanda Foxworth

Cartoons: Rich Tennant (www.the5thwave.com)

Composition Services

Project Coordinator: Jennifer Theriot

Layout and Graphics: Carl Byers, Andrea Dahl, Lauren Goddard, Denny Hager, Stephanie D. Jumper, Barbara Moore, Heather Ryan

Proofreaders: Laura Albert, Leeann Harney, Jessica Kramer, TECHBOOKS Production Services

Indexer: TECHBOOKS Production Services

Publishing and Editorial for Technology Dummies

Richard Swadley, Vice President and Executive Group Publisher

Andy Cummings, Vice President and Publisher

Mary Bednarek, Executive Acquisitions Director

Mary C. Corder, Editorial Director

Publishing for Consumer Dummies

Diane Graves Steele, Vice President and Publisher

Joyce Pepple, Acquisitions Director

Composition Services

Gerry Fahey, Vice President of Production Services

Debbie Stailey, Director of Composition Services

Contents at a Glance

Table of Contents

Introduction

● ●

*T*hink back to the Internet circa 1994. (Or just watch while I trip down Memory Lane.) In those heady days, Web pages consisted mostly of personal collections of favorite links. Not many people recognized it, but the Web was a revolutionary force of self-expression and global connection. Yahoo! emerged to catalog all those personal pages and was itself pretty revolutionary. More upheavals followed: e-commerce, instant messaging, MP3, Google. And now, blogging.

Blogging is throwing the Internet forward and backward at the same time. Forward into a new era of consumer empowerment, and backward to the grass-roots spirit of the early Web. The popularity and influence of Weblogs have stolen the spotlight from established media powerhouses. Blogging has taken back the Web.

One of the most influential online research organizations estimated in mid-2005 that a new blog was created every 5.8 seconds. Fortunately, there's no such thing as missing the boat (or the rocket), so if you haven't yet created your first blog, now is the perfect time. Blogging is the perfect antidote to highly commercialized, blandly consolidated Web sites. You can have a great site, be part of an amazingly dynamic global community, and, if you play your cards right, attract a devoted audience.

About This Book

My intent in these pages is to reveal the total world of blogging. That total world includes the following:

- ✔ Understanding exactly what a blog is
- ✔ Knowing how to get a blog
- ✔ Being aware of the potential pitfalls
- ✔ Finding an effective blogging style
- ✔ Smoothly joining the blogging community
- ✔ Searching for blog content and tracking topics
- ✔ Detailing specific blog programs and services
- ✔ Trying fancy blogging techniques such as moblogging and podcasting
- ✔ Using RSS to be a master blog reader
- ✔ Possibly making a few dollars with a blog

Many people, even those who think they know all about blogging, are astonished to learn what a wide-ranging subject it is, laden with possibilities.

New bloggers have innumerable choices. No single book can illuminate all the blogging programs, Weblog services, and feed aggregators, as well as the wide assortment of related technologies. In narrowing the choices offered in this book, my criteria were quality and popularity, with an emphasis (perhaps surprisingly) on the latter. Most new bloggers get their feet wet in one of the popular social networks or one of the big-name hosting services. People follow the advice of friends and acquaintances, so to some extent I follow along those paths. Naturally, the popular services are usually popular for good reasons. Regretfully, I could not find space to describe some great resources, programs, and services that have not yet gained widespread usage. I left out one blog program that I use and love, because I concluded that its features would not serve readers enough to justify many pages of description. But you will find an introduction to blogging at any level, from the most simple to the brain-teasingly complex, in these chapters.

Conventions Used in This Book

I wanted to include the Basel Convention on hazardous waste minimization in this book, but my inability to find Basel on a map brought that idea to a dead end. So, instead, I have settled for the following simple conventions that you find in these pages:

- ✔ When I use an important term for the first time, I *italicize* it. Of course, slanty letters aren't really very helpful, which is why there's a glossary at the back of the book.
- ✔ Web addresses, also called URLs, look like this: www.typepad.com.
- ✔ A few chapters discuss code (HTML, CSS, and PHP) that underlies Web pages. When I must cite an example of such code, it looks like this:

```
# ObjectDriver DBI::postgres
# Database <database-name>
# DBUser <database-username>
# DBPassword <database-password>
# DBHost localhost
```

How to Use This Book

Literacy is required, plus the ability to turn pages.

What You're Not to Read

I forbid you to read trashy novels from the supermarket. And although I'm less adamant about this, I prefer you stay away from Portuguese limericks. I'm just trying to protect you.

Nothing in this book will cause you harm (except for the carpet nails attached to page 129 — good luck with them), but some sections might not scratch your itch. This isn't one of those books where, if you skip something, you'll never understand the subject. Although there *is* a very important paragraph somewhere in the middle of the book . . . I don't remember which one, unfortunately. Good luck with that, too.

Read contents; the chapter titles map out the subject matter of this book. Stick to the subjects you need. Parts I, II, and III are progressively more challenging. Part IV is interesting, with Chapter 13 being the one I would *least* advise you to skip. Part V is useful for everyone, but is definitely optional. If you intend to read Part VI, I feel so sorry for you. Really; get help.

Foolish Assumptions

First, I assume you appreciate self-indulgent banter and silly asides. Attempted witticisms do nothing but distract you from the useful stuff in this book, and I assume you're okay with that. If you're not, talk to my editor. She probably doesn't rein me in enough.

Beyond assuming your tolerance of the occasional funny, I do assume a basic facility with computers, Web browsers, and the Internet. Being a creative act, blogging requires a lot of clicking and typing. You should be familiar with Web forms and their inevitable check boxes and radio buttons. You must know how to position the mouse cursor in a Web form before typing in it. Familiarity with e-mail should put you at the right level. If you are shy about operating a browser or viewing Web pages, you might want to get a beginner's Internet book under your belt or take some quick tutoring from a friend before launching into blogging.

That warning delivered, let me say that my mother, with basic Internet experience and no e-mail, got up and blogging in less than a day and loves it.

How This Book Is Organized

Words. Sentences. Paragraphs. Pages. Chapters. Parts. It's a thing of beauty.

Part I: The What, Where, Why, and How of Weblogs

The three chapters in Part I present a bird's-eye view of the entire blogging landscape. Here you glean not only what a blog is (it's amazing how many people don't really know, even if they read blogs) but also what elements typically go into a blog, from entries to archives, from comments to RSS feeds. The information in this part summarizes, illuminates, and points you to later chapters that explain more completely how it all works.

Also in this part (Chapter 2, specifically), I identify the four types of blog services covered in this book and begin to compare them in a way that helps you decide which level contains your comfort zone.

It might seem presumptuous to consider blogging a lifestyle, but this part gladly presumes just that, and outlines the perks and pitfalls of that lifestyle. You don't have to be a full-time blogger to gain insight into the blogging mindset from Chapter 3.

Part II: Starting a Blog Today

Part II gets right to it, helping the eager first-time blogger find the quickest path to publishing a blog. Chapter 4 explores MSN Spaces, a social network that includes an attractive blogging platform. Chapter 5 focuses on another social network — Yahoo! 360, which provides one of the simplest starting points for the beginning blogger. Blogger.com, the subject of Chapter 6, is by some measurements the world's most popular blogging service and is populated by many newcomers trying out their first blogs. Chapter 7 details TypePad, a full-featured blog service subscribed to by many serious bloggers.

Part III: Installing Your Own Blog Program

The chapters in Part III are the most challenging of the book, but I don't assume any special knowledge. Any ambitious reader can reach an advanced power-blogging state by taking these chapters one step at a time.

Of the five chapters in this part, Chapter 8 is the most important for any reader curious about using a self-installed blogging program. The self-installed programs, which get installed on a server (not on your PC), offer unmatched power and features, along with a steeper learning curve than the hosted blog services. Installation is the hardest part, and Chapter 8 covers the principles encountered when installing any of the big blog programs.

Movable Type and WordPress are the two server-installed programs covered in this book, and each gets a chapter that clarifies how they work after installation. Then I move on to Radio UserLand, a blog program and service that is installed on your PC and connects to a server where your blog actually lives. That setup is unique, and Chapter 11 explains it completely.

Finally, Chapter 12 covers the best of both worlds: power-blogging software that somebody else installs for you, in specialized Web hosts whose accounts come equipped with Movable Type or WordPress ready to go.

Part IV: Total Blog Immersion

My hope is that you become profoundly hooked on blogging in Parts I, II, and III, and then thirst for more information and cooler things to do with your blog. Part IV explores blog culture, blog revenue, podcasting, photos, video, music, and — most importantly — syndicated feeds. Ah, the feeds. Please don't neglect Chapter 13, the first chapter of this part. Feeds are important not only because they make it easy for a global audience to read your blog, but also because fluency with feeds makes it possible for you to follow a global network of blogs and other news sites. Feeds tie together the two sides of blogging: creating blogs and consuming blogs.

Podcasting is a hot topic as I prepare this manuscript, and it will no doubt be hotter as you read it. Thousands of podcasts exist, but millions of people don't know how to get started. Chapter 16 advises you on a handful of services that can get you started.

Part V: The Part of Tens

This part carries on the *For Dummies* tradition by providing selections of blog search engines and directories as well as blogging resources for your browsing pleasure. The Part of Tens is always a fun portion of the book to write and, I hope, fun to read.

Icons Used in This Book

Britney Spears is my icon. I would do anything to see her, meet her, touch her . . . I'm sorry, I slipped into a bizarre alternate reality in which I was a 15-year-old girl with eyeliner. I hope to revisit that reality some day. In the meantime, let's discuss more meaningful cultural artifacts, such as the little pictures in the margins of this book.

Tips are particularly useful nuggets of information.

This icon represents paragraphs that embody a fear of being forgotten. They seem to be crying "Remember me! Remember me!" It's pathetic.

I don't use this icon much because, honestly, I don't know much technical stuff. When I do think of something technical, I'm hideously proud of myself and rattle off gibberish tediously. Don't indulge me when I get like that. These paragraphs can safely and beneficially be skipped.

This icon pops up when your computer is about to explode. It doesn't happen often — every few chapters, maybe. To prevent computer shards flying about the room, read the marked paragraph slowly and carefully, and then drink a cup of prune juice. The efficacy of prune juice in settling down an explosive computer is unproven, but I'm a great believer in the calming effects of squished fruit.

Where to Go from Here

Only one in a hundred readers will read this book straight through, cover to cover. Oddly, that is the exact percentage of the book-buying public that spontaneously bursts into flames. Coincidence? If self-immolation isn't on your agenda for the next week, take the safe route and skip a chapter here and there. Your selection of content in these pages will be determined by your blogging experience level, your ambition, and your curiosity. Beginners probably should read the first three chapters. Then, to get blogging quickly, focus on Chapters 4–7. Chapters 8–12 are for aspiring power bloggers with a hunger for the big, Humvee-type programs. Those chapters could be starting points for readers with the most experience.

A more theoretical reading plan starts with Chapters 1–3, and then skips to Chapters 13–17; that body of material packs a lot of understanding without diving much into the plain mechanics of blogging. And "The Part of Tens," is excellent reading while on the phone with an in-law, in the bathroom, or when sitting in a plane avoiding conversation with your seatmate.

Part I

The What, Where, Why, and How of Weblogs

The 5th Wave   By Rich Tennant

"I'm sorry. I'm answering email right now.
And since when does the Taco Bell
Chihuahua have a blog anyway?"

In this part . . .

Many people have heard of Weblogs (blogs), but not many people can say what they are. The three chapters in this part define blogs at length and with crystal-clear illumination. Peruse these chapters, and you'll know more than most teenagers — and that's really saying something. Chapter 1 describes exactly what a blog is and isn't, and familiarizes you with essential blogging terms and concepts. Chapter 2 sketches the options available to you as a future blogger looking for a first home. The understanding gained from this chapter will serve you well throughout the book. Chapter 3 is about the blogging lifestyle. Perhaps you didn't know there was a blogging lifestyle. Wait until you start blogging. Specifically, this chapter deals with the daily rhythms of writing a blog, self-promotion, and maintaining a tidy blog.

By the end of Part I you will be primed to choose a blogging platform or service and to immerse yourself in the encompassing pleasure of daily blogging.

Chapter 1

Understanding Blogging at Last

Consider some amazing measurements. (I'm talking about measurements of blogging, not the size of Donald Trump's hair.) According to some sources, about 70 million Weblogs existed in mid-2005. One respected research company reported that 6 percent of the U.S. population had created a Weblog and that 16 percent of the population read blogs. Another study in the summer of 2005 put the number of blog readers somewhat lower, but discovered something amazing about those people who did read blogs: about two-thirds of them didn't know what a blog was.

Ever since the lead-up to the 2004 U.S. presidential election, Weblogs have been in the news. Many articles reporting on the blog phenomenon take a stab at defining them, but these halfhearted attempts don't go far in educating the masses of people who are a bit puzzled by the whole "blog thing." Are blogs 21st-century news outlets? Fund-raising gimmicks? Online diaries? Self-expression for teenagers? Are they Web sites or something different? Are bloggers journalists, columnists, or celebrities, or can anyone be a blogger? Is there money in it? Many people have heard of blogs and even read them but don't really know what they are.

As for creating a blog, despite the millions who have already started one, millions more don't know where to begin. They hear that it's easy, but nothing is easy without a nudge in the right direction. This book provides that productive push toward the easy answers and also explains more challenging solutions for ambitious readers who want greater control over how their blogs look and operate. This chapter sets the stage by defining Weblogs and blogging from every angle, and then touching down on all aspects of the *blogosphere,* from new ways to read other people's blogs to terms you should know (such as *blogosphere,* which simply means the universe of blogs and bloggers).

There's a refreshing piece of news in all this: Kids don't necessarily know more than you do about blogs and blogging. The subject is fairly new, even to them. Many kids do blog, but starting a blog in one of the easy services doesn't, by itself, give anyone an overview of the whole scene. So this book — and even this chapter — might give you enough knowledge to teach the nearest teenager a thing or two about the Internet.

Let's get to it.

The Truth about Blogs

With a provocative headline like that, you might expect a scandalous revelation, such as, "Weblogs Slept with American Idol Contestant." But no, this section just answers the question: "What the heck is a blog, anyway?"

First and foremost, don't be confused by my interchangeable use of Weblog and blog. *Blog* is simply a contraction of *Weblog*. However, people who write blogs are called *bloggers* — never Webloggers. Blogging is a verb; Weblogging is the utterance of an ill-informed person. (Also, don't buy into the clueless two-word extraction *Web log*.)

Glad we straightened out those basic terms. Moving on to understanding what a blog is, the answer is best divided into a technical part (don't worry, it's easy to grasp) and a practical answer. The first illuminates some nuts-and-bolts facts about blogs; the second reveals how you can use that information.

The technical answer

First of all, a blog is a Web site. Don't let anybody tell you that Web sites and Weblogs are different creatures. To be clear, though, a Weblog is a *type* of Web site. It follows, then, that all Weblogs are Web sites, but not all Web sites are Weblogs.

Note that a blog is a Web site, not an entry on that Web site. Some new bloggers say, "I wrote five blogs today." Actually they wrote five entries in their blog.

So, what distinguishes a Weblog from other sites?

Weblogs have a certain type of software running in the background. This answer might seem obscure, but that software is the hidden key to blogs. In fact, blog software is *so* useful that it has spawned the blogging revolution with its millions of new sites. So what is this powerhouse that lies behind blogs, and how does it make blogs different from other sites?

Here is the crucial power of blogs: They make it easy to frequently add content to a Web site. Blog programs and ready-to-use blogging services cut out the laborious and technical traditional process of building a Web site and adding pages to it. Consider what a site owner needed to do before blogs were available:

1. To create a single Web page, a site owner had to gain some familiarity with HTML (hypertext markup language, the underlying code of all Web sites). The choice was to write out the code by hand (fairly difficult) or use software that made page-creation a little more intuitive. Design skills were needed and the software could be expensive. Ready-made templates eased the pain somewhat, but building a single page the old way was never as easy as blogging.

2. After creating a single-page, old-style site, the owner had to get it up on the Web. Usually, this meant using an internet system called FTP (file transfer protocol), which is somewhat like the My Computer program in Windows but operates across the space between two computers. (See Figure 1-1.) Using FTP, the owner could upload newly created or altered pages to his or her site, which resided on an Internet computer. After the transfer, the new page became "live" and could be viewed by visitors to the site.

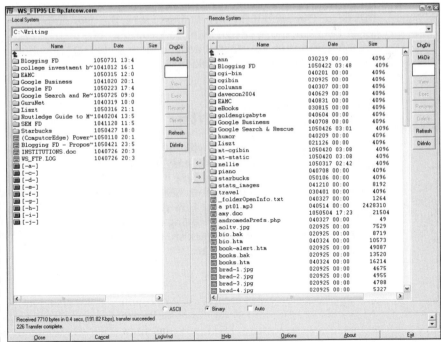

Figure 1-1: FTP programs enable uploads of new pages from a home computer to a Web site.

Note: I use the past tense in the preceding steps, but the fact remains that most sites today are not blogs, and their owners still go through the old page-creation and FTP processes to update them. I don't want to imply that those methods are obsolete. But I do want to emphasize that the HTML and FTP system is like lifting weights compared to the ease of blogging, which can be likened to lying in a hammock. Escaping the arduous manual update system is one major reason blogging has taken off.

To summarize: Creating a nonblog Web site is hard, and the difficulties discourage frequent updates. Blogging is easy, and blogging software encourages frequent site updates. Creating a blog page doesn't need to be any harder than writing and sending an e-mail or posting a message to an online discussion forum. In fact, these three tasks — blogging, e-mailing, and posting a message — follow the same basic three steps:

1. **Go to a Compose screen.**

2. **Type something brilliant (or not).**

3. **Click a Send (or Post) button.**

Figure 1-2 illustrates the My Blog Compose Entry screen in Yahoo! 360, one of the simplest blog services. As easily as sending an e-mail, bloggers add content to their sites. More than that, the new content is neatly organized within the Web site, and it contains all the design elements and navigational features that occur throughout the site. In most cases, the user didn't have to lift a finger to create those design features. Beautiful, informative, fun, up-to-date, personal Web sites are created with no more technical know-how than is required to chat with the grandkids in e-mail.

The practical answer

The preceding section reveals what blogs are technically: Web sites powered by certain software that makes it easy to add stuff to the site. A more specific understanding of that software (how it works and what forms it takes) awaits in the next section of this chapter. Here in this section, I want to discuss the practical definition of a Weblog. How do people use a blog? This is where you find a definition of blogs and blogging that you can talk about with friends or at a party, without appearing geekish. Of course, if you *are* a geek, there's nothing wrong with appearing so.

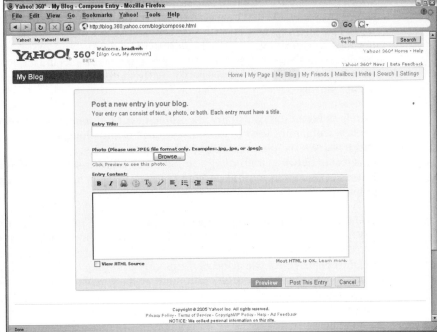

Figure 1-2:
Composing
a blog entry
is no more
difficult than
writing an
e-mail. This
is Yahoo!
360, an easy
blog
service.

Blogging software encourages frequent updating of the Web site. And frequent, easy updates result in the following typical blog characteristics:

✔ **Fresh content on the site:** Many bloggers update their content every day or several times during the day. Even weekly updates result in a fresher Web site than most nonblog personal sites.

✔ **Personal content:** When given the opportunity to self-publish on a daily basis, most people reach into their own lives for content. Many blogs are like personal, public diaries.

✔ **Newsy content:** Other bloggers take a less personal approach, keying their updated content to news items or pages on other sites. These blogs can still have a personal slant, especially if the blogger offers comments on the news or outside pages. These commentary blogs typically use lots of links to those other pages so visitors can see the source material as well as the commentary.

One aspect of blog software that influences the practical definition of blogs is that new content is usually dated. (See Figure 1-3.) Every new page created by the blogger is stamped with the date and time that it's added, supporting the idea that Weblogs are online diaries. (The dating feature can be disabled or altered in some cases, but most people don't bother.) In fact, many news stories about Weblogs define them exactly that way, as online diaries or online journals.

Purely personal blogs usually *are* online diaries, intended to be read by a few friends and family. Less personal examples of the blogging genre, such as those written by journalists, might be called professional diaries. A connection exists between *journaling* and *journalism.* Professional blog journalism has a personal quality, and personal blog journaling sometimes has a professional quality.

You might think that blogs are always solo efforts. They usually are, but there are notable group blogs, such as the famous BoingBoing (`www.boing boing.net`) and The Huffington Post (`www.huffingtonpost.com`). Teamwork can ease the grind of frequently updating the blog. But blogging lends itself to individual publication and self-expression. Most blogs are run by individuals and, to some extent, are about their owners.

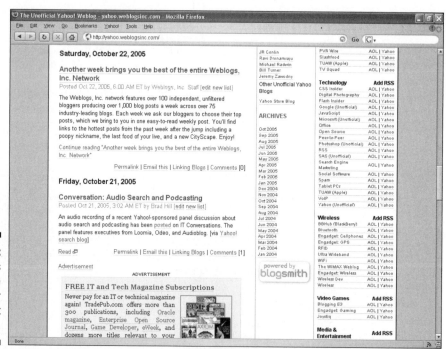

Figure 1-3: Most blogs organize their content by date.

Many types of blogs have been created, with many unimagined types to come. Following is a list of blog types an active reader can easily find. Weblogs have no official categories or designations, so I use the following names descriptively:

✔ **Personal diaries:** This is probably the most common blog type. Many individuals start blogs without knowing exactly what they'll do with them; the pleasure of self-publishing is enough by itself. Visitors to these blogs are often greeted with content along the lines of "Here's what I did today." (See Figure 1-4.) Some celebrities reveal themselves in personal blogs; Rosie O'Donnell has achieved post-TV fame with her idiosyncratic stream-of-consciousness blog entries (www.rosie.com).

✔ **Professional diaries:** These sites are better known than personal diaries, but scarcer. More and more professionals are choosing to maintain blogs alongside their actual jobs. These include journalists, who get lots of publicity for softening their objectivity in the more opinionated blog space — when their publishers allow them to do so. Blogging can turn a journalist into a columnist, and some newspapers and magazines forbid their writers doing so. Professionals in other fields blog to the great edification of wide readerships. John Battelle, a technology expert who helped start *Wired* magazine, has a blog at www.battellemedia.com. Alex Ross, the classical music critic of *The New Yorker,* keeps a blog called The Rest Is Noise (www.therestisnoise.com) in which he writes informally about his concert adventures. Movie producer Peter Jackson kept a detailed blog diary with film clips during his making of *King Kong* (www.kongis king.net). In these and many other cases, the blogs humanize their writers and offer a glimpse into their professional lives.

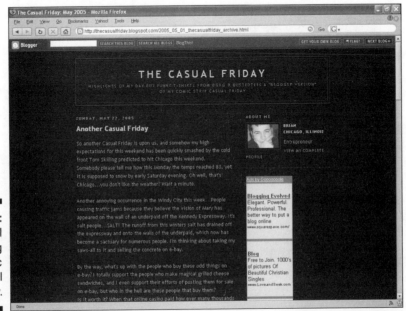

Figure 1-4: The Casual Friday blog is a public personal diary.

✓ **Institutional blogs:** Companies are jumping on the bandwagon with mixed results. Blogging, though versatile, is a fragile genre of online publication. Inauthentic voices, or any bogus attempt to be cool, reveal themselves immediately in the blog format. But many examples are invaluable; one corporate blog I check all the time is the Yahoo! Search blog (www. ysearchblog.com), written by the engineers who create the Yahoo! search engines. Yogurt maker Stonyfield Farm tentatively started with one corporate blog and now operates four of them (www.stonyfield. com/weblog), making the corporate site a destination for parents, women, and kids. Corporate blogs are written sometimes by company executives (one of the Stonyfield blogs is written by the owner) and sometimes by employees hired as bloggers.

✓ **Topical blogs:** Blogs exist on nearly every subject under the sun, including politics, technology, Starbucks (see Figure 1-5), sports teams, music, cars, and all manner of current events. Topical blogs range from hobby sites to full-fledged professional ventures supported by advertising. Political blogs hit the mainstream in 2004, leading up to the American presidential election. Some of those bloggers, such as Markos Moulitsas of The Daily Kos (www.dailykos.com), became media stars. Celebrity has descended also on a few gossip bloggers, notably Ana Marie Cox of Wonkette (www.wonkette.com). Many topical blogs deal with the day's news in a general way, linking to Web articles and commenting on them. The best and most active of these publications have become alternate news sources.

Figure 1-5:
Topical blogs cover every possible subject under the sun. This one is all about Starbucks.

✔ **MP3 blogs:** These musical journals include actual music in the form of downloadable MP3 songs. In many cases, the recordings are sent to the blogs by independent musicians hungry for exposure.

✔ **Fiction blogs:** Not many blogs are complete fabrications, but I've run across some entertaining examples. One beauty was the fictional blog of Darth Vader (`darthside.blogspot.com`), which revealed a previously unimagined sensitive side of the great dark lord. That blog was discontinued, leaving many mourning readers in its wake, and the author started a serialized blognovel called *Simon of Space* (`simonofspace.blogspot.com`). Another ongoing literary blog, not exactly fictional but reading like a novel in daily installments, is the diary of Samuel Pepys. The actual diary was written and published in the 1600s and is faithfully reproduced as if Pepys was blogging it now (`www.pepysdiary.com`). Toymaker Mattel has durable doll Barbie writing her own blog (see Figure 1-6). Caesar started a blog (`www.sankey.ca/caesar/index.html`), but the great Governor of Gaul let it peter out.

This list doesn't consider multimedia blog efforts such as *podcasts* (see Chapter 16), *vlogs* (video blogs), audioblogging (see Chapter 17), and blogs devoted mostly to photos. Written blogs can be anything from sparse *link blogs* (many links to outside sources, little commentary) to provocative *think blogs* (fewer links, tons of opinion), from occasional hobbies to obsessive avocations. If you have something original to say, blogging can possibly be your rare ticket to fame. For most people, it's a ticket to fun and the satisfaction of self-expression.

Figure 1-6: Barbie has her own fictional blog.

Understanding Blog Mechanics

Now you know that a Weblog is different from other Web sites because of specialized software running in the background. You know many of the uses of blogs, from online diaries to amateur news sites, from professional diaries to fiction. In this section, I talk about how the software works in the background, and the tools it puts on your screen. I won't get too technical; the purpose of this section is to describe the mechanics and terminology of basic blogging so every reader understands the layout of a typical blog.

The many blog programs and services (see Chapter 2) sport similar features. At the heart of all blogging, from the ready-to-go platforms requiring no work on your part to the self-installed monsters described in Part III, is *content management*. The phrase sounds corporate and boring and daunting, but it's just a concise way of describing how blogging makes updating your site easy. Content management is the heavy lifting performed by blog software. You write something; the software puts it on the site in the correct place.

Entries, posts, indexes, and archives

In the context of blogging, content management almost always means organizing the site by backwards chronology. In this way, your most recent writing appears first. As visitors continue reading your updates, they work backwards in time. Each piece of content is called an *entry*. When you write a blog, you *post* entries, and those posted entries are sometimes called *posts*. (The word *post* derives from Internet message boards, where online communities chat by means of publicly posted messages.) Each posted entry is stamped with a date and (usually) time. The front page of the blog contains recent entries, with the most recent at the top. Many blogs are organized with big daily headers that group each day's posts.

Blog software makes easy business of posting entries. The interface is usually similar to the Compose screen you use for e-mail. You write in that screen, and then click a button marked Post or Post Entry. The software uploads the entry to the blog, putting it above previous entries on the home page, and assigning it a date and time stamp. The software also assigns the entry its own page, so that each entry has a dedicated URL (Web address).

In some instances, bloggers make the software put short entry excerpts on the home page (called the *index page*), saving the entire entry for the dedicated page. With that arrangement, readers can skim short bits of many entries on the index page, clicking through to a dedicated entry page when they want to read an entire post.

Even in blogs where the entire entry is published on the index page, a dedicated page is created — that unique URL enables bloggers to promote individual entries by sharing links to those entries. Creating a series of dedicated pages is how the blog software maintains an *archive* of everything written.

Whew. This little section packs a lot of information, and all of it is important. Here is a summary of the general process of blogging:

1. The blogger writes a blog entry.

2. The blogger posts the new entry.

3. The blog software uploads the new entry and fits it into the Weblog chronologically. Part or all of the entry is placed on the blog's index page (the home page of the site), and the entire entry is also archived on its own page with a unique URL.

4. Visitors see the index page first, where they can skim recent entries in reverse chronological order. They can click through to individual entries on individual pages.

More about archives

The preceding section explains that blog programs create a unique page for each entry. The two reasons for this are linkability (when you want to point to a specific entry) and continuity — the unique pages are an archive of the entire blog. Archiving is important. You might think that the immediacy of blogs makes past entries obsolete, but the opposite is true. Blogs represent a history of a person's writing.

It can be fascinating to dive into a blog's past, and most software encourages visitors to do that by linking to archived posts in a variety of ways:

- On the index page, at least a few days' worth of entries are presented.

- A "recent entries" column is often displayed on the index page's sidebar, listing recent posts that aren't on the index page.

- Deep archives are often listed by month, by year, or by both, somewhere on the index page. A calendar format is sometimes used.

Figure 1-7 shows one blog's archives listed both by category and by date. Archived entries are particularly useful in professional diaries and topical blogs, where you might want to research article links and commentary opinion from months or years ago. This brings up a question: If blogging is so new, how can archives stretch back for years? The fact is, blogging *has* been around for many years; it has only recently hit a tipping point of popularity. I started my first blog in 2002 and considered myself a newbie among experienced hands who had been blogging for a few years already. As you surf from blog to blog, you'll encounter some impressive archives.

Common blog elements

Chronological entries and archives would be enough for a basic blog, and indeed, a few blogs eliminate all other elements from their pages. (See the Russell Beattie Notebook at `www.russellbeattie.com`.) Most blogs, though, incorporate these standard features:

- **Author byline:** A byline above (or below) each entry is less important if you're the blog's only writer than in group blogs. Still, many blogs carry that byline as a default setting in the blog software.

- **Permalink:** Short for "permanent link," this link takes the visitor from the index page to the entry's unique page. Figure 1-8 illustrates a permalink below a blog entry.

- **Blogroll:** The blogroll is not a requirement, but it is a tradition to list the blogger's favorite blogs in a sidebar. The blogroll is usually common to every page of the blog, so visitors can see your favorite blog destinations no matter where they enter your blog. Blogrolls make the blogosphere somewhat incestuous, with many topical blogs all linking to each other. Having one's blog included in a high-profile blogroll is an honor and can deliver lots of traffic to a previously little-known blog.

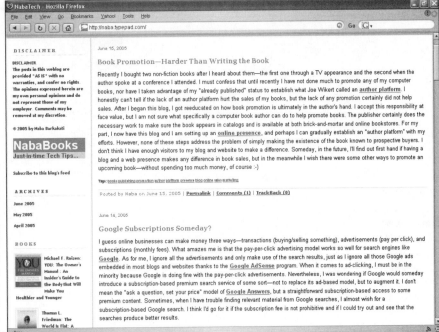

Figure 1-8:
The
permalink,
comment
link, and
TrackBack
link reside
below each
entry of
this blog.

✔ **Categories:** Some blog programs allow the blogger to assign categories to blog entries. These categories are listed in a sidebar, so that visitors can restrict their reading to a category of interest. It's not unusual for one entry to be tagged in multiple categories.

✔ **Comments:** Comments are written by visitors to your blog and are presented below your entry on that entry's unique page. On the index page, a Comments link sends visitors to that unique page, scrolled down to the first comment (see Figure 1-9). Many blog programs allow the comments function to be turned off, so visitors cannot talk back. Some blog experts believe that the presence of comments is a defining feature of a Weblog. I disagree with this restrictive view; I have operated no-comment blogs, and I visit some wonderful blog products in which readers can only read, not talk. But it is true that the blogosphere would be fundamentally altered if there were no comments anywhere. Comments are a crucial part of what I call the *macrologue* — far-flung group discussions across many blogs. Chapters 3 and 14 explore the macrologue in more detail.

✔ **TrackBacks:** TrackBacks are related to comments but are trickier to understand. Chapter 3 makes TrackBacks absolutely clear. For now, know that TrackBacks offer a way to put a link to your blog entry on someone else's blog. TrackBacks link blogs together in the macrologue.

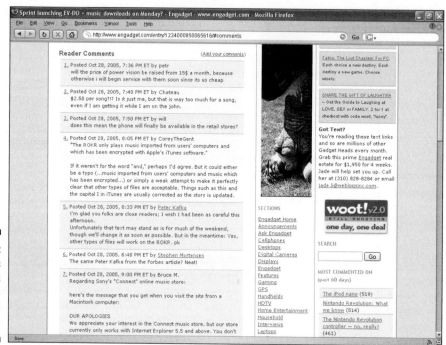

Figure 1-9:
Comments
give blogs
a conver-
sational
quality.

A final element common to most blogs is the syndication link, which can take several forms and is worthy of a thorough discussion. That discussion occurs in Chapter 13, which dives into the important topics of *RSS* (really simple syndication) and *newsreaders.* The take-away point for now is that many people read blogs in newsreaders, not by visiting the blog sites. Newsreaders pull the content of many blogs into one window. Within a newsreader, each blog is called a *feed.* These newsreaders are mostly free and can be stand-alone programs that you download to your computer or Web-based services that you visit from any computer.

Making your blog's content available as a feed is crucial. Fortunately, this fairly technical method of distributing blog entries is effortlessly handled for you by nearly all blog software. Using RSS and other syndication formats has become so simple that this book doesn't spend any space explaining how to create syndication links from scratch. (For the technical stuff, see *Syndicating Web Sites with RSS Feeds For Dummies,* published by Wiley.)

The Design and Appearance of Blogs

Veteran blog readers notice that Weblogs have a characteristic appearance, beginning with the date headers, which indicate the blog's chronology. Also, blog services provide a few templates used by thousands of sites, so many of those blogs resemble each other. These templates are page designs that make the site attractive with no work on your part. Without templates, Web site designers spend hours, days, and weeks creating the content spaces and navigation sidebars that make up a typical Web page. With prebuilt templates, you just select a site design and start blogging.

Templates not only define the colors of your pages but sometimes also determine how your archives are presented, the format of your date and time stamp, and other details that affect your visitors' experience. These details are sometimes configurable, and personalizing them is a worthwhile effort.

The existence of templates doesn't mean that you can't tweak, or even completely reimagine, the design of your blog. Some blog platforms allow total personalization, but starting from scratch is challenging. Most beginners (and, really, all those who prefer creating content to creating design) prefer preconfigured design choices. And because many users of popular blog services don't even bother exploring all the available template choices, the top designs are commonly used. As a result, most blogs created with Movable Type (Chapter 9), TypePad (Chapter 7), Blogger.com (Chapter 6), and other services are instantly recognizable.

If you care about your site looking different from thousands of others, dig deep into the menu of templates. In many cases, the template can be changed in midstream; when you do that, every page of your blog is changed over to the new design.

Chapter 2

Blogging Options

Chapter 1 defines Weblogs and illuminates the basic elements of a blog: entries, the index page, comments, TrackBacks, archives, blogrolls, and categories. That chapter was all about the question, "What is a blog." This chapter asks the question, "Where will you blog?"

I don't get into evaluating specific blog services and programs in this chapter; those comparisons occur in Parts II and III. This chapter uncovers categories. You can operate a blog in a multitude of online places, using four main methods, or *platforms*. This chapter identifies those platforms and spells out their strong and weak points. Well, no point beating around the bush; here they are:

✔ Social networks

✔ Blog services

✔ Self-installed blog software

✔ Web hosts with preinstalled blog software

Your main choice is whether to host the blog yourself or have a blog company do it. By "host," I don't mean "write." You'll be the one writing your blog no matter where it lives. The hosting decision is about whether you install the blog software or use a service with the software already running. Most people choose the latter because it's easier. Adventurous and technically inclined people choose the self-installed options because they are more powerful.

By the end of this chapter, every reader should have an idea of which direction to go. Many people start blogging impulsively, with the first solution they come across. That's fine, but a little thought at this stage can set you up for a more satisfying experience in the long run.

Itching to blog

Want to get started quickly? Of course you do. You've got a lot to blog about. Just keep in mind that with blog services, the quickest start usually delivers the fewest features. I suggest reading through the following sections to decide how steep a learning curve you're willing to climb.

You can be blogging minutes from now. When my mother wanted to start a blog, I set her up in one of friendliest environments because I knew she didn't want any hassle. If you're the same way, and don't even want to know about alternatives, skip to Chapters 4 and 5. The social networking platforms described in those chapters (MSN Spaces and Yahoo! 360, respectively) include blogging and blaze a quick path to your first entry.

If you think a pure-blog service might better serve your blogging mission, read through this chapter. These pages survey the social networks in a general way, as well as more sophisticated platforms and programs.

Blogging in Social Networks

Chapter 5 details three social networks that contain blog services. But the question arises: What is a social network, anyway? That brings up a further question: Why does the author of this book keep asking questions? Which leads to a final question: Are we stuck with this guy? Yes. Yes, you are.

Social networks are online community sites that link people together. Some amount of personal information is usually shared in an effort to present a profile that other members can get to know. This profile can be nudged along by questionnaires, or by making it easy to create lists of favorite things, or just by providing space to type and upload stuff. Various community features are offered, such as photo sharing, instant messaging, and invitation-only circles of friends. Figure 2-1 shows my page on Yahoo! 360, covered in Chapter 5. If you squint, you can see pictures of my dog, the start of one blog entry, my shared feeds, and a quote that I "blasted" to my friends.

Blogging at these sites fits in with the overall tone of instant chumminess. Nearly always, blog content in social networking services is personal, like a diary. You see a lot of chit-chat blogging in these clubs. But the truth is that you can use any blog space for any purpose whatsoever. It is my informal observation that serious topical blogging usually occurs in the pure-blog services that don't offer all the communal, meet-and-greet features. Pure-blog services frequently offer a more sober, uncluttered, professional presentation of the blog.

Joining a social network is profoundly easy. Usually, you just fill in a Web form to establish a username and password combination. This registration form might gather some personal information for your profile or give you a chance to invite online friends to join you in membership. (See Figure 2-2.) Fill it in, click a link, and it's off to blogdom.

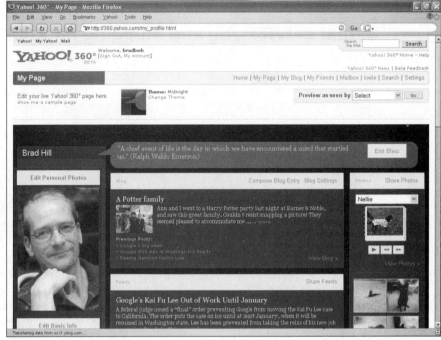

Figure 2-1:
Social networking combines blogging with community sharing features.

Figure 2-2:
Signing up at Live-Journal, a blog-friendly social network, is quick and easy.

Social networking and blogging for kids

Teens have taken to blogging and social networking in a big way. Like many Internet services adopted by the youth market, blogging has come under the gun of concerned parents decrying the dangers of posting personal information online. True; there are risks in revealing addresses, phone numbers, and even real names (not fictional screen names) in any public online environment. But this issue is hardly new and not unique to blogging. Parents should administer all aspects of a child's online citizenry.

Some social networking services attract huge numbers of kids. These sites become hangout spots where kids feel they must be seen. They put up pages, write blog entries, post photos, instant message each other, and in other ways have a fine time frolicking in the Internet playground. Xanga and MySpace.com are two such destinations. Xanga requires users to be at least 13 years old; in MySpace the age barrier is set at 16. Young kids routinely and successfully lie about their ages; that's one fact of life parents should know. Kids of all ages should certainly be counseled about remaining unlocatable in public online communities. Addresses and phone numbers should never be posted. Full names (first and last) should be avoided, especially if the user's home town is mentioned. Many kids upload photos and can be recognized by their friends that way; screen identities can also be shared privately. Underlying these details should be a general parental awareness of social networks, how they work, which ones are being used, and how they are being used.

Alarmism and panic, though, as you sometimes read about in newspaper stories, is uncalled for. Actual harm resulting from online stalking is exceptionally rare. Harm to a child is always tragic, but the very few instances resulting from millions of teen blogs and social networking pages make it clear that blogging is safer than walking down the street. It's probably safer than eating cafeteria food.

Taken as a group, social networks are the easiest and the cheapest (often free) platform on which to blog for the first time. So what's the issue? Why not recommend them and be done with it? When will I stop asking questions? Social networks are primarily about socializing and secondarily about blogging. The blogs included in these services tend to be merely one of many devices used to connect personally with friends and make new friends. You can make the blog the centerpiece of your social network presence, but if you're more interested in blogging than in sharing photos and chatting, a pure-blog service might be more appropriate.

To be specific, social networks sometimes lack standard blogging features found on more serious Weblog platforms, such as entry categories and configurable archives. Just these two examples are important enough, if you're writing for the ages, to seek outside the social networks. At the time of this writing, podcasting is out of the question in the social networks. (See Chapter 16 for more on podcasting.) Owning your own domain (www.my-immortal-blog. com) is generally not possible. Mobile blogging (called *moblogging*) might not be available. You cannot run ads to make a few bucks on a social network page (although the service might run its own ads on your page).

None of these detriments matter to casual bloggers who are in it for the fun of self-expression in an online community. But they do matter to those who are more ambitious about presenting content in an organized and undistracted manner and who might eventually want access to sophisticated features.

It is usually impossible to transfer a blog from a social network to another platform. So if you start blogging in a social network and later move up to a full-featured blogging platform, you will most likely lose your old entries.

Blogging and Nothing but Blogging

For the determined blogger, one step up from social networks leads to a blog service without the cozy community games such as friend lists and member-only e-mails. In this book, I cover two such services: Blogger.com (Chapter 6) and TypePad (Chapter 7).

The fanciest of the blog hosts have evolved into fairly powerful and sophisticated vehicles for mounting and maintaining a determined blog. The free services tend to be a little stripped-down compared to those that charge a modest monthly fee. Both Blogger and TypePad have become rampantly popular. My observation is that Blogger.com has more personal-diary blogs (see Figure 2-3), and TypePad attracts topical bloggers with a specific agenda (see Figure 2-4). But you can find plenty of crossover.

Figure 2-3: A Blogger.com diary blog, detailing one person's quest to become an astronaut.

Figure 2-4:
A TypePad
blog,
offering one
person's
news
commentary.

Blog hosts provide the specialized blogging software and the server space that holds your blog entries. You don't need to bring anything except a desire to blog and (in some cases) a little money. The Web address (URL) of your blog usually includes the name of the hosting company, like this: *mylife.bloghost.com*. Blogger and TypePad also both offer an option for owners of their own domains, such as www.*my-blog*.com.

The High Road: Self-Installed Blogging Programs

Installing sophisticated blog software in your own server space (leased from a Web hosting company) is the most cost-effective way to get full-throated blogging power over a long period. This method is also the most challenging way to start blogging. I don't mean scratch-your-head challenging, I mean tear-your-hair-out challenging. Grown-men-weeping sort of challenge. Self-installation of a blog is like building an SUV.

Technical sorts who are accustomed to installing programs across computers think nothing of setting up blog software. And there is definitely satisfaction in mastering the hardships and driving that SUV down the blogging highway. I created my first blog in Greymatter, which presented a thorny installation and setup challenge to my feebly technical brain. (Greymatter isn't used much anymore.) I poured hours into mastering a basic understand of server databases and hand-coding design templates (see Figure 2-5). If you do it once, it will never be so difficult again, even if you switch from one blogging program to another.

Chapter 8 explains the principles and basic routine of installing blog software on a server. It doesn't make sense to document the exact installation process of the programs covered in this book, because each is similar to the others but different in the details. So, Chapter 8 sets you up for any installation you might attempt by explaining how these programs work and what you need to find out about your Web host. Then the chapters devoted to individual programs cover a post-installation rundown of features. These chapters also point you to online installation help.

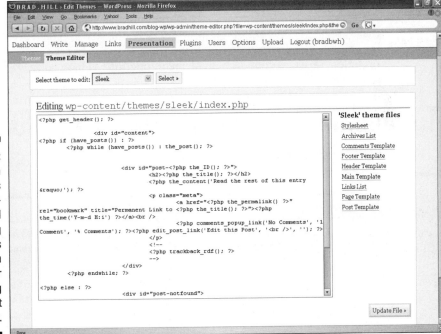

Figure 2-5:
Design templates in self-installed blog programs give you control over every blog element. But it's not easy.

Web Hosts with Blogging

In Chapter 12, I identify Web hosts that offer preinstalled blog programs — either Movable Type (described in Chapter 9) or WordPress (described in Chapter 10). Web hosts normally specialize in serving Web sites at registered domains owned by the Webmasters of those sites. For example, you might register and purchase the `www.sleepyzzzz.com` domain, and then build a Web site located at that URL. A Web host would store the site pages on its computer and display them to people who visit `www.sleepyzzzz.com`.

Some Web hosts attract blogging customers by preinstalling powerful blog programs such as Movable Type and WordPress, so the users don't have to wrestle with difficult installations. These packages, paid by the month or year, represent the most expensive way to blog, but you get a lot for your money: powerful blog software perfectly installed and ready to use.

A blog program called Radio UserLand is a different and, in this book, unique type of blogging solution. Described in Chapter 11, Radio UserLand does require installation by the user, but it's a desktop installation, not a Web-server installation. Installing Radio UserLand is on the same technical level as installing a new instant messaging program, a new browser, or a new productivity application on your computer. Once installed, you blog by typing entries into the program, which then uploads them to Radio UserLand's server and provides the usual content management functions of blog software.

A Comparative Look at Blogging Options

Table 2-1 compares the four blogging options identified in this chapter.

Table 2-1	Comparing Blog Platforms			
	Social networks with blogging	Hosted blog-only platforms	Self-installed blogging	Web hosts with preinstalled blogging
Cost	Free or under $5/month	Free or under $15/month	Free or one-time license fee ($50–100)	$5–15/month
Difficulty	Easy	Easy to moderate	Difficult	Moderate to challenging
Features	Basic	Basic to moderate	Sophisticated	Sophisticated

	Social networks with blogging	*Hosted blog-only platforms*	*Self-installed blogging*	*Web hosts with preinstalled blogging*
Domain ownership	No	Yes	Yes	Yes
Design choices	No or templates	Templates that can be modified	Templates that can be modified	Templates that can be modified
Blogosphere networking	Feeds and comments	Feeds and comments; possible TrackBacks	Feeds and comments; possible TrackBacks	Feeds and comments; possible TrackBacks
Storage	Not always known	100 megabytes to unlimited	500–2000 megabytes, depending on the Web host	500–5000 megabytes, depending on the host
Ads for income	No	Yes or no	Yes	Yes
Photos	Yes or limited	Yes	Yes	Yes
Moblogging	Yes or No	Yes	Yes or no	Yes or no
Podcasting distribution	No	Yes	Yes or no	Yes or no
Traffic reporting	No	Yes or no	Usually (depends on Web host)	Usually (depends on Web host)

A couple of notes:

- ✔ **Storage:** This category refers to the amount of server space reserved for your blog. If you're paying for your blog service, you can sometimes get more storage by paying more money. For text-only blogs (no photos, videos, audio clips, or podcasts), 100 megabytes (the low end) can go a fairly long way. But start piling in photos — and more videos or audio — and you'll hit that ceiling before long.

- ✔ **Ads for income:** Chapter 15 explores the revenue possibilities of blogging. For the most part, those possibilities consist of running ads on your blog site. You can do this in several ways, from Google's contextual ad service to banner-ad brokering.

✔ **Photos:** Most blog services allow the inclusion of a photo in a blog entry, but some platforms make it surprisingly difficult. Another issue is whether the service provides photo albums for showcasing your photos in a special page design. See the individual chapters in Parts II and III for more information. Also take a look at Chapter 17, which includes a comparative chart detailing photo services.

✔ **Traffic reporting:** Most Web hosts allow their users to monitor the number of visitors to the site. Those statistics usually include page-by-page accounting of visitor *hits* (visits to that page) and other metrics, such as the number of unique visitors to the site. Blog traffic measurement can operate the same way and is almost never available in social network sites. Blog measurement is tricky because many readers are not visitors but receivers of the blog's syndication feed (see Chapter 13). The traffic of those feeds is notoriously difficult to measure, and most hosts (blog hosts and hybrid hosts) don't even try.

Chapter 3

Living the Blogging Lifestyle

In This Chapter

▶ Avoiding burnout while staying productive

▶ Deciding on your blogging style

▶ Setting a conversational tone with blog comments

▶ Finally understanding TrackBacks, really

▶ Looking for yourself in blog search engines

▶ Promoting your blog

*T*o be honest, the title of this chapter notwithstanding, blogging needn't be a lifestyle. Casual hobby, fun escape from the offline world, convenient method of connecting with friends and family — many types of blogging never threaten to disrupt the basic patterns of daily life.

But something about blogging, like keeping a diary, becomes important and seems to become alive. Some people know they want to blog seriously even before they start. Others are surprised by how much they love it as they get involved. This chapter is about some of the issues that arise in daily, determined blogging.

Also in this chapter is (I hope) the most detailed, complete, and understandable explanation of TrackBacks. TrackBacks are an important part of the daily blogosphere macrologue (see Chapter 1) and an important part of self-promotion. TrackBacks are notoriously difficult for newcomers (and even old-timers) to understand. If you have heard of the term and experience the white noise it can stimulate in the brain, your dark days are nearly over. This chapter will set you free.

Read on for a discussion of blog stress and how to avoid it, comments, TrackBacks, following the ripples of your blog in the blogosphere, and promoting your blog in specialized sites.

The Rhythms of Blogging

Here's the truth: Blogging is a grind. A joy, to be sure, but difficult to sustain over the long haul. Creating frequent entries can seem like a chore. Of course, nobody is putting a gun to your head. At least, I don't suppose so; if somebody *is* putting a gun to your head, you have bigger troubles than deciding what to write about.

The pressure in blogging is the need to blog often and to keep the blog going over weeks and months. It's easy enough to blog often for a short while (usually at the start), and it's easy enough to blog infrequently for a long period. But putting the two together is harder than most people realize when they are contemplating their first blog. There's the imaginary gun to your head again: Nobody can force you to post entries every day or continue your blog for the rest of your life. But because the definition of a blog is a Web site that makes it easy for the owner to make frequent updates (see Chapter 1), the underlying point of most blogs is to write in them often. And to accumulate an historical archive of those writings. That's two points. Oh, and to get readers; that's three. Oh! And to keep those readers. Lots of points, all related in a way this section makes clear.

Different paces for different cases

Coping with blog stress is a matter of pacing. As with any other endeavor, diving in too fast at the start invites burnout. The tendency is to believe that you must keep up whatever pace you start with, which might be ten entries a day. That pace would be loads of fun for the first three days, then a bit of pressure for the next three days. After two weeks you'd wish you had never picked up this book, and after a month you'd be on a ledge threatening to jump.

First, switch to decaf if you're attracted to ledges. Second, you don't have to maintain a manic posting tempo if you went overboard in the first week. Third, don't go overboard in the first week. Fourth, spend a bit of time contemplating what you want to accomplish with your blog and how much effort it will take.

"Accomplish?" you might be thinking. "I'm not into accomplishing. I just want to have an easy Web site and put up pictures of my kids." Well, there you go. You've contemplated your blog's purpose and formulated a mission statement. This particular mission is fairly relaxed and should not inspire dramatic leaps.

Personal journals are the most easygoing sort of blog. More ambitious are topical blogs in which the link-and-comment style takes its pacing cues from daily news. If your topic is Loch Ness monster sightings, you might not have much to say on a daily basis. But hordes of technology blogs, political blogs, current events blogs, and many other newsy blogs compete with each other to stay up to date. Forget up to date; they compete to stay up to the minute. That's where the pressure comes in: covering all the news and covering it without much lag.

Another reason to be speedy with a topical blog goes beyond sheer competitiveness. Several blogs chattering about the same subject, with comments and links flying back and forth, form a big, multisite conversation on the topic — what I call the *macrologue* (see Chapter 1). Participating in the macrologue requires reading it and writing into it every day, more or less.

The rhythms of readership

The quest for readership, like the quest for topical currency, differs from one type of blog to another. Here again, personal diaries often don't have readership ambitions equal to topical blogs. If you are writing for close friends and family, you can rely on your audience to check your space from time to time and delight in the occasional new entry. But if you're writing for a broader readership of strangers who also follow other blogs in the same subject area, leaving holes in your posting schedule might cause your blog to drop off your audience's radar. Devoted blog readers like frequently updated content.

As a general rule, if more than one weekday passes with no new entries, the blog risks losing momentum. If that seems harsh or exaggerated, you might be underestimating the voracious content appetite of blog addicts. Fortunately, some exceptions apply:

- ✔ Most bloggers dial back on the weekends, which are exempt from the news cycle. Conversely, casual personal interest bloggers might swing into high gear on the weekends after slacking during the week.

- ✔ Respected blogs have more leeway; their readers are willing to wait for posts because the content is worthwhile and influential.

- ✔ Customs be blasted, you can do whatever you want.

Volume equals traffic

To understand the fickle nature of blog readers, you must understand their information-soaked lifestyle. The most active blogosphere participants make a daily (or more frequent) circuit of their favored sources by one of three means:

- ✔ They visit and read blogs.
- ✔ They view blog feeds in newsreaders, looking at each feed separately. (See Chapter 13 for more on feeds and newsreaders, and see Figure 3-1 in this chapter.)
- ✔ They use newsreaders that merge their feeds into one big feed that, when refreshed, shows the most recent posts from all the feeds.

The first option is the most prevalent. Even though feeds are becoming more popular, and I believe they will eventually be used by nearly everyone who reads online, most people at the time of this writing have no idea what they are. The third option, using a specialized newsreader that can merge feeds on command (such as Rojo), is rare indeed. It is my favorite option, and I discuss it in Chapter 13.

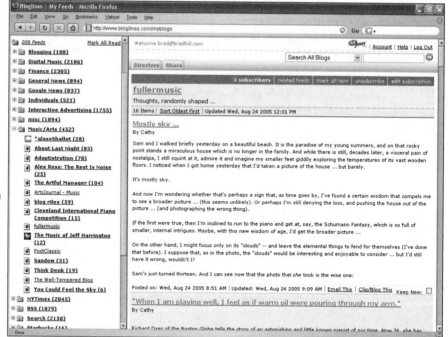

Figure 3-1: Active blog readers look at individual blog feeds in a newsreader like Bloglines.

The point here is about ebbing and flowing readership. When readers take the trouble to visit your site, which consumes more time than receiving a feed of your site in a newsreader, they get discouraged if you haven't posted any new entries since their last visit. Naturally, after coming up empty a few times, they might stop visiting. I don't mean to imply that quantity is more important than quality, but a decent blog with few posts will have a smaller readership than a decent blog with many posts. Volume brings in traffic. Keeping that traffic requires good quality and a steady pace.

I know this principle — volume encouraging steady readership — is true from my own experience both as a blogger and as a consumer of blogs. In the latter case, my daily routine is all about slogging through more content than I can possibly absorb. I use two main newsreaders, each containing more than 200 feeds divided into more than a dozen folders. One folder contains the essentials: feeds from blogs and other information sources that I must read every day. The feeds that make it into the elite group are the ones that I've learned, over time, always deliver fresh content. Those feeds also offer high-quality content, but the constant flow of entries is essential.

Posting to the rhythm of your readers

Posting at least one entry each weekday is a good benchmark for attracting and holding a readership. Composing five blog entries per week is a manageable minimum for most serious bloggers covering a newsy topic. Many topical blogs post content more prolifically, and many personal blogs are more relaxed about it all.

If you do post once or more a day, you might want to consider the rhythm of blog readership. Many people hit their newsreaders first thing in the morning, either at home or at work. I like to get some topical content up and live by 8:00 a.m. eastern standard time. Obviously, this early-morning writing schedule isn't practical for everyone, especially those who live in earlier time zones such as on the West Coast of the United States. Those folks can effectively practice an evening schedule, posting entries that go live after the East Coast has gone to bed; that writing will enjoy rush-hour readership the next morning. I like to post at night for European readers, who live five to eight hours ahead of my time zone.

Spacing can be as important as pacing for those who post a lot. If you write several entries each day, all composed before you head for work, it can be advantageous to spread out those entries. If you can't sit at the computer all day blogging, you can use a blogging platform that allows post-dating entries. This feature allows you to write an entry at 8:45 a.m. and set it to appear to readers at 2:00 in the afternoon or even the next day. When writing a multipart daily series, I have sometimes composed the entire thing at one sitting and then post-dated the entries to appear at the same time for several consecutive days. Spreading out your entries encourages readers to keep checking your site or feed, lest they miss your latest gem.

Finding a Voice

The Weblog medium is a personal medium. Nearly all bloggers — even professional bloggers and corporate bloggers — write with some kind of a personal voice. Of course, diary-style blogs are *all* personality; their purpose is not to deliver news or comment on it. But even newsy blogs are often written in the first person when delivering commentary ("Greenspan's predictions might turn out to be justified, but I think it's more likely that somebody spiked his drink."). Those that maintain a more objective formality (no "I") still offer opinion. Blogs are rarely purely journalistic efforts. Even stiff blogs publish entries that read more like opinion columns than newspaper articles.

So, in the wide range of editorial attitudes from intimate to professionally opinionated, you must decide what your voice will be. This isn't a time for angst; your best bet is to write naturally. Your blog should showcase the real you. That could mean writing in sentence fragments, stream-of-consciousness rhapsodies, polished prose, verse, chatspeak, or whatever writing style you'd use in an e-mail to your best friend. (Figure 3-2 shows Rosie O'Donnell's idiosyncratic blog style.)

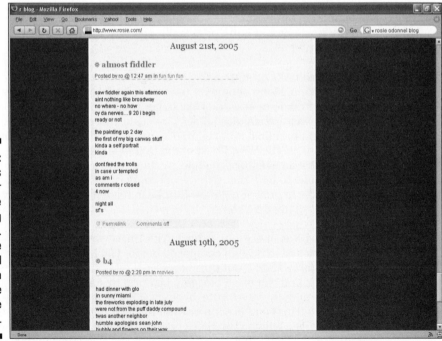

Figure 3-2:
Your blog's voice, or style, can be anything you like. Rosie O'Donnell writes in a unique verse shorthand.

If you're launching a topical blog, your selection of voice is also an editorial decision. Will you balance your entries toward objective filtering of news or your personal commentary? Will you link to stories about which you can be critical? Is unabashed enthusiasm your style? Do you want to project an acerbic persona or a gentler voice that readers trust to recommend items of interest around the Web? Serious or funny? Deep or superficial?

 One editorial attitude that particularly characterizes blogs is called *snark*. Snark can be sarcasm, ill temper, scathing criticism, cynicism, or any combination of grouchy attributes. Snarky writing is like a badge of honor for many bloggers, but more than that it represents a certain know-it-all informality of the genre. An unrelentingly snarky voice can be tiresome, but you should feel that snark is always available when you feel strongly about something — especially when you feel strongly critical.

The entire idea of "finding a voice" might not appeal to some readers. It's a bit nebulous. If defining a personal style isn't important to you, it's not important, period. Your blog might develop a distinct tone over time, or you might start out effortlessly being exactly yourself (not the easiest trick in writing) and stay that way. Nothing in this section is a requirement.

Using Comments in Your Blog

You might not realize it until you get deeper into your blogging lifestyle, but bloggers spend an amazing amount of time tracking the influence of their blogging. That means attempting to locate other blogs citing their work and figuring out who is talking about them. Blogging isn't only about writing; it's about inducing other people to respond, either on one's own blog or in another blog. The macrologue, the big blogging conversation I describe in Chapter 1, encourages bloggers not only to participate but to hope for an influential role in that conversation and compete for it.

Let me be clear. It is mostly topical blogs that join the influence race. Their owners are serious about blogging, and they track their ripples on the blogosphere. Casual bloggers — diarists, families blogging together, teens blogging in social networks, and many other bloggers — don't bother with techniques of self-infatuation. Later in the chapter, I cover self-promotion, which is closely related to self-tracking. It's all about attracting attention, for those with a taste for attention.

If your blog accepts comments (most blogs do), the comments you receive are the most direct indications that people are reading and responding to your stuff. Tending to your comments — reading them, responding to them as you feel moved to, and clearing out the irrelevant ones — occupies some time in the blogging lifestyle. The degree to which you're willing to attend to your comments can determine the extent to which your blog becomes a conversation forum and the style with which you write entries.

To a large degree, comments are solicited by bloggers who write in a conversational style or even directly request comments. The old "What do you think?" directed to the readership at large is a request (a somewhat desperate invitation, at that) for feedback. Some bloggers run polls and surveys to get some traffic flowing in the comments section. Well-known bloggers attract comments simply because people want to talk to them or because a comment that contains a link to the commentor's blog is a promotional gambit (see Chapter 14). Figure 3-3 shows the start of a long comment discussion on the blog of well-known blogger Jeremy Zawodny. Note that Jeremy participates in the conversation, which contained 19 comments one day after the entry was posted.

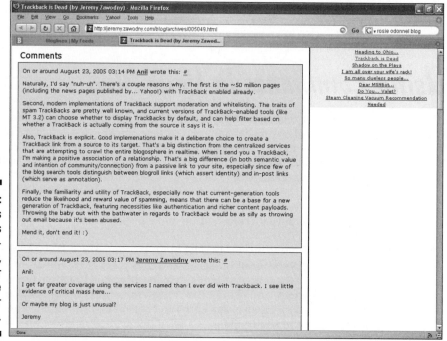

Figure 3-3:
Comments make blogs conversational forums, to whatever extent the blogger wants.

The degree to which you respond to comments can also set the tone. Bloggers who quickly answer comments and lead discussions usually get more comments than bloggers who essentially lecture to their audiences and leave comments unanswered. But there should be no judgment of that approach; some bloggers prefer to let readers talk among themselves. It's a matter of personality, really. If you're a conversational type who enjoys group discussions, you'll find a way to encourage participation from your readers. If you are quieter, your writing style will probably encourage reading but not responding. If comments make you uncomfortable, simply turn them off. (Some blogging services do not allow you to disable comments.)

Beyond comments, I want to cover two other, more elaborate, ways that bloggers track their influence in the blogosphere: TrackBacks and blog search engines.

Understanding TrackBacks

TrackBacks offer a unique way for you to know that other bloggers are aware of your work and are responding to it on their own blogs. The TrackBack is also one of the trickiest concepts for new bloggers to understand. Heck, even veteran bloggers haven't necessarily untangled what a TrackBack is, thanks to overly technical and indecipherable explanations on the Web. The subject is a bit loopy (literally, as you'll see), but I mean to illuminate TrackBacks with crystal clarity to every reader.

TrackBack basics

The meaning of TrackBacks can be encapsulated a few ways, because they mean different things to different people. I am listing a few descriptions here in case they prove useful to remember as you read through this section. If they don't juice your brain right now, it's not a problem. If you read steadily through the next few pages, you will understand TrackBacks perfectly.

So, TrackBacks are

- A way for two sites, each running a blog, to communicate with each other
- A form of remote commenting, allowing multiple bloggers to have a conversation spread out among their sites
- A way for one blogger to insert a link to his or her blog on another blog

The availability of TrackBacks

If you are already blogging, you might be looking at your software or blog provider while reading this section, saying "What the heck is he talking about? I don't see any option for TrackBacks." Perhaps your language is even stronger. Perhaps instead of "option" you are saying "danged option." Curb your temper and let me explain.

TrackBacks were invented by SixApart, one of the major blog software and hosting providers. (SixApart operates Movable Type, TypePad, and LiveJournal, which are all covered in this book.) TrackBack was introduced in August, 2002. SixApart intended, and still would prefer, that its TrackBack feature become standard equipment in all blog platforms and services. TrackBack is an open standard and costs no money to implement. It attains greater usefulness as more blogs have it available. But many blog platforms do not use the feature, and therefore many blogs do not display TrackBacks and cannot track back to other sites.

Currently, none of the social networks covered in this book (including SixApart's LiveJournal) allow TrackBacks; neither does Greymatter and Blogger.com. Among the platforms covered in this book, Movable Type, TypePad, WordPress, and Radio UserLand all include TrackBack as an option.

Keep in mind that a TrackBack is a communication between two sites, so *both* sites must be empowered with the TrackBack feature for it to work.

Each of the preceding statements is true. You might get the drift, from the name *TrackBack,* that something is . . . well, being tracked back, like following bread crumbs to a starting location. That is exactly right. TrackBacks put bread crumbs (a link, actually) from a second blog back to a first blog.

At this point, it's useful to imagine two blogs. Actually, more than two blogs can participate in a TrackBack conversation, but each single TrackBack occurs between just two blogs. So, we have Blog A and Blog B. These two blogs are similar, in that their entries are about the same subjects and their authors each read the other blog daily. As you examine how TrackBacks work in this section, you will alternately place yourself in the role of Blogger A and Blogger B. TrackBacks represent a two-way street, and bloggers who use them travel in both directions.

In our scenario, Blogger A posts first; Blogger B posts second. Here is what happens without explaining all the details (details are coming soon):

1. Blogger A posts a really good entry on Blog A. The entry is titled "How to save the world."

2. Blogger B reads Blogger A's post and is impressed. Blogger B wants to spread the word about Blogger A's great entry, and at the same time he

has some thoughts of his own about how to save the world. Blogger B could leave a comment on Blog A, but instead . . .

3. Blogger B goes to his own blog and writes his commentary as a blog entry on Blog B. This new entry is called "Does the world need saving?" Blogger B cites Blogger A's entry ("How to save the world") by embedding a link to it in the text of "Does the world need saving?" and also plants a TrackBack to Blog A. The TrackBack is invisible to Blog B's readers, but . . .

4. A TrackBack listing appears on Blog A, below the "How to save the world" entry on that entry's unique page. The TrackBack listing contains Blogger B's entry title ("Does the world need saving?"), a snippet from the posted text of Blogger B's entry, and a link to that entry.

The TrackBack is complete. (See Figure 3-4.) The two blogs are linked: Blog A's readers can follow the TrackBack link to Blog B's entry ("Does the world need saving?"), and Blog B's readers can follow the embedded link to Blog A's entry ("How to save the world") *if* Blogger B embedded that link (which he did in the preceding series of steps).

Figure 3-4: TrackBacks are listed below the blog entry to which they refer, and link to another blog.

TrackBacks are circular and benefit both blogs only if the second blogger puts in a link to the first blog. The TrackBack planted by Blogger B *is not visible* to readers of Blog B and does not function as a link to Blog A. The TrackBack listing on Blog A is visible and offers an automatic link to Blog B. As you can see, the TrackBack mechanism is partly invisible and automated. When Blogger B plants the TrackBack to Blog A, the two blogs (the software running the two blog sites) communicate with each other behind the scenes. It's as if this conversation was happening:

> **Blog B:** Hey, Blog A! My blogger just planted a TrackBack in me, pointing to your guy's entry. Something about saving the world — I don't know. These messianic types are too heavy for me.

> **Blog A:** Yeah, I've been taking a lot of TrackBacks on this one. All right, let me have it.

> **Blog B:** Here's the information, including my entry that my blogger is coupling with the TrackBack. You'll put the TrackBack in the right place, as always?

> **Blog A:** What am I, a newcomer? Yeah, it'll go right under his blather about saving the world, and I'll link it back to your entry. What is that, anyway? The world wouldn't need saving if everyone watched more cartoons.

> **Blog B:** Don't ask me; I don't read this stuff anymore. Just put in the TrackBack and let me go back to my archives, would you?

> **Blog A:** Not a problem. Oh geez, here come some more. He *had* to save the world at 8:00 in the morning.

> **Blog B:** Yeah, well, good luck with that.

Visitors to Blog A see the "How to save the world" post and, below it on the page, TrackBacks and comments. The page, taken as a whole, is both a statement from the blogger and a discussion among the readers. The blogger might and might not be posting comments in response to readers. Several TrackBacks might be listed, each from a different blog. Each TrackBack displays a line or two of comment, taken from that blog's entry, and a link to the full entry.

Visitors to Blog B see the "Does the world need saving?" post that contains an embedded link to Blog A's "How to save the world" post. For some visitors, Blog B's citation of Blog A's entry is their first encounter with Blogger A's statement. These visitors, entering the macrologue at Blog B, might think of Blogger B's entry ("Does the world need saving?") as the primary jumping-off point of their own participation in the big discussion; they might and might not visit Blog A. They could leave comments on Blog B or return to their own blogs to write entries inspired by the work of Blogger B. The TrackBacks associated with those comments (if the bloggers choose to plant TrackBacks) are placed on Blog B, linking to new entries on Blogs C, D, E, and so on. So the networked conversation expands into a complex web of discourse.

This is the blogosphere.

The tricky task of following your own conversations

Between comments and TrackBacks, many bloggers become deeply and happily enmeshed in far-flung blog conversations. Because every blog is a click or typed URL away from every other blog, geography doesn't matter; only shared interests are important. Involved blogosphere jockeys can spend as much time commenting and backtracking as posting original entries. The problem is keeping notes on it all. Comments are more ephemeral than TrackBacks. One of the great values of the TrackBack is that it brings the conversation (or portions of it) to *your* blog, where you can more easily follow it.

When you leave a comment on another blog, you must remember to visit that entry page (where the comments are listed below the entry) again if you are to follow the conversation. A few blog programs offer RSS feeds for comments, distinct from the RSS feed that distributes entries. (See Chapter 13 for a full discussion of RSS and feeds.) With a comment feed added to your newsreader (a program that brings entry streams from many blogs to one window), you can check for responses to your comment quite easily, as part of your daily reading. But comment feeds are rare. WordPress, covered in Chapter 10, offers them. But using WordPress doesn't help you; other bloggers must be using software that offers comment feeds, and not many do.

TrackBack specifics

Let's return to Blogger A and Blogger B, shortly after Blogger A posted his "How to save the world" entry. We know about the conversation spawned from that entry, but we haven't seen exactly how it was accomplished. The specific actions of the two bloggers are the final pieces of the TrackBack puzzle that clarify how it works.

In the sidebar titled "The availability of TrackBacks," I mention that both bloggers must be using a blog program or blog service that supports the TrackBack feature. By this I mean each program or service must enable the display of TrackBacks (that would be Blog A in our example) and the planting of TrackBacks (that would be Blog B). Blog B takes the step of planting the TrackBack, which then appears on Blog A; both blogs must be TrackBack-enabled. Any blog in which you can plant a TrackBack can also display them, and vice versa; there is no such thing as a blog program or service that can travel only one direction of the TrackBack street.

Now, here's what happens with the details filled in:

1. Blogger A posts a remarkable entry called "How to save the world." His blog automatically posts the entry, establishes space below it for incoming TrackBack listings and comments, and posts a *TrackBack URL*. (A URL is a Web page address.)

2. Blogger B sees Blogger A's excellent entry and wants to promote it on his blog, while also commenting on it and notifying Blogger A that he has done so. Blogger B decides to write an entry on Blog B and plant a TrackBack.

3. Blogger B copies the TrackBack URL from the entry page on Blog A. He could jot it down on a piece of paper, but instead he sensibly highlights it and uses Ctrl+C to copy the address into the Windows clipboard.

4. On Blog B, Blogger B brings up the Compose Entry screen of his blog program or service. Before writing his entry, Blogger B pastes the TrackBack URL into a special field (a box into which something can be typed or pasted) for TrackBack URLs. He uses the Windows keyboard command Ctrl+V to paste the TrackBack URL.

5. Next, Blogger B writes his entry and titles it "Does the world need saving?" In this entry, Blogger B embeds a link citation to the "How to save the world" entry page in Blog A. Blogger B copies and pastes the page URL in the same way that he did the TrackBack URL. The TrackBack URL and page URL *are different.* It is important to realize and remember this last fact.

6. Blogger B posts the "Does the world need saving?" entry. Immediately and invisibly, Blog B uses the TrackBack URL to *ping* (communicate with) Blog A.

7. Blogger B's TrackBack is listed on Blog A, below the "How to save the world" entry. The TrackBack contains a line or two of the "Does the world need saving?" entry, plus a link to that entry.

Many people are confused by the fact that the TrackBack URL *is not* the address of the entry page on Blog A. When that confusion exists, bloggers attempting to plant a TrackBack make one of two mistakes:

✔ Using the TrackBack URL as a live link in their entry text

✔ Using the page URL in the TrackBack field

Oops. The TrackBack URL must be placed in the special TrackBack field, and the page address (of Blog A) displayed in the browser's destination bar should be used for the link inside Blog B's entry.

Remember, none of this is possible in blogs that do not have the TrackBack feature. This, too, is a common confusion. New bloggers spend hours trying to make a TrackBack happen by copying and pasting the TrackBack URL everywhere they can. TrackBack is a specific software *protocol,* and if your blog platform doesn't use it, you can neither create nor display TrackBacks.

The blight of spam

If you use e-mail, you know about spam, or junk mail. Actually, spam is more than just unwanted advertisements for sex-enhancing drugs in your Inbox. Spam is a broad term for any intrusive and irrelevant commercial placed anywhere online. In blogs, spam rears its hideous head mostly in comments and in TrackBacks.

As with e-mail spam, comment spammers and TrackBack spammers are amazingly sophisticated. The best and most prolific of them use automated software that rips through blogs polluting their pages with irrelevant and sometimes disgusting notices. Fighting spam is a significant part of any blogger's lifestyle, if that person's blog exists outside a social network. (Social networks can protect their members from spam to a certain extent.) The problem reaches desperate proportions at major blogs, where substantial resources are deployed mounting technology to thwart spambots — and those solutions almost never work perfectly. Many high-profile blogs hopelessly switch off their comments and TrackBack fields, which is a loss to the blogosphere.

Extreme pessimists say that TrackBack has been killed by spam and comments have been assassinated too. But average folks engaging in casual, avocational blogging are not nearly as troubled by what is often a minor and occasional nuisance.

Obsessing with Blog Search Engines

TrackBacks serve a few purposes. First, they assist the blogosphere's macrologue, or blog-to-blog dialogue. Second, they offer a promotional tool for the blogger who places a TrackBack link on another blog (it's Blogger B in the preceding example who benefits promotionally). Third, they furnish content to the blog upon which they appear (Blog A in the preceding examples) and let all visitors know that the blog entry is important and discussion-worthy. Like ripples on a pond, TrackBacks spread the macrologue outward.

Whether or not they have TrackBacks enabled on their blogs, many bloggers track their influence on the blogosphere in another way, by checking Weblog search engines. Did I say checking? I should have said obsessing over — in some cases, anyway. Bloggers caught up in the quest for influence and reputation spend altogether too much of their time tracking their words in blog-specific engines. What makes these engines so beguiling is their dedicated focus on blog entries and their ability to unearth who is talking about whom. In this regard, blog-specific engines are like giant TrackBack machines, allowing users to find citations to their blog entries.

Generic search engines such as Google and Yahoo! also index blog entries, which turn up mixed into their search results. In fact, one might argue that Google and Yahoo! do a better job finding blog content than the blog-specific engines do. That's not exactly true, but it is true that the big engines do a better job organizing and ranking search results, eliminating poor results or shoving them out of sight. The problem with using Google or Yahoo! to find blog citations is that blog results are mixed in with all the other Web results, and there is no way to break them out onto their own results page. Many a blogger has called for Google or Yahoo! to set up a blog-specific engine that would benefit from the excellent algorithms and ranking systems that govern their general search results.

The easiest and most common way to examine one's own influence in the blogosphere as reflected in a blog search engine is to enter the URL of an entry page into the engine. It's a simple process, and here are the steps using the BlogPulse engine as an example:

1. **Bring up an entry page in your blog.**

   Ideally, this entry should be an important one and perhaps one that has received some comments.

2. **Copy the page URL.**

   The page URL appears in your browser's destination bar. Highlight it and use Ctrl+C.

3. **Go to BlogPulse.**

   The address is `www.blogpulse.com`. (See Figure 3-5.)

Figure 3-5:
The home page of BlogPulse, a blog search engine.

4. **Click once in the keyword box below the Search the Blogosphere banner.**

   Clicking once in that box clears it; then it is ready to receive your page URL.

5. **Paste your page URL in the keyword box.**

   Use Ctrl+V to paste.

6. **Click the Go button.**

The most disappointing result of this search is no results. That means that no other blog has cited your blog entry — at least, no other blog searched by BlogPulse during the time since you posted the entry. Although most blog search engines claim lightning-quick search cycles, it doesn't always seem that way. Allow a full day since your post before assuming the engine has crawled the blogosphere. Remember, too, that although bloggers move fast to stay current, many citations are two, three, or more days behind the post they are citing. So if your search results are unsatisfying, try again tomorrow.

Next up are a few of the most-used blog search engines. Quality of results varies hugely from engine to engine and from search to search. For a long time, Technorati ruled the blog-search business; it still enjoys loyalty, but many bloggers have become frustrated by chaotic search results and have moved on. Most blog search engines are portals of blog information that offer more than just pure search. Poke around BlogPulse for some interesting and innovative presentations of blogosphere activity. And when you are purely searching, remember that you can enter plain keywords into the search box; you don't have to enter a URL.

Following are four major blog engines:

- **Technorati (www.technorati.com):** The godfather of blog searching, Technorati indexes a database of about 16 million blogs, as of this writing. Older entries are harder to find than newer ones; if an entry no longer resides on the blog's index page (because newer entries have pushed it off), that entry's status is reduced in Technorati's index ranking. (Figure 3-6 shows Technorati search results.)

- **Feedster (www.feedster.com):** With the tagline, "Who's linking to whom," Feedster is perfect for blogosphere addicts. Fast, with extremely useful results, Feedster enjoys a loyal following. Click Links for a dedicated URL-citation lookup.

- **BlogPulse (www.blogpulse.com):** BlogPulse is spectacularly imaginative when measuring the blog universe and is worth visiting even if you are not searching. When you are searching, keep in mind that the index contains nothing older than six months.

Figure 3-6:
Technorati
displays
search
results for
the URL of a
blog entry;
each result
cites that
page.

> ✔ **Bloglines (www.bloglines.com):** One of the foremost Web-based RSS
> newsreaders (see Chapter 13), Bloglines also functions as a major
> searching destination. Owning perhaps the deepest archive of any blog
> engine, Bloglines never throws anything out. However, it crawls only
> blogs whose RSS feeds are subscribed to by at least one Bloglines user.
> That means that if a quality blog, read devotedly by many people, does
> not happen to have an RSS subscriber using the Bloglines newsreader,
> that blog is not crawled or indexed by the Bloglines search engine.

Promoting Your Content

Participating in the blogosphere's macrologue, by writing comments and
planting TrackBacks, is the most organic way to promote your blog. These
techniques do not promote gratuitously or purely for selfish gain. Instead,
promotion is garnered by virtue of worthy discourse. If you have things of
value to say, people start visiting and subscribing to your feeds. Continued
participation in the blogosphere discussion is important to maintaining a
high profile.

You can promote individual blog entries also in more direct ways. As I mention in Chapter 14, flagrantly promoting your entries on other blogs, either with comments or irrelevant TrackBacks, is inadvisable. Doing so merely ruins reputations and repels visitors. Don't put a link to your blog entry in a comment on somebody else's blog, unless you've written a whopping, brilliant comment that justifies citing your own work. Even if you are whopping and brilliant, the tactic is off-putting.

The next two sections describe sites at which entry-specific promotions are appropriate.

Digging for traffic

Digg (www.digg.com) is an experiment in collaboratively filtering Web content. Stop rolling your eyes; I'll explain. *Collaborative filtering* is a way of finding high quality through group intelligence. The theory is that mobs are smart even if the taste and intelligence of individuals vary. Get enough people to vote Yes or No about something, and the cream rises to the top. (Unsatisfied election voters disagree, of course.)

Digg invites users to submit Web pages, which get categorized and put on long lists. Those lists continually have new pages added to them. When submitting, you can add a short comment or summary of the page. New items stay on the first page of the list until they get pushed to later pages by the continual influx of newer items. Once pushed off, an item's visibility diminishes. At any time during this marching process, Digg visitors can click through to the item's page (or not), and "digg" the item by clicking a special link. A tally is kept of the number of times the item is "dugg." After a certain threshold is reached, that item is moved to Digg's home page (see Figure 3-7), where it receives tremendously more visibility. Front-page Digg items generate tons of traffic to their pages.

Some bloggers submit every single one of their entries to Digg, hoping for the one that clicks hard and delivers throngs of visitors. (Remember from Chapter 1 that each blog entry resides on a separate page with its own URL.) Even a modestly dugg item can generate substantial traffic. There is not a one-to-one correspondence of diggs (votes for the item) and visits to the item's page; to the contrary, it is nearly inevitable that the item's page receives much more traffic than reflected in the "dugg" number.

Here again, in Digg as on a blog, some discretion is advisable. Digg users can comment on any submitted item, and if the item is lame by the Digg standard of cool, the submitter is likely to get flamed. Because everyone's submissions are collected onto a single page, it's quite possible to ruin your reputation by making trivial submissions that waste time and Digg space. Digg's purpose is to showcase the best of the best; it is everyone's responsibility to focus on quality whether voting or submitting.

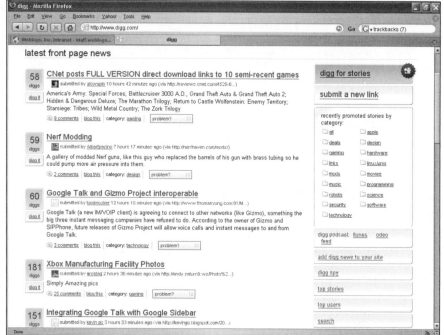

Figure 3-7: Digg showcases popular Web pages, including blog pages, as determined by site users.

Del.icio.us links

Del.icio.us (the URL is `del.icio.us`) is not only the most difficult-to-type Web address in history but also a popular social tagging site. *Tagging* is a way of organizing many items into categories such that each item can inhabit many categories. Instead of creating categories like boxes, and dumping items into those boxes, tagging starts with the item and assigns it several (or just one) descriptive tags. Visitors to a tagging site can click any descriptive tag to see all items that have been assigned that tag.

As a voting system, Del.icio.us is not as organized as Digg (described in the preceding section). But Del.icio.us preceded Digg and has a strong following. Instead of submitting items (Web pages or blog entries) for group voting, in del.icio.us, you keep a personal store of favorite pages (actually links to pages), each of which is tagged. Del.icio.us provides a *bookmarklet* (a button for your browser) that lets you save any page you visit with a single click. Once saved and tagged, a page becomes publicly viewable in the del.icio.us site. Others might click through to your saved page and save it themselves in their own del.icio.us cubbyholes. Each saved page displays the number of times it has been saved by the entire community (see Figure 3-8). As in Digg, success breeds success; most people are more curious about popular pages than unpopular pages. The result of a popularly saved page is lots of traffic to that page.

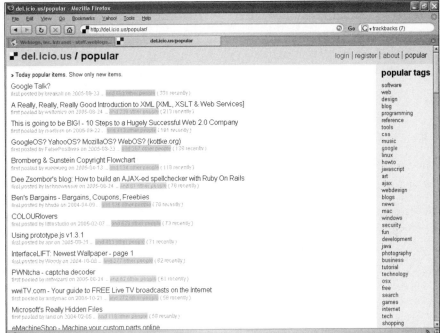

Figure 3-8:
Del.icio.us
uses group
saving and
tagging to
determine
page
popularity.

With no comment system to discourage poor submissions, as in Digg, nothing stops bloggers from saving their entries — perhaps even all their entries. I don't encourage obsessive promotion of this sort, though; you'd end up spending more time promoting entries than writing them.

Part II
Starting a Blog Today

The 5th Wave By Rich Tennant

"You want to know why I'm mad? I suggest you read my latest blog post titled, 'Why an Obsessive Control-Freak Husband Should Never Pick Out Bathroom Tile Without Asking His Wife First'."

In this part . . .

This collection of chapters puts you on the fast track to your new blog. That's not to say the fast track is the best track. You must decide if the quick-and-easy services represented in these pages are right for you, or if the more elaborate, powerful, and difficult blog programs described in Part III are in your destiny.

Chapters 4 and 5 cover two social networks (MSN Spaces and Yahoo! 360, respectively), which combine blogging with other community features. Chapter 6 moves on to Blogger.com, a popular service for first-timers. The blogs offered there are easy to set up but lack some features found elsewhere. Chapter 7 examines TypePad, a paid service that provides a generous suite of blogging tools.

It makes sense to look at the chapters of Part II before signing up anywhere. But if you do sign up quickly at one of these services, the corresponding chapter will help you make the most of it.

Chapter 4

MSN Spaces

● ●

In This Chapter

▶ Discovering the ease and beauty of MSN Spaces

▶ Making your space your own

▶ Basic blogging in MSN Spaces

▶ Adding pictures and creating photo albums

▶ Recapping the MSN Spaces experience

● ●

Social networks are fun and communal and easy, and the full-tilt development of these sites has improved them tremendously since the old days of laborious site-building. Personality and sharing are the foundation stones of social networks. These free services are not exclusively about blogging, or even primarily about blogging in some cases, but the services covered in this chapter and the next do include fairly robust blogs. For casual bloggers who have no interest in speed bumps or learning curves, fairly robust blogs are plenty robust enough.

Perhaps I'm underselling the blog experience here. MSN Spaces, described in this chapter, and Yahoo! 360 (Chapter 5), each delivers the basic tools you need to put up a blog, update it as frequently as you like, show it to your friends everywhere, syndicate your entries with feeds (see Chapter 13 for more on feeds), and include photographs. In addition to the blogs, social networks encourage sharing details about yourself, your interests, your experiences, and your life. Social networks love lists, and they want you to love them, too: lists of your favorite music, favorite books, favorite Web sites. Through lists we shall become a big family; that's the idea here.

Because of their intense personal quality, social network blogging is all about *you*. Of course, you can write an online personal diary on any blog platform, but social networks tromp on more impersonal services when it comes to presenting a high-personality site. As a result, most social network bloggers are casual and informal about blogging — unlike the dead-serious and high-powered topical bloggers that tend to gather at TypePad, WordPress, Movable Type, and Radio UserLand. (But as I repeat throughout this book: You can create any type of blog with any type of blog service. No restrictions.)

In exchange for ease, social networks trade power. Every one of them sacrifices some feature that a loyal user of the fancier programs takes for granted. In this chapter and the next, I touch on four important areas:

- ✔ **Customization:** How easy is it to personalize the social network space with custom colors, layouts, lists, and other content? How much variety and distinctiveness are possible?

- ✔ **Blogging:** How complete are the blogging tools? How effortless is it to write and post an entry?

- ✔ **Features:** What distinguishes one social network from the other, and from other blogging alternatives? Whether in the blog section or in other tools, every social network provides features that set it apart.

- ✔ **Ease:** Perhaps most importantly, how simple is it to sign up, launch your site, and play with your site every day?

These four considerations are brought to two of the most popular blog-oriented social networks: MSN Spaces and Yahoo! 360.

MSN Spaces Overview

MSN Spaces is Microsoft's contribution to social networking and blogging. *MSN* (which stands for Microsoft Network) contains the company's extensive suite of interactive Web sites and its dial-up home Internet service. The home page of MSN Spaces is located here:

```
spaces.msn.com
```

Starting on that page, click the Sign Up button and follow the instructions for establishing your own space. Figure 4-1 illustrates a newly created space before it is touched by eager hands ready to customize and post blog entries. Note the ad at the top; that advertisement (or others like it) is there to stay. MSN Spaces is free to you; the price you pay is to display ads for Microsoft.

MSN Spaces has an international flavor thanks to Microsoft's global marketing. There's lots of youth in Spaces, but this is not a kids' service or a teen hangout. Spaces is also a colorful service, thanks to the many bold themes available. (An MSN Spaces *theme* is a color design.)

After a more-tedious-than-average sign-up process, MSN Spaces becomes easy to use and extremely gratifying. Some aspects of the service — especially uploading and displaying pictures — are impressively well designed and blessedly easy to use.

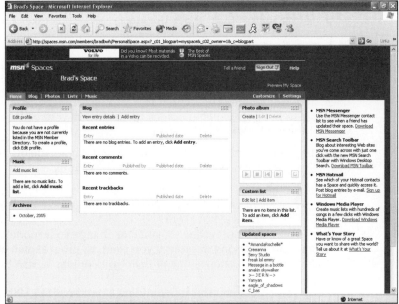

Figure 4-1:
A newly minted MSN Spaces site, ready to be personalized.

The best and most innovative features of MSN Spaces kick in for users of the Internet Explorer (IE) browser, version 6. (Click the Help menu and select About Internet Explorer to determine which version you have. Upgrading the browser is free.) Firefox is the browser of choice in this book; nearly all the screen illustrations show Firefox. In many cases, when reviewing online services, I react harshly when the user is pushed into using IE. In this case, I recommend IE for the incredible ease and usability it brings to MSN Spaces. MSN Spaces doesn't stop you from using another browser, but the experience is not remotely as pleasurable. Therefore, Internet Explorer is the default browser for this section of the book; all the examples and instructions assume that you are using IE.

Customizing Your MSN Space

Before blogging, you might want to customize your space. If you're like me, you'll have trouble keeping your hands off the slick drop-down and click-and-drag goodness of the customization tools. Don't even think about looking at page code, seeking hidden menus, or jumping through exotic hoops as in some other blog services. MSN's customization tools are things of beauty and a delight to use.

Designing your page

In MSN Spaces, you customize your space in three basic ways:

- **Choosing modules:** Modules contain your blog roll and other lists, links to your photo albums, blog archives, your profile summary, the blog itself, and other chunks of content that can be arranged on your page. You choose not only which modules to display on your page, but also where they are located on the page.

- **Choosing a layout:** MSN Spaces offers six page layouts using one, two, or three columns. Your modules go in those columns.

- **Choosing a theme:** Themes are color schemes. At the time of this writing, MSN Spaces offered 81 interchangeable themes.

MSN Spaces is built to be played with; you can change your modules, layout, theme, and module positions whenever you want, as often as you want. Flexible and fun customization is one of the strong points in MSN Spaces.

The following steps walk you through building a personalized MSN space:

1. **Go to your MSN space site.** Your new MSN space is located at a URL like this: spaces.msn.com/members/*your-space-name*.

2. **If you are not in Edit mode, click the <u>Edit Your Space</u> link.**

   Your MSN space has two modes: Edit and Preview. A link just above Customize lets you toggle between them. When in Edit mode, the link reads <u>Preview My Space</u>. When Previewing, the link reads <u>Edit Your Space</u>. In Preview mode, you see the site just as visitors see it, with no editing controls, except for the <u>Edit Your Space</u> link, which gives you back your blogging and customizing controls. This easy switch is powerfully convenient — and should be imitated by other services.

3. **Click Customize.**

4. **Click the Layout tab, and then click a layout to select it.**

   A drop-down menu (see Figure 4-2) displays the available column layouts available for your space.

5. **Click the Modules tab, and then click a module to add or remove it.**

   Your space is equipped with default modules, but you can remove them or add others.

6. **Click the Themes tab, and then click any theme to select it.**

   Figure 4-3 illustrates the drop-down menu of Themes. Remember that there are two pages of themes — maybe more by the time you read this. To see the second page, click 2.

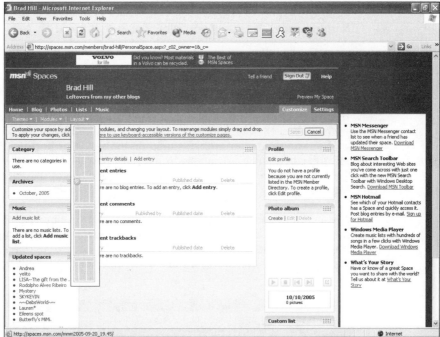

Figure 4-2:
Select a
page layout
from the
drop-down
menu.

Figure 4-3:
Select a
theme for
your space
from two
pages of
colorful
choices.

7. Click the Save button.

Nothing is locked in until you click that Save button.

8. Click the <u>Preview My Space</u> link to see what your page looks like without any editing controls visible.

This view is how your space looks to visitors.

Now that you've added some modules to your page, you should try repositioning them. You can put your blog module in the middle of the page or in a sidebar. You can drag your archives module to the top or bottom of its column. You can, in fact, arrange your modules any way that suits your fancy. No other blog service covered in this book comes close to the ease of page building provided by MSN Spaces. You simply must try it.

To move a module around on the page (see Figure 4-4), simply grab the top of it with your mouse cursor (click with the mouse and hold down the button) and drag it (move the mouse). Throw it across the page from one sidebar to another. Bury it at the bottom of a stack of modules or highlight it near the top.

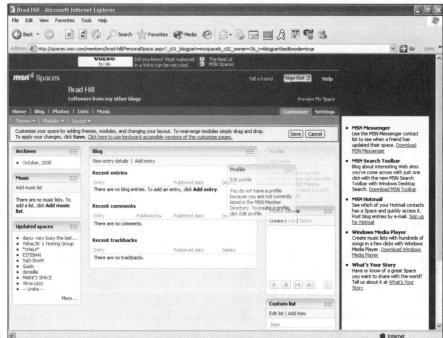

Figure 4-4:
The Profile
module
is being
dragged
across the
page.

You must click the Save button to lock in the new positions of your moved modules. Also, you must use the Internet Explorer browser to drag modules.

Module placement is tied to your layout choice. If you're unsatisfied with how your modules look no matter how much you drag them around, try starting fresh with a new layout.

Making other space settings

Click Settings (next to Customize) to see several groups of settings that affect your space and your blog:

- Space Settings is the page where you set your space's title and description.

- Blog Settings is where you decide how many entries appear on the first page (every entry also gets its own page) and whether comments are allowed on entry pages.

- Permissions is where you make the blog public or private.

- E-mail publishing is where you determine settings that enable you to post a blog entry from any e-mail account. Many more sophisticated blog services allow this type of remote posting; bravo to MSN for putting it in.

- Storage keeps track of how much of your allotted memory your pictures are taking up. More on pictures later in this chapter. Each MSN space gets 30 megabytes of storage.

- Statistics reveals measurements to your space and shows which pages have been visited.

Blogging in MSN Spaces

Writing blog entries in MSN Spaces is straightforward and painless.

1. **In your blog module, click Add entry.**

2. **In the Title box, enter an entry title.**

3. **Compose your entry, adding any formatting you want.**

   The formatting controls resemble those in many e-mail services, some instant message programs, and Word and other writing programs. (See Figure 4-5.) Click the Paragraph, Font Style, and Font Size menus to see those choices. Run your mouse cursor over the icons to see their functions. The Insert Search Link feature creates a link to MSN Search, using the highlighted word (or words) as the search query.

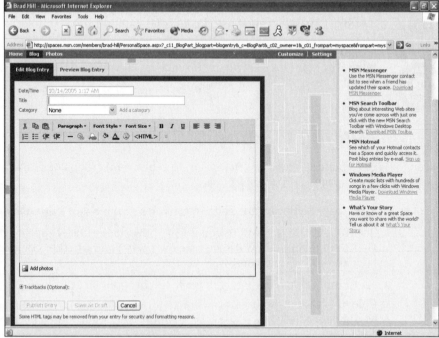

Figure 4-5:
Writing a
blog entry
in MSN
Spaces is
like writing
an e-mail.

4. Assign a category to the post.

This step is optional. Either choose from the drop-down menu of preset categories or use the <u>Add a category</u> link to create one. Categories help sort your blog entries and become useful when you have many posts. It's a good idea to start using categories early if you are going to use them eventually.

5. Click the Publish Entry button.

You can save entries in progress for later completion with the Save as Draft button.

Note that TrackBacks are allowed in MSN Spaces. See my detailed description of TrackBacks in Chapter 3. The short explanation is this: TrackBacks let you refer to somebody else's blog entry and leave a link to your post on the other person's blog. To use the feature here, click the small button next to TrackBacks (Optional) and then enter the TrackBack URL from the other person's blog.

As you compose your entry, use the Preview Blog Entry tab to see what your formatting choices look like. On the other hand, if you don't use the formatting icons, there's not much point is previewing the post.

Note: Unlike some other blog services, you cannot pre-date or post-date entries. Manipulating the date is a feature not often found in social networks.

Editing and deleting blog entries are common tasks, and MSN makes them more accessible than many competing networks. Click the X corresponding to any blog entry in your blog module (when in Edit mode) to delete the entry. Click any entry title to edit that entry. Your blog module must be positioned in a wide column (as in Figure 4-6) to see entry titles and the corresponding deletion Xs.

Sharing Photos in MSN Spaces

You can probably tell that I like MSN Spaces. But the best is yet to come. MSN has fabulous photo features. Fast, friendly, fabulous photo features. This service makes it unusually easy to upload, display, and even touch up your digital photos. Pictures are automatically compressed — which would be a "so what?" fact except that the compression helps you fit more pictures in your allotted space. You can create as many photo albums as you like. The Photo Upload Control tool streamlines the addition of multiple photos like you wouldn't believe. And in the end, your photos are presented on your Spaces page as a slide show.

Figure 4-6:
When in edit mode, your full blog entries are hidden to reveal editing links and delete controls.

The individual features I rave over are not unique to MSN Spaces; other services allow photo albums, provide upload tools, and display slide shows. But total packages as delightful as this one are rare. If photo sharing is a priority for you, you're going to like this.

You don't have to use the MSN Photo Upload Control uploading tool, but I recommend it. The following steps walk you through installing it (could hardly be easier) and starting to use it for all uploading to MSN Spaces:

1. **In the Photo album module, click Create.**

2. **Enter an album title.**

   The default title is the date. Highlight that title and type over it. Unless, of course, you want the photo album's title to be the date it was created.

3. **Click the <u>Add photos</u> link.**

   A window pops open, offering something called MSN Photo Upload Control. Could no one think of a less intimidating name for this thing? Sheesh. Still, it's a great little program.

4. **Click the Install Now button.**

5. **If a verification pop-up appears, click its Install button.**

   The installation is fully automatic and takes less than ten seconds over a high-speed connection. Figure 4-7 shows the Photo Upload Control immediately after installation, awaiting your instructions.

Figure 4-7:
The Photo
Upload
Control
program
immediately
after being
installed.

6. **In the Photo Upload Control window, select a photo album from the left sidebar.**

   The left pane of the uploading window shows your computer's folders. The interface is the same as in Windows Explorer. Click your way to a folder containing pictures that you'd like to include in your Spaces photo album. The pictures in that folder display in the main upload pane.

7. **Run your mouse cursor over any picture to see the option icons.**

   Photo Upload Control lets you perform basic editing tasks on a picture, such as brightening it, increasing the contrast, and rotating it. (See Figure 4-8.) Clicking the center icon brings up the editing controls, as shown in Figure 4-9. Click the View Thumbnails button to return to the folder view.

Figure 4-8:
Roll your mouse over a photo to reveal the rotation controls and a link to more editing controls.

Figure 4-9:
You can brighten, darken, and alter the contrast as well as perform other photo edits before uploading.

8. **Click the pictures you want included in the photo album.**

   Click Select All to tag all pictures in the folder for upload. Selected pictures are checked in the upper-left corner. Click again to deselect any picture.

9. **Click the Upload Now button.**

   MSN Spaces automatically compresses your photos (leaving them unchanged in your computer) and uploads them to your new album. The Photo Upload Control window disappears and your browser reappears, displaying the newly created album in edit mode. (See Figure 4-10.)

10. **If you want to retitle any photo, click its caption and type a new title.**

    You can also rename the album.

    Renaming a picture in the Add Photos window does not rename the photo's file name in your computer. You can have two names for any photo: one in your computer, and one in your MSN Space photo album.

11. **Click the Save and Close button.**

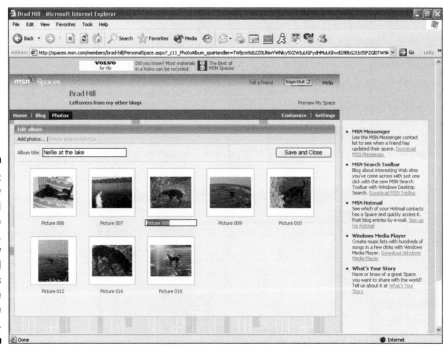

Figure 4-10:
A newly uploaded photo album. Rename any individual pictures before saving the album.

After creating a photo album, you might want to rearrange your modules or even choose a new layout style. The reason for this consideration is that the photo album module contains a fancy and effective slide-show control that invites your visitors to browse through your photos right on your main page. They can click through to a full-page presentation of the photo album, but a large, prominent photo album module is a convenience to your visitors and is great to look at. Try using a layout with wide sidebars and putting the album in one of them. Just a thought. Figure 4-11 shows a page design that puts the Photo album module in a wide main column and shoves the blog into a sidebar. That's a dramatic example of showcasing the photo module. As you can see, narrow blog modules show not full entries but links to entries.

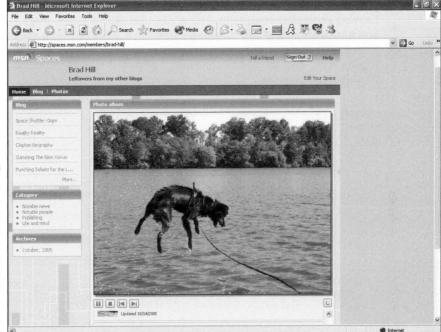

Figure 4-11: A whopping-big photo album module shoves the blog module to a narrow sidebar. It's a look.

MSN Spaces Recap

MSN Spaces is a mix of careful, thought-out design and restrictive demands on the user and visitor. Well, one restrictive demand, which is the required use of Internet Explorer to access and view the best parts of the Spaces service. Not only are module dragging and the Photo Upload Control tool unavailable in other browsers, but your visitors do not see photo slide shows in other browsers. So for Spaces to come alive, you and your visitors need to use IE. You might prefer IE anyway, but the results you get with it are not necessarily visible to your viewers. This dichotomy reveals the underside of Internet site design: What you think you're showing people might not be what they're seeing.

Leaving aside that complaint, I must say that MSN Spaces offers an effortless and fun site-building and blogging experience. MSN has hit a sweet spot combining serious tools and entertainment value. The results are attractive in any browser, and anybody can create a personal statement in Spaces that can be shown off proudly.

Chapter 5

Yahoo! 360

Yahoo! 360 was started in March 2005 as a blog and community site with a few unusual and interesting innovations. Yahoo! is a gigantic suite of Web sites, online communities, and services. It's hard to imagine anyone being online for one year (or one month) and not touching the Yahoo! empire, even inadvertently. Yahoo! publishes news, hosts Web sites, runs auctions and personal-ad services, stores photos, was the Web's first major directory and is still one of the three most important search engines, operates music services enjoyed by millions, hosts a gigantic online chatting platform, is one of the world's largest e-mail providers, and has the world's most popular personalized home page service. The Yahoo! domain (`yahoo.com`) is consistently — month after month, year after year — the first or second most-visited Internet destination.

There's a reason I'm promoting Yahoo!'s resumé. The beauty of Yahoo! 360 is that it ties together some parts of the Yahoo! platform and throws them onto your page with little effort on your part. That means if you have ever uploaded pictures to Yahoo! Photos (`photos.yahoo.com`) or to Flickr (a photo-sharing site owned by Yahoo!), you can put those photos on your Yahoo! 360 page with a click or two — no further uploading. If you have ever written a review of a restaurant in Yahoo! Local (`local.yahoo.com`), you can easily have that review displayed on your 360 page.

This type of integration, or bundling — easily making your Yahoo! stuff appear on your 360 page — is just beginning, and will get more developed, with more options, over time. Yahoo! 360 is already nicely integrated with Yahoo! Messenger, the instant messaging program. That means you can see which of your 360 friends is online at any moment. If you use Yahoo! Groups — another social network that does not include blogging — you can post messages to your groups from your 360 page.

Yahoo! 360 is neither pretty nor ugly. It is plain; the focus is more on smooth functionality than on dazzling appearance. Just before this book was finished, Yahoo! added color schemes called Themes to 360, but I didn't see many people using them. Perhaps too much time had gone by without theme choices, and inertia had set in. Anyway, you can change colors but not the layout style, so Yahoo! 360 pages look similar, one to another, except for the content loaded into those spaces. That content is a mix of what you write and your photos.

Getting Started in 360

Yahoo! 360 is a free service available to anybody with a Yahoo! ID. If you don't have a Yahoo! ID, stand in the corner. Then, abashed, return to the computer and get yourself a Yahoo! ID. Simply go to the Yahoo! 360 home page:

```
360.yahoo.com
```

There, click the Sign Up link, fill in the boxes on the next page, and click the I Agree button.

Me-centric, Not We-centric

That is how one observer described Yahoo! 360 soon after it opened. All social networks give you your own space, but they are about the whole membership. Yahoo! 360 is more about you, and it gives you ways of reaching tentacles into the membership. The best example of the me-centric approach is the navigation bar that stretches across the top-right of your 360 space. No matter how many times you click away from your own page — to a friend, then to that friend's friend, then onward to the pages of strangers and their friends — that navigation bar remains in place, keeping you one click away from your own space. When you click away you're not really traveling outward in a straight line; you're traveling in a tight circle around your home base. That is me-centric.

Home page and My Page

I joined Yahoo! 360 when it first opened and was immediately confused by one little point. I hope to spare you the same confusion by straightening it out here. The potential confusion exists between two pages in your 360 space: Home and My Page.

Home is a page that only you can see. It gives you quick links for adding photos, composing a blog entry, and inviting a new friend. More important, Home is the page upon which your friends' additions appear. New stuff from your friends gets pushed to your Home page. Your new stuff gets pushed to the Home pages of your friends.

My Page is how other people see you in Yahoo! 360. Other people can also see your blog page and friends page and other pages, but My Page is your summary of yourself to the public. My Page contains everything you have created and want to share: photos, lists, and the start of your most recent blog entry.

Here's a tip. Use the drop-down menu on My Page labeled Preview as Seen By to display My Page as it is seen by different groups: everyone, friends, friends of friends, certain categories of friends, and so on. Because you can assign content blocks as visible or invisible to different groups and categories, My Page alters depending on who is looking at it. The Preview menu is a great way to see you as others see you. Click the Go back to Edit My Page link (on the left side of My Page) to return to edit mode.

There is more to the me-centricity of Yahoo! 360. The service specializes in keeping you in touch with your circle of friends. When you put a new piece of content in your space — a blog entry, let's say — Yahoo! 360 can *push* that new piece onto the pages of your friends. This feature might seem pushy . . . well, it is pushy, but pushy in a good way. Everyone involved has agreed to this, and it's an enjoyable, essential part of the 360 experience. This pushy system provides effortless contact among circles of friends. You can even fine-tune who sees what by categorizing your friends and restricting certain contributions to specific categories. Conversely, you can broaden your reach by assigning new blog entries to the pages of friends and *their* friends.

Because circles of friends, with you in the center, are so important, Yahoo! 360 relies on an invitation system. Yahoo! is less concerned with mashing strangers together than with making connections easier for already existing friendships. Click the Invite link in the navigation bar to view the invitation page (see Figure 5-1), where Yahoo! makes it easy to bulk-invite your existing friends from the Yahoo! Address book and Yahoo! Messenger.

Friends exist in 360 as overlapping public circles. Everyone can see anyone else's friends and the pictures they have (optionally) uploaded to represent themselves. (See Figure 5-2.) A portion of large friend circles appears in the right sidebar of any member's page. You can focus on any member from a friend list, seeing that person's page and issuing an invitation to join each other's circles.

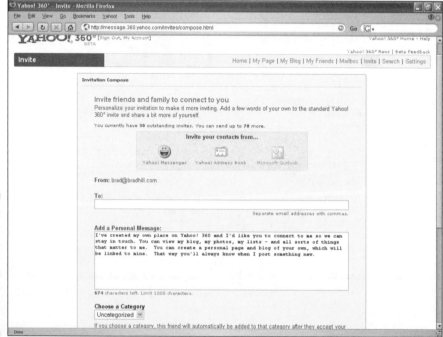

Figure 5-1:
Use this page to send invitations to a friend or a group of contacts.

Figure 5-2:
Yahoo! 360
is built on
groups of
friends;
everyone
can see
other
members'
friends.

The Yahoo! 360 Page

The main page elements of Yahoo! 360, like those in MSN Spaces (see Chapter 4), are customized content modules (though they aren't called that in 360 and can't be dragged around the page as in Spaces). There are five main chunks of content, and a few others that dedicated users enjoy discovering. The five big items are these:

✔ **Blog:** Naturally, your 360 blog is a major portion of your 360 space.

✔ **Blast:** This fun feature is a short bit of text, perhaps an announcement or a famous quote, that gets "blasted" to your friends' pages. The blast is meant to be the briefest and most transient of your sharings. (See Figure 5-3.) When I get into the mood, I offer an inspirational short quote in the blast and change it daily. I lose my momentum after a while, then later start it up again.

✔ **Photos:** You can add a photo to a blog entry, though the formatting of photos in entries is not flexible. You can also share photos uploaded to Yahoo! Photos or Flickr. Both those services are free to use (Flickr offers a premium account that cost $25 a year at this writing).

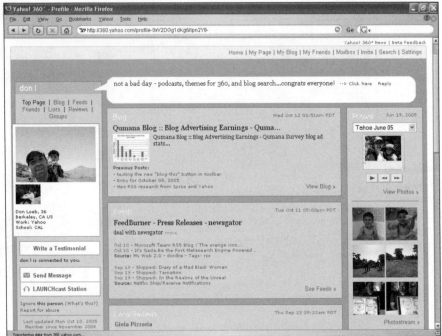

Figure 5-3:
A Yahoo!
360 blast
floats above
a member's
page.

✔ **Friends:** It might seem silly or insulting to think of your friends as "content," but because everybody's list is public, checking on the friends of friends is part of 360's appeal.

✔ **Lists:** Like most social networks, Yahoo! 360 encourages the creation of lists, such as lists of books, movies, and music. List items are linked to everyone else who shares that item. For example, I put kayaking and dogs as two of my interests (even though my dog won't get into my kayak, making it hard to blend those interests). Each item links to a grand list of other Yahoo! 360 members interested in that item (see Figure 5-4). That list is a search result, and the page includes tools for narrowing the search by member age and proximity to your location. You can determine who sees each of your lists: friends, friends plus their friends, friends plus their friends plus *their* friends, or just you. It's kind of like mingling at a party.

Blogging in 360

Writing a blog entry in Yahoo! 360 benefits from one of the simplest and most reassuring interfaces around. (See Figure 5-5.) The title box is filled in for you with the current date, but you can change that by highlighting it and typing over it.

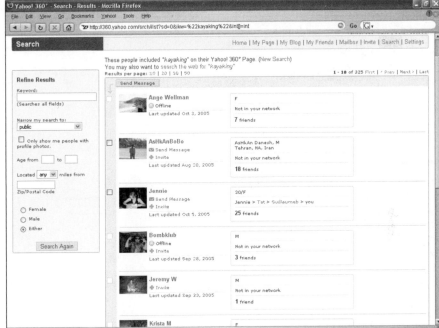

Figure 5-4:
Click any
interest to
find out who
else is
interested in
that topic.
Then
narrow the
search on
the left.

Use the Browse button to upload a picture to include in your entry. Only one picture is allowed per entry, and you have no control over its position, which is atop the written portion of the entry. (See Figure 5-6.) The photo uploaded to your entry is also compressed and might come out smaller than the original in your computer. Nothing you can do about that, either. Before posting, click the Preview button to see what your entry will look like.

Blogging in Yahoo! 360 is ridiculously easy. Casting my mind over the range of programs and services profiled in this book, I think Yahoo! 360 would get the award for easiest blog tool or perhaps share that distinction with Blogger.com. Yahoo! 360 doesn't offer the range of features that Blogger does, which makes 360 either undesirable or preferable, depending on your need for simplicity.

When my mother surprised me by expressing her interest in starting a blog, I nudged her toward Yahoo! 360, thinking it would provide the most hassle-free on-ramp to the blogosphere. I'm happy to report that she is still at it, writing a gem of a nature blog called "Out There," shown in Figure 5-7.

Figure 5-5:
Yahoo!
360 makes
blogging
straightfor-
ward, with
few compl-
ications or
enhance-
ments.

Figure 5-6:
A blog
entry with
an added
photo. The
picture is
always on
top and
cannot be
moved.

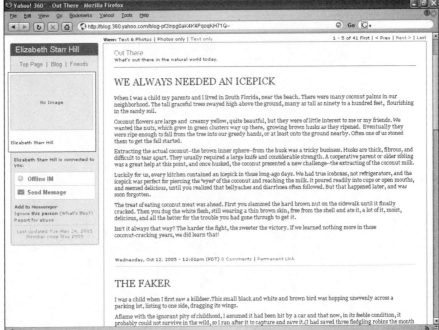

Figure 5-7:
My mother's
blog in
Yahoo! 360.

Photos in 360

Yahoo! 360 is a photo-oriented community, yet there is no direct uploading of pictures to your page except for blog entries. Peculiar, isn't it? The reason for this omission in the photo department is Yahoo!'s desire to utilize Yahoo! Photos and Flickr, the company's two photo-sharing services. If you have photos already uploaded in either place, simply click Add Photos on your Home page in 360, and follow the easy-click instructions for displaying those uploads in Yahoo! 360.

If you don't have any pictures stored in Yahoo! Photos or Flickr, you need to upload your photos at one of those locations. Yahoo! Photos is here:

```
photos.yahoo.com
```

Flickr is here:

```
www.flickr.com
```

Yahoo! Photos is a plain photo repository service without any community features. Flickr is a photo-sharing community, where pictures are located by means of a tagging system and shared rampantly. Flickr is ragingly popular; people who use it, love it. I use both, and Figure 5-8 shows my 360 page with albums from both sites appearing in the sidebar.

Figure 5-8:
Photo albums from Yahoo! Photos and from Flickr can appear in a Yahoo! 360 sidebar.

The Yahoo! 360 Upshot

Yahoo! 360 strikes an attractive balance of community features and blogging features. The blogging is simple to the extreme, which is a solid advantage to newcomers. More ambitious bloggers with a knack for designing pages might be bored with the sameness of 360's spaces. Yahoo! 360 is a great place to establish yourself and then drag in all your friends. The service is easy enough for everybody, and its keep-in-touch nature, with new items being pushed onto friends' screens, encourages lots of communication. Blogging is definitely just an item on the buffet here; you could have a good 360 experience without ever writing a blog entry. For more serious (yet still easy) blogging without the social perks, I would head for Chapter 6 and Blogger.com.

LiveJournal: A classic social network

LiveJournal (or LJ as its devotees call it) is an open-source social site operated by SixApart, the company behind TypePad and Movable Type. What does *open source* mean? Simply that the underlying software can be developed by anybody. As a result, some third-party programs have been developed that enhance the LiveJournal experience.

The big question for new LJ users is: Should I get the free or paid version? At the time of this writing, a paid LiveJournal account costs $19.99 for a year or $3 a month. A free version is also available. I recommend starting with a free account; you can upgrade at any time. Advertisements are not displayed in either type of account. Free accounts give you most of the basic LiveJournal tools, including blogging, a profile, and limited uploading of pictures. You can customize the appearance of your LJ page to some extent, but a paid account gives you more control and better tools, including remote posting and a photo-organizing tool called ScrapBook.

LiveJournal is full of features meant to emphasize who you are and what you like. Each blog post can be tagged with your mood and what music you're currently listening to, for example. Every member can upload small pictures that can be selectively attached to blog posts for an extra dash of personality. Another excellent feature that enhances community is the threaded commenting in LiveJournal. Unlike most other blog systems, which list comments in strictly chronological order, LiveJournal comments are displayed by discussion, so you can see who is responding to whom.

The blog entry-writing page in LiveJournal is stark, neither getting in the way nor enhancing the blogging experience. In its default mode, this page offers a bare subject box and entry box. You can manipulate the date and time to place the page before or after the present time in your blog chronology. The rich text option adds standard formatting controls above the entry box.

LiveJournal stumbles badly in the customizing and page-design departments. The complex, obscure, unexplained series of options is a nightmare. Previewing design changes does not always work, and in those instances you must choose new designs blindly, and then choose again if you don't like the result. Comparing this tangle of frustration with newer tools in MSN Spaces, TypePad, Blogger.com, and WordPress is, frankly (and with apologies to the LJ community), laughable.

Millions of people use LiveJournal and feel great loyalty to the network. Give LiveJournal a whirl if you're curious and enjoy tinkering. Or, join up if you have a friend in LJ. Otherwise, If you're new to blogging and new to social networking, LiveJournal could easily thwart your enthusiasm. The service doesn't do a good job of holding newcomers' hands and walking them through to a satisfying product. In the contemporary blogging scene, easier, prettier, better options exist for the newcomer.

Chapter 6

Finding a Home in Blogger

. . . .

. . . .

A ll roads lead to Blogger, it sometimes seems. Blogger.com is the first stop on the blogging highway for innumerable newcomers. Here are three good reasons for Blogger's popularity:

✔ Blogger is free.

✔ Blogger is unlimited; there is no restriction on the number of blogs you can have or the number of pictures you can upload.

✔ Blogger is easy. Advertising "push-button publishing," Blogger gets you up and posting faster than any other service.

You might think that I am making a whole-hearted recommendation of Blogger. There is much to recommend it, but Blogger has drawbacks, too. Despite its user-friendliness, Blogger has the soul of a geek and sometimes makes simple tasks unnecessarily complicated. One complaint: the difficulty of adding sidebar content such as a blogroll. Blogger makes you stick your hands into your site's code to do that, which is why so many Blogger sites don't display blogrolls.

Blogger stands somewhere between social networks (see Chapters 4 and 5) and TypePad (see Chapter 7). Blogger offers some of the community tools that are characteristic of social sites such as Yahoo! 360 and MSN Spaces. For example, each listed interest in your Blogger profile links to search results showing everyone else in Blogger with that interest — one of the bedrock features of social networks. But Blogger lives up to its name and is a more blog-intensive, blog-centric service than the social networks. Blogger is primarily about blogging, not primarily about meeting people.

This chapter makes a detailed survey of Blogger's most important features. If you haven't yet chosen a blogging service and are drawn to Blogger by its friendly reputation and no-charge service, you might want to read through this chapter to make sure it's the right choice for you.

The Blogger Look

Because Blogger offers relatively few (but fairly attractive) templates, many blogs are instantly recognizable as belonging to Blogger. One example is "Blogging For Dummies" — hey, wait a minute! That's not my blog. (See Figure 6-1.) It belongs to Jeff Sievers, who started the blog as a how-to about blogging. It has more recently evolved into a general diary about everything from politics to the repeated breakdowns of Jeff's car. I thought it would be fun to put his site in the book, and Jeff agreed. See it live, here:

```
drumacrat.blogspot.com
```

Jeff's blog has the typical Blogger look; that template and similar ones with different colors are much in use. If you scroll down the page, you might notice that there is no visible feed link. (See Chapter 13 to find out everything about RSS and feed links.)

The lack of a visible feed is another drawback to Blogger. However, Blogger uses a common feed link that you can simply add to the end of any blog's home-page URL:

```
/atom.xml
```

Using Jeff Siever's Blogger site as an example, the feed link is this:

```
drumacrat.blogspot.com/atom.xml
```

Blogger uses an alternative to the RSS feed format called Atom. Atom feeds work just like RSS feeds in the important ways. Atom feeds display blog entries just like RSS feeds in a feed newsreader. Blogger's choice of Atom has nothing to do with the lack of a feed link on Blogger blogs. The missing feed link is simply a design choice at Blogger — inexplicable, perhaps, but there it is. If you use a feed-enabled Web browser (such as Firefox), Blogger feeds appear in the browser just as reliably as on pages that *do* contain feed links. Firefox finds the feed link in the page's code, where it lurks invisibly.

A site that deviates from the typical Blogger look is the one that belongs to guitarist and recording artist Ottmar Liebert. (See Figure 6-2.) His site is located here:

```
www.ottmarliebert.com/blog/
```

Figure 6-1:
Jeff Siever's blog uses a popular Blogger template.

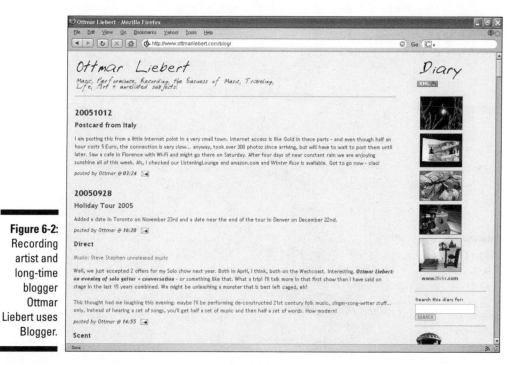

Figure 6-2:
Recording artist and long-time blogger Ottmar Liebert uses Blogger.

Notice that Ottmar Liebert hosts his blog at his own domain, `ottmar liebert.com`, not at Blogger's free hosting domain, `blogspot.com`. Liebert takes advantage of Blogger's free FTP service, which enables Webmasters to use Blogger templates and tools while keeping the blog on their own domain. In this chapter, I assume that most readers want to host their blog on `blogspot.com`. If you prefer the FTP option, choose it during sign-up, or choose it after sign-up on the Settings, Publishing page of the control panel. (You'll know much more about the control panel by the end of this chapter.)

Note that Ottmar Liebert streams photos from Flickr, which is a photo-sharing site that allows members to tie their photo collections to their blogs. Read Chapter 17 for more about Flickr. Read also Chapter 5, which describes how Yahoo! 360 makes the Flickr tie-in especially easy. While you're at it, read *Huckleberry Finn*. It's good for you.

As a final example, check out the This Is Not Art 05 Moblog located here:

```
tina05.blogspot.com
```

A *moblog* is a mobile blog, where entries are posted remotely using portable computers, PDAs, or cell phones. Many moblogs are rich in photos, and pictures are the point here. Notice in Figure 6-3 that the blog's template is similar to Jeff Siever's (see Figure 6-1), but with a different color scheme. It is instantly recognizable as a Blogger blog.

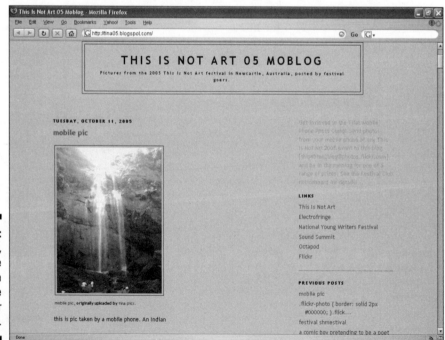

Figure 6-3: A moblog, or mobile blog, using a recognizable Blogger template.

Getting Started with Blogger

You must start an account with Blogger to begin blogging, but your account is completely free. Furthermore, one account gives you a theoretically unlimited number of blogs. Each blog has a theoretically unlimited amount of space for entries and photos. I say "theoretically" because I have heard of restrictions being placed on accounts that are overused. No published restrictions exist, and with normal use even active bloggers should be able to expand their sites without constraint.

Starting up is easy. This section walks you through the path of least resistance: the easiest way to start posting entries in Blogger. You can make changes to your account, and to your blog, later. In later chapters (covering TypePad, Movable Type, WordPress, and Radio UserLand), I recommend doing some blog setup before starting to write. With Blogger, which is designed as "pushbutton publishing," I advise pushing those buttons and getting your blog published without delay (except for a few small settings). Then, later in this chapter, I describe how you can customize, personalize, and otherwise exercise other blog settings.

Here we go. Go to the Blogger site:

```
www.blogger.com
```

Then, follow along with these steps:

1. **On the Blogger home page, click the Create Your Blog Now button.**

2. **Fill in the username, password, display name, and e-mail address; select the Terms of Service acceptance box; and then click the Continue button.**

   The username and password log you into your Blogger account when you want to post entries or change blog settings. The display name, which can be changed later, appears on your blog. The e-mail address does not necessarily appear on the blog but is used for communication between Blogger and you.

3. **Fill in a name and address for your blog.**

   You can give your blog any title at all, and you can always change it. The blog's address is partly determined by the Blogger host, which is located at `blogspot.com`. This means that your blog address will be `yourblog.blogspot.com`. Simply type what you want that first word of the address to be; it doesn't need to be the same as your blog title or display name. So, if your blog is titled *Random Deep Thoughts,* your address could be `joesmith.blogspot.com` (which would make sense only if your name is Joe Smith).

Note the Advanced Setup option; I am ignoring that option for now. Use it if you have your own domain that resides on a Web host. You can use Blogger tools to operate the blog on your Web host.

4. **Fill in the Word Verification, and then click the Continue button.** The word verification step ensures that you are a real person, and not a software robot. Because, yes, software robots do try to create Blogger accounts.

5. **Select a template by clicking the radio button below one of the designs.**

   The template determines the color theme and design layout of your site. Click the <u>preview template</u> link below any template to see a pop-up window illustrating a sample blog in that design.

6. **Click the Continue button.**

   You might have to wait a few seconds at this point, as Blogger creates your blog template and plugs in your information. Before you can recite the complete poems of Robert Frost, a page jubilantly declaims, "Your blog has been created!" You'd think Blogger had cured the common cold. Anyway, click the Start Posting button to . . . well, start posting.

After following these steps, you will have created a blog. It's that painless. Perhaps that's enough for one day. If you put aside this project for now, you can return to it at any time by visiting the Blogger.com site and logging in using the Username and Password boxes in the upper-right corner. Doing so presents the Dashboard page (see Figure 6-4); here, Blogger displays news about the service and hints for using it better. On this page, also, are direct links to editing your profile, changing your password, adding a photo to your profile, and — most important to daily blogging — creating a new post and accessing your other Blogger controls.

Drill this into your brain and thank me later: The Dashboard is where you access your profile information. Don't ask me why Blogger does not put your profile settings inside the control panel along with all the other settings. I have no idea why not. If you do ask me, my eyes will become glassy and I'll start humming "Desperado." To get to the Dashboard, click the <u>Back to Dashboard</u> link near the upper-right corner of the control panel. In the Dashboard screen, click the <u>Edit Profile</u> link to see your profile settings.

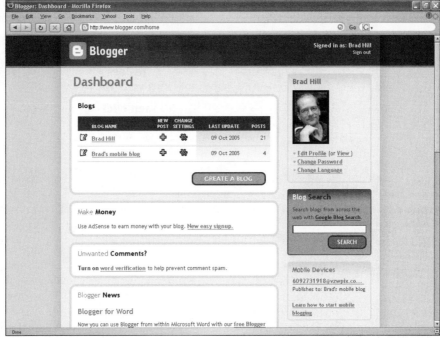

Figure 6-4:
The
Dashboard
in Blogger
displays
Blogger
news and
links to
editing your
profile.

Three Crucial Settings

I'll get to posting in a bit. First, you should address three default settings in your new blog. I don't mean that you must change the settings, but you should be aware of them before you start writing entries into your blog. Follow these steps to review these crucial settings:

1. **Go to Blogger.com and sign in to your account.**

2. **Click the Change Settings icon.**

   Blogger displays the Basic page of your Settings tab (see Figure 6-5).

3. **Use the Add Your Blog to Our Listings drop-down menu to make your blog public or private.**

   The default setting is Yes; this means that your blog is included in the Blogger directory and might be included in Blogger's list of highlighted blogs. Select No if you prefer keeping the blog private, either temporarily while you build up some entries and practice your Blogger skills or permanently.

4. **Click the Save Settings button.**

   You might have to scroll down the page to see this button. You must save changes you make to any page in the Settings tab before moving to another page; otherwise, your changes will revert to previous settings.

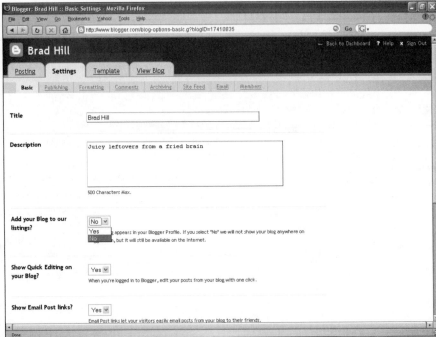

Figure 6-5:
You might
want to visit
the Basic
Settings
page before
starting to
post entries.

5. **Still in the Settings tab, click the <u>Formatting</u> link.**

6. **On the Formatting page, use the Show Title drop-down menu to deter-mine whether your entries are individually titled.**

   Curiously, this setting is defaulted in the No position, meaning that there is no Title box available when you write an entry. Consequently, when this option is set to No, your blog contains no message titles. Such a design might be to your taste, but I find it odd and recommend changing this setting to Yes. When you do so, the Title box appears on the page on which you compose entries. Then, you have a choice with each entry: create a title or not.

7. **Click the Save Settings button.**

8. **Still in the Settings tab, click the <u>Comments</u> link.**

9. **On the Comments page, use the Comments radio buttons to choose whether your entries will allow comments.**

   The default here is Show, which allows visitors to leave comments on your entry pages.

10. **Click the Save Settings button.**

Now you are ready to blog!

Writing and Posting Entries in Blogger

With your basic settings ready to go (see the preceding section), you might want to write and post an entry. That's what it's all about. If you're in your Blogger control panel (where the Settings tab is), a single click gets you to the page where you compose an entry. If you're entering Blogger after being away from it, go to Blogger.com and sign in, and then click the name of your blog on your Dashboard page. Clicking your blog name takes you to the control panel.

Composing an entry and publishing it

However you get there, follow these steps to write and post your first blog entry. Doing so is just about as easy as sending an e-mail:

1. **Click the Posting tab.**

   You are delivered to the Create page within the Posting tab — just where you want to be. (See Figure 6-6.)

2. **Enter a title for your blog post.**

   As noted in the preceding section, you must select an option that puts a title field on the Create page. If you don't, you can't title your entries.

Figure 6-6:
This is where you write and publish new blog entries.

3. **In the large box, type your entry.**

   Don't worry about being brilliant, profound, or even interesting. You can delete or edit the post later.

4. **Click the Publish Post button.**

That is all there is to writing and posting a blog entry in Blogger. Well, those are the basics. Other features are available. Note the icons and drop-down menus just above the entry-writing box. You might be familiar with similar controls if you use e-mail in AOL, Gmail, or another system where you can select fonts, colors, and other formatting options. Run your mouse cursor over the icons to see their labels. Here is a rundown of Blogger formatting choices:

✔ Use the Font and Normal Size drop-down menus to select a typeface and type size, respectively. If you're uncertain what this means, experiment! Remember, nothing gets published on the blog until you click the Publish Post button.

✔ Use the b icon to make **bold** text. Simply select any text you've already typed, and then click the icon. Alternatively, click the icon, start typing (even in the middle of a sentence), and then click the icon again to end the bold formatting.

✔ Use the i icon to make *italicized* text.

✔ Use the T icon to change the color of your text. Again, this control may be used on words within sentences. The truth is, most people don't insert colored text into blog posts. Blogs are more about the writing than fancy and useless formatting. Bold and italic text makes a point; colored text rarely does.

✔ That little chain icon next to the T icon is the link icon; use it to insert a link to an outside Web page. Highlight any word or group of words, and then click the link icon and type (or paste) a copied link into the pop-up box. (See Figure 6-7.)

✔ The alignment icons line up your text as follows: on the left (with a ragged right edge), in the middle (ragged on both sides), on the right (with a ragged left edge), or with full justification (even on both sides). The default setting is left alignment (the icon shown in the margin of this book), and there is little reason to change it.

✔ Use the numbered list and bulleted list options to create indented lists in your entry. The list you're reading right now is a bullet list. The list before this is a numbered list.

✔ The blockquote option creates an indented portion of the entry that many people use when quoting material from another site. Figure 6-8 illustrates a blockquote.

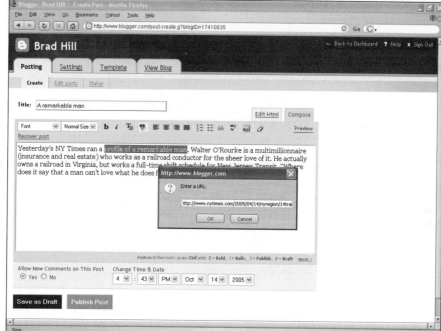

Figure 6-7:
Copy an
address
from a Web
site, and
insert a link
to it in your
blog entry
using the T
link icon.

Figure 6-7:
Copy an
address
from a Web
site, and
insert a link
to it in your
blog entry
using the T
link icon.

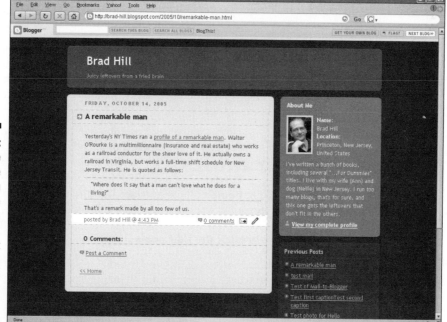

Figure 6-8:
The
blockquote
formatting
feature
highlights a
quotation.
The exact
formatting
depends
on the
template.

- ✔ The ABC icon represents a spell-check feature.

- ✔ The small picture is for adding images; I get to that later in the section called "Inserting a photo in an entry."

- ✔ The rightmost icon, which looks like an eraser, removes formatting from any portion of highlighted text.

That's it for the formatting. Tempting though these one-click options are, try not to gunk up your blog too much. I mean, it's your blog; do what you want. But most people don't like having their eyes savaged by colored text, weirdly sized characters, bizarre fonts, or willy-nilly bolding and italicizing. Sorry to be a sourpuss, but use formatting with discretion.

You might notice a second tab above the entry-writing box, labeled Edit Html. Use this tab if you prefer to manually code your formats with HTML tags. HTML specialists can also use HTML tags that are not represented by the format icons just described. When you want to check your hand-coding efforts, click back to the Compose tab. You can toggle between the two, editing your code and checking it.

The Preview link invites you to see what your entry will look like. Unfortunately, it does no such thing. That link displays a composed and formatted version of your entry, but it does not display it in your blog's template design. Because the page on which you compose your entry shows all the formatting choices you make, the Preview link seems pointless to me. So my tip is: Ignore it (the Preview feature, not the tip).

Note two final features on the Create page. First, use the Yes and No options to determine whether comments will be allowed on the entry you're writing. You can use this setting to override the global setting you made in the preceding section. Second, use the Time & Date menus to alter the accurate time of the post. You can place the entry in the past or the future (more on why you might want to do this in a moment), and the blog will sort it accordingly in your archives and index page.

Editing your entries

Blogger makes it easy to edit or delete entries. To edit an entry, you use the same basic tools as those for writing a new entry. Proceed like this:

1. **In the Posting tab, click the <u>Edit posts</u> link.**

2. **On the Edit posts page, click the Edit button corresponding to any entry.**

   (See Figure 6-9.) Use the drop-down menu to select how many published entries appear on this page. You see only the titles, not the full entries.

3. **Alter your entry using the familiar writing and formatting tools.**

   See the preceding section for details on these tools.

4. **Click the Publish Post button.**

You have an opportunity to change the date and time of the changed entry. The default setting of the Time & Date menus is the original moment of the entry's publication. If you're updating previous information, you can bring the time and date up to the present. If you're merely correcting a mistake, standard blogging protocol calls for leaving the entry in its original chronological placement.

To delete an entry, go to the Edit Posts page and click the Delete link corresponding to any entry. Blogger displays the post and asks whether you really want to delete it. Click the Delete It button. A deleted post cannot be recovered.

Figure 6-9: Use this page to select entries for editing.

Inserting a photo in an entry

Including a photo in a blog entry is not a problem in Blogger. The photo can come from your computer or from a Web location, the former being more common. Blogger can upload the photo from your machine, store it on its computer, and resize it for display in the blog entry (a big picture could stretch out the entry grotesquely). Visitors who click the resized picture see the full-sized photo on another page.

Follow these steps to insert a picture in a Blogger entry:

1. **In your control panel, click the Posting tab.**

2. **On the Create page, type an entry title and begin writing your entry.**

   It doesn't matter when you insert the photo in the entry-writing process. The photo can come first, or the writing, or a portion of the writing.

3. **Click the Add Image icon.**

   To find the Add Image control, run your mouse over the formatting icons. A pop-up window appears to handle your picture selection and upload. (See Figure 6-10.)

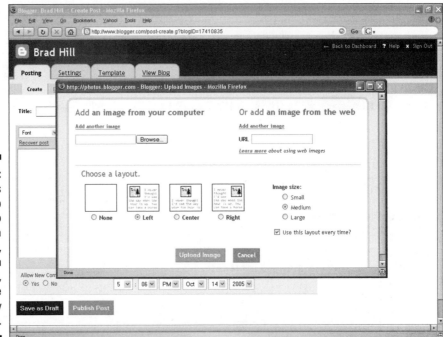

Figure 6-10: Use this pop-up window to select a picture, place it in your entry, and choose a display size.

4. **Click the Browse button to select a picture from your computer.**

   If you're inserting a picture found on the Web, copy that picture's location (Web address) in the URL box.

5. **In the File Upload window, click the image file you want to insert and then click the Open button.**

6. **Back in the Blogger pop-up window, choose a layout by clicking a radio button.**

   The layout selections let you determine whether the picture is positioned to the left of the entry's text, to the right of the text, or centered above the text.

7. **Select an image size.**

   The size selections are vague: Small, Medium, or Large. I always use the Small setting, so the picture doesn't dominate the entry. Readers who click the picture see it in full size on a new page.

8. **Click the Upload Image button.**

9. **In the confirmation window, click the Done button.**

   Back on the Create page, you can see your uploaded photo in the entry box. Now is a good time to complete your writing of the entry, if necessary.

10. **Click the Publish Post button.**

    You can use this process to insert multiple pictures in a blog entry.

Personalizing Your Blogger Blog

You've made basic settings and you've posted at least one entry. Your blog is launched. However, you can do more to make it unmistakably *your* blog. Blogger personalization consists of choosing a site design (which you already did but can change at any time), creating a personal profile that's displayed on a unique page, and setting a few formats. You can also change the title and description of the blog at any time. Let's get started finding these features.

Switching Blogger templates

Blogger templates determine the color scheme and layout design of your blog. Templates are interchangeable. You can switch from one to another with a few clicks, and the changes ripple out through every page (except the Profile page) of your blog.

Blogger offers a modest selection of templates — about thirty at the time of this writing, and certainly more than Blogger showed you during sign-up. Follow these steps to see how your blog looks with a whole new design:

1. **In your Blogger control panel, click the Template tab.**

2. **In the Template tab, click the <u>Pick new</u> link.**

3. **On the Pick New page (see Figure 6-11), click any template picture to see a full-size sample of that template.**

   The sample opens in a new browser window and illustrates what an active blog looks like.

4. **Close the sample browser window.**

   You don't want it hanging around your screen forever. Leaving it open doesn't affect the template selection process, but closing it reveals the original browser window that you use to select a template.

5. **Click the Use This Template button below your selected template.**

   Your selected template can be the one you just previewed or any other one.

Figure 6-11: Choose from a few dozen design templates. You can change templates at any time.

6. In the pop-up verification window, click OK.

This pop-up window warns that if you switch templates, you will lose any customizations to your old (current) template. These customizations are not the settings in the control panel that I have discussed to this point, or those I discuss later in this section. Blogger is referring to customized code inserted into the template's CSS stylesheets. Don't know what I'm talking about? Good; the warning doesn't apply to you.

7. Click the Republish button.

Republishing the blog forces the template change to propagate through the entire site. If you were to view your Blogger site before republishing, it would show the old template. If your blog has many entries, republishing could take a minute or two. New blogs republish in a few seconds.

8. Click the <u>View Blog</u> link to see your newly designed site.

The question is, how often should you change your template? Frequent changes are disconcerting to regular visitors. But occasional changes keep the site fresh for you, who must look at it more often than anyone else. Every few months, at the most, is an appropriate guide. It doesn't hurt to ask your readers for feedback before and after the change.

Republish, republish, republish

This sidebar is about republishing — could you tell? I am hammering on this point because it is a frequent source of confusion among Blogger users, and I forget about republishing myself sometimes.

Here is the point: In Blogger (as in many other blog services), saving changes is not the same as publishing changes. I'm not talking about posting entries here. The changes I'm talking about are in the Settings and Template tabs of the control panel. Those pages allow you to make global changes that affect many, or all, pages of your blog. A three-stage process effects those changes:

1. Make the changes.

2. Save the changes.

3. Republish the blog.

Even though a Republish button is displayed on your screen after step 2, it is not particularly big and people overlook it. If you don't do step 3, the changes don't appear in your blog and you might rip your hair out wondering why Blogger isn't showing your changed settings. If your hair is ripped out already (from long experience with computers), you might gnash your teeth. If your teeth are ground down (from even longer experience with computers), you might start lashing out at family and friends. If everyone already hates you — oh, never mind. Just don't forget to republish your blog!

Building your Blogger profile

Perhaps the most important personalization work you can do on your Blogger blog is creating a profile. The Blogger profile is a page dedicated to who you are and what you like. The profile page is attached to your blog but resides outside the chronological organization of the blog. Your profile never appears on the blog's index page. Visitors view your profile by clicking the View my complete profile link in the blog's sidebar. Figure 6-12 shows my Blogger profile.

The profile can be as complete or sketchy as you want, within the options provided by Blogger. A profile setup page is where you determine what information about you appears. You can make it easy, or not so easy, for people to contact you. Specific and direct contact information, such as your address or phone number, are not profile options.

Profile options are not part of the main control panel; perhaps you have already noticed that there is no Profile tab in the control panel. This confusing wrinkle might be why many bloggers in the system have blank profiles. You access your profile setup page through the Blogger Dashboard. Remember the Dashboard from earlier in the chapter? No? Were you too busy shredding your brain with caffeine to notice? Wait — that was me. Anyway, here's the step-by-step for finding and setting your profile choices, starting from scratch:

1. **Go to Blogger.com and sign in to your blog account.**

2. **On the Dashboard page, click the Edit Profile link.**

   The link is in the right sidebar.

3. **On the Edit User Profile page, fill in the options you'd like to appear on your profile page.**

   Figure 6-13 shows the Edit User Profile page. You need to scroll down to see some options.

4. **Click the Save Profile button.**

   It's at the bottom of the page.

5. **Click the View Updated Profile link to see your profile page.**

   You can amend and alter your profile as much as you like, whenever you like.

An interesting option on the Edit User Profile page might give you pause. It also might give you indigestion, because Blogger does not make the feature particularly easy. I'm talking about the feature that lets you add a picture to your profile. The next section clarifies how to do that.

Figure 6-12:
A Blogger profile. Mine, in fact, only slightly altered from reality.

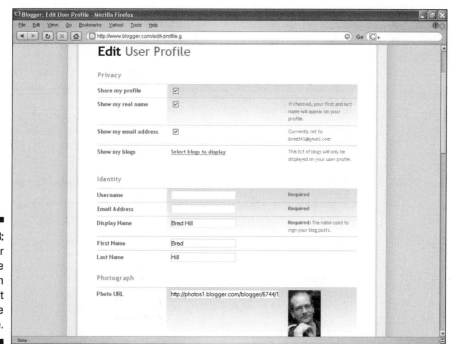

Figure 6-13:
Set your profile information on the Edit User Profile page.

Adding a photo to your Blogger profile

Blogger lets you put a photo in your profile, but makes it outrageously complicated. Most blogging services provide a Browse button for finding a photo in your computer and adding it to your profile. Perhaps you've seen those buttons in certain sites. Blogger puts that button in other places. Yet Blogger persists in tormenting its users with a convoluted method of adding a profile photo.

Here is the problem. Notice, on the Edit User Profile page (refer to Figure 6-13), that Blogger offers to include a photo — *if it is already on the Web.* The option asks for a "Photo URL." That means Blogger wants the Web address of a photo that has already been posted online. Quite likely, you have a photo of yourself on your hard drive and have never before uploaded that photo to a Web site. (If you have posted the photo on another Web site, plug the URL into this option and be done with it.) This is where Blogger should put the Browse button, enabling you to locate the photo in your computer and upload it to your Blogger profile. But noooo.

Enough complaining. There is a way around Blogger's cumbersome and user-hostile insufficiency. I intend to make the profile-photo process crystal clear. If you are familiar with HTML tags, you'll have no trouble with this. If not, don't back away. Take this process one step at a time, and you'll complete it with surprising ease. Here we go:

1. **On the Edit User Profile page, click the <u>Dashboard</u> link.**

   You need to back out of the Edit User Profile page and return to the Dashboard — your starting point when first signing in to your Blogger account. You can get there also by clicking the <u>Home</u> link at the bottom of the Edit User Profile page.

2. **On the Dashboard page, click the New Post icon.**

   As you can see, adding a profile photo has something to do with creating a blog entry. We are going to use the Create page to upload a photo from your computer to Blogger. This tactic is roundabout, but effective.

3. **On the Create page (in the Posting tab), click the Add Image icon.**

   Clicking causes a pop-up window to appear; the same window you used to insert a picture in a blog entry (see the preceding section).

4. **Using the Browse button, select an image from your computer.**

   At last, there is the Browse button. Better here than nowhere. At this point you are following the same steps as those when choosing a picture to insert in a blog entry. The difference this time is that you are *not* going to actually post the blog entry. We are going through this charade to upload the picture and get it into your profile.

5. After selecting your photo and layout, click the Upload Image button.

It doesn't matter which photo display size you select — small, medium, or large. Remember, you are not going to actually post this entry. Whichever setting you choose, the full-size photo is uploaded from your computer to Blogger.

One important note: The Blogger profile does not accept photo files larger than 50 kilobytes. That is a small file and an inexplicable limitation. Photo files in blog entries can be any size, but not so with the profile photo. Using Windows Explorer, right-click your photo file and select Properties to check the file size. This size has nothing to do with the size selections (small, medium, or large) in the uploading window. Blogger always uploads the full file size, even when altering the display size (small, medium, or large).

6. In the confirmation window, click the Done button.

7. Back on the Create page, click the Edit Html tab.

Before clicking this tab, you can see your uploaded photo in the entry-writing box. When you click the Edit Html tab, that photo disappears and is replaced by a few lines of code.

8. Highlight the URL address of your photo.

This step is the trickiest part, so put down your potato chips and read carefully. In most cases, the photo URL appears twice, on the second and fourth lines of code — but different screens show the code in different ways. You are looking for a Web address that begins with `http://` and is entirely enclosed in quotation marks. If your photo is in the common JPG format, the final part of the address is `.jpg`. Highlight the entire address *but don't highlight the quotation marks.* Figure 6-14 illustrates the HTML code and the highlighting.

9. Use the Ctrl+C keyboard command to copy the highlighted address to the Windows clipboard.

10. Click the <u>Back to Dashboard</u> link near the upper-right corner of the page.

You are finished with the Create page; you have what you came for — namely, an uploaded photo and its address. Now you can abandon the entry like a sack of rotting potatoes. (The entry, not you.)

11. On the Dashboard page, click the <u>Edit Profile</u> link.

12. On the Edit User Profile page, use the Ctrl+V keyboard combination to paste the photo URL into the Photo URL box.

13. Scroll down and click the Save Profile button.

14. Click the <u>View Updated Profile</u> link to see your newly photo-enhanced Blogger profile.

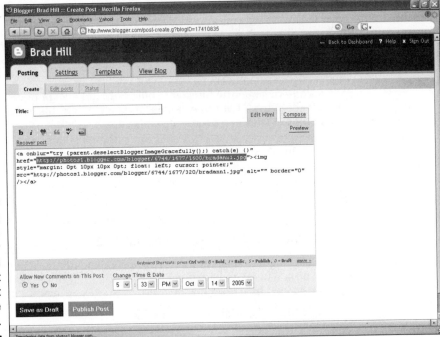

Figure 6-14:
Highlight the URL of your photo, and then paste it into the Edit User Profile page.

The photo appears in your blog sidebar under the About Me heading, in addition to appearing on your profile page. Blogger automatically sizes the photo to fit in the sidebar. A small version is displayed on the profile page, too; when a visitor clicks that picture, a fill-sized version is displayed on a new page.

Audioblogging in Blogger

Believe it or not, you can put your actual voice right into a Blogger entry. Doing so is free to all Blogger users and fairly easy. Blogging in audio is called *audioblogging,* and Blogger uses a service called Audioblogger (located at www.audioblogger.com). Once you get the hang of putting an audio message in a blog entry, you can also place one in your profile page.

How does it all work? First you establish an account with Audioblogger (again, it's free). Then you call a phone number to record your voice entry. Your recording, up to five minutes in length, is automatically posted to your blog within seconds after you hang up. The entry consists of an audioblogging icon; visitors click the icon to hear your recording. The audio file is recorded in MP3 format; to hear it, a visitor must have MP3-playing software on his or her computer. (Such software is installed on nearly all computers built in the last several years.) When someone clicks the audio file icon in your blog entry, that software opens and plays your voice entry.

Some people use audioblogging as their main, or sole, type of blog post. Others use it occasionally and support each audio entry with written text. You are free to experiment. You might use it only once, or you might fall in love with blogging in this manner. Follow these steps to set up a free Audioblogger account:

1. **Go to Audioblogger.**

2. **Click the Start Audioblogging Now button.**

3. **Log in with your Blogger username and password, and then click the Continue button.**

4. **Select the blog in which you want to audioblog from the drop-down menu, and then click the Continue button.**

   If you have just one Blogger blog, the selection is obvious.

5. **Enter your phone number, type a four-digit identification number, and then click the Finish Setup button.**

   Entering a phone number does not restrict you to that number when audioblogging. But you must remember that number as an identifier, even though you also create a four-digit ID number. Consider the username plus password combination required in most Web site registrations. In Audioblogger, you can think of your phone number as your username and the four-digit number as your password. You might have to wait a few minutes while Audioblogger completes your setup.

At the end of this setup, you might see a confirmation screen, and you might see a page of incomprehensible gibberish. No fooling. But even if you see gibberish, chances are good that your Audioblogger account was set up satisfactorily. Try an audio post *before* you repeat the setup process.

To make an audio entry, call up the Audioblogger dial-in number:

```
1-415-856-0205
```

Use any phone, and have your entered phone number handy. Audioblogger's robotic assistant asks for that phone number as a kind of username, and then asks for your PIN as a kind of password. In both cases, you use the phone's keypad to enter the numbers. When robot-guy cues you, speak your blog entry, and then press the phone's pound key (#) to end the message.

If you have a cell phone, put the Audioblogger phone number in your phone's memory. Then you can post an audio entry from anywhere, at any time, without having to recall the number.

Your audio entries (see Figure 6-15) are editable just as your written entries are. The audio entries appear on the Edit Posts page along with text entries. You cannot edit the audio, however. You can add a title — I try to do this as soon as possible, because audio entries get posted without titles. And you can add text that explains or enhances the audio.

You can add an audio file to your Blogger profile page. Doing so is no easier than jumping through hoops to add a photo — as I describe in the preceding section. In fact, the process is pretty much the same:

1. **Create an audio entry using Audioblogger.**

   Your recording should be appropriate for the profile page — perhaps a brief welcoming message divulging a bit about you or the blog.

2. **In your Blogger control panel, click the Posting tab.**

3. **Click the Edit posts link.**

4. **Click the Edit button corresponding to your newly created audio entry.**

5. **Click the Edit Html tab.**

6. **Highlight the audio file's URL.**

   The URL address ends in .mp3 and is enclosed in quotation marks.

Figure 6-15:
An Audio-blogger entry. Clicking the icon opens the viewer's default program for playing MP3 files.

Audioblogger and Audioblog

Two audio blogging services are named similarly, and operate similarly, so they are sometimes confused. Audioblogger is paired with Blogger.com, and is free to Blogger users. Audioblog is an independent service that charges a monthly fee for phone-in recording and posting to blogs on any platform. You can use Audioblog with Blogger, but you must pay that monthly fee ($4.95 at the time of this writing).

One advantage of Audioblog over Audioblogger is that it creates MOV files instead of MP3 files, and posts the MOV files in a miniature player right in the blog entry. Most browsers have no trouble playing these audio entries without the need for another program to open. That seamless performance is a convenience to your readers. If you intend to audioblog seriously, the somewhat more sophisticated service offered by Audioblog is worth considering.

7. **Press Ctrl+C to copy the address.**

8. **Click the <u>Back to Dashboard</u> link near the upper-right corner of the page.**

9. **Click the <u>Edit Profile</u> link.**

10. **Press Ctrl+V to paste the address into the Audio Clip URL box.**

11. **Scroll down and click the Save Profile button.**

Your audio clip is now featured as a playable link and icon on your profile page. It does not play automatically when a visitor lands on your profile page; the visitor must click it, just as with an audio blog entry.

E-mailing Entries to Blogger

Blogger has developed a beautifully simple method of posting entries by e-mail. Using this feature means you can avoid logging into your Blogger account to write a post. This feature is convenient for people who keep their e-mail running on the computer screen all the time. Because e-mail is always handy, posting through that program or Web interface is quicker than signing in to Blogger.

The service is called Mail-to-Blogger, and it works only with text messages — no pictures. You simply create your own personalized e-mail address on Blogger's computer, and Blogger assigns all mail received at that address to your blog. When you send an e-mail, Blogger makes the e-mail title a blog entry title, and the body of the e-mail becomes the entry text.

Follow these steps to set it up:

1. **In your Blogger control panel, click the Settings tab.**

2. **In the Settings tab, click the Email link.**

3. **On the Email page, create your special address in the Mail-to-Blogger Address box.**

   You need to think of just one word, because most of the address is set and unchanging. The first part of the address is your account username; the last part of the address is the `blogger.com` domain. You need to put a word in between, as shown on the page, and it's best to use a word that you easily remember — perhaps *blog*. Or *entry*. Or *pickadilly*. Notice the BlogSend Address box. Put an e-mail address in there if you want to be notified of your mailed entry being posted.

4. **Click the Save Settings button.**

   You do not need to republish the blog.

5. **In your e-mail program or interface, address an e-mail to your special e-mail address, title and compose the e-mail, and send it.**

   The body of your e-mail becomes that text of your blog entry.

6. **Check your blog for the entry's appearance.**

   It can take up to a minute for the mailed entry to be posted.

You can use the Mail-to-Blogger feature from any connected computer and e-mail program in the world. It doesn't even have to be your e-mail; Blogger doesn't know or care who owns the e-mail account sending the entry to your special address. That's why it's important to keep your special address secret. Anyone who knows it can post to your blog. If that happens, change the secret word on the Settings, Email page.

On the Road with Blogger

Mobile blogging, or *moblogging* (the generalities of which I discuss in Chapter 17), is supported nicely in Blogger Mobile. Blogger Mobile is a free service included in a standard free Blogger account; you don't have to sign up for it separately. You must, however, go through a set of steps to get it working for you; once through those steps, moblogging to Blogger is easy. You can take a cell phone that has a built-in camera (a camera phone) and Internet connectivity, snap a picture, send the picture to Blogger, and have it posted to your blog — all in seconds. You can send text, too, or a mix of text and a picture.

Blogger Mobile uses an unusual but effective method of starting a mobile blog path for each user. You can start a new blog in your account for mobile posts, or you can assign mobile posts to an existing blog. (I step you through the exact process here.) First, you send a picture from your cell phone to a generic, public e-mail address:

```
go@blogger.com
```

This e-mail address rejects incoming pictures from non-cell locations. In other words, you can't use your normal computer e-mail address (such as an AOL, Hotmail, Yahoo! Mail, Gmail, Comcast, or Earthlink address) to remotely post pictures through go@blogger.com. Blogger Mobile works with entries sent from Verizon, AT&T, Cingular, Sprint, or T-Mobile accounts.

When go@blogger.com receives your first mobile post, it instantly creates a blog for it. That's right — Blogger builds an entire blog around one entry and assigns it a blogspot.com Web address.

At this point, the new blog doesn't belong to anybody, even though it displays your entry. You have to claim the new blog to your account, either keeping it as a separate blog or assigning the entry (and future mobile entries) to an existing blog in your account. Blogger Mobile sends a *claim token* to the cell phone that sent the entry — that would be your cell phone. You enter the claim token on a special Blogger Mobile page and take control of the new blog. At that moment, you can make the new blog disappear and put the first entry into an existing blog or keep the new blog and rename it.

That's the general process; here are the specific steps:

1. **Send a text message or picture to go@blogger.com.**

   Check your camera phone's user manual to find out how to send pictures to e-mail addresses. Within a minute (at most) of sending, Blogger Mobile sends back a text message containing a claim token. That message is sent to your cell phone, not to your computer e-mail.

2. **Read the text message sent to your cell phone by Blogger, and write down the claim token.**

   The claim token is a short string of letters and numbers. Blogger also sends the Web address of the new blog created around your first entry; you can visit the blog but can't access its controls until you claim it as yours.

3. **In your computer browser, go to go.blogger.com.**

4. **Type your token in the Claim Token box, type the correct word in the Verification box, and then click the Continue button.**

   The Mobile Blog Found page appears, showing your Blogger sign-in username.

5. **Click the <u>Continue as this user</u> link.**

6. **On the Claim Mobile Blog page, choose to keep the new blog or switch to your existing blog, and then click the Continue button.**

In this example, I am keeping the new blog, not switching. If you do switch, your mobile post is transferred to the existing blog, and future mobile posts go to the existing blog. Of course, you have access to that blog's controls. Keeping the new blog (not switching) separates mobile posts from regular posts, for better or worse.

7. **On the Name Your Blog page, select a blog title and domain address, and then click the Continue button.**

   Naming and addressing the blog should remind you of how you first started in Blogger. Name the blog whatever you want. The address will be something like `mymobilepics.blogspot.com`. You type only the first part of that address; `blogspot.com` is the default and unchange-able domain.

8. **On the Choose a Template page, click the radio button below your selected template design, and then click the Continue button.**

9. **On the You're Done page, click the View Blog Now button.**

   You're off and running with a new mobile blog. (See Figure 6-16.)

Now that your mobile blogging setup is complete, you can continue sending pictures, text, and pictures-plus-text entries from your camera phone to `go@blogger.com`. Blogger Mobile knows that incoming entries from your phone belong to your Blogger account, and directs them to the blog you selected.

Figure 6-16: A moblog using Blogger Mobile. Use the Edit Posts page to change and add titles.

Chapter 7

Creating a TypePad Blog

*T*ypePad is a commercial blog service with fairly powerful site-building and entry-writing tools and no installation hassle. Your blog, and the control screens through which you operate the blog, all reside on TypePad computers, not your computer. You pay a monthly or annual fee for a chunk of server space and access to the administrative controls. Three levels of service offer three levels of power and flexibility.

TypePad is operated by the same company that created Movable Type (see Chapter 9) and the social network LiveJournal (see Chapter 5). TypePad holds down the middle ground between the other two, with Movable Type being the most advanced product. Movable Type is a powerful Web-publishing application, and TypePad bears the unmistakable resemblance of a younger sibling. TypePad blogs look somewhat like Movable Type blogs and share many features. TypePad is enormously easier to manage, from start to finish.

Easier, but not necessarily easy. If TypePad is a stripped-down version of Movable Type, you can also think of it as a bulked-up alternative to Blogger. com (see Chapter 6). I think most people would regard Blogger.com as the easier blogging platform, but the two services — TypePad and Blogger — stand at roughly the same place in the blog-service hierarchy. If you're looking for a dedicated hosted blogging platform, you should read both this chapter and the Blogger chapter before deciding which to use.

Signing Up with TypePad

Although I am putting sign-up information near the beginning of this chapter, you might want to look through the chapter first to see whether you like the look of TypePad. By this I mean not only the look of TypePad's control screens but the look of TypePad blogs currently in publication. The descriptions and screen shots in these pages give you a good idea of the blogging experience through TypePad. Here are three sites that show off a few results:

✔ **Ed in Europe (`http://edineurope.typepad.com`):** A travel blog, Ed in Europe combines written entries with plenty of photos, thereby making good use of TypePad's integration of text and images. (See Figure 7-1.)

✔ **The Cathrows (`www.thecathrows.com`):** This family blog is all about the pictures. The Cathrows use what's called a mixed media layout to emphasize their photo albums; the blog contains no written entries at all except a welcome message on the home page. (See Figure 7-2.)

✔ **The 80/20 Rule (`willsheward.typepad.com`):** Will Sheward writes a serious current events and opinion blog from Germany (in English). His thoughtful and articulate work is all text, no photos. (See Figure 7-3.)

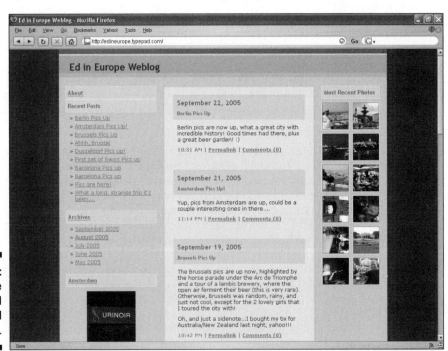

Figure 7-1: Ed in Europe is a mixed text and photo blog.

Figure 7-2:
The Cathrows produce a family photo blog using a mixed media layout.

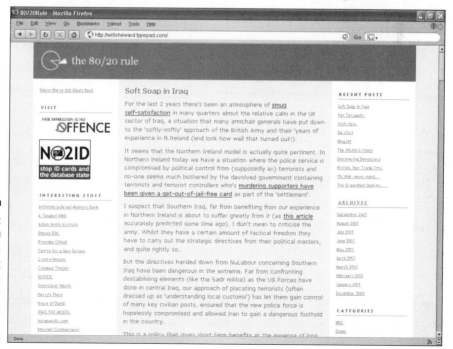

Figure 7-3:
The 80/20 Rule is an all-text opinion blog with plenty of commentary.

To see more representative TypePad blogs, go to the TypePad site and browse through the list of recently updated sites.

Starting your TypePad account

TypePad usually offers a free 30-day trial. To get started, go to the main site:

```
www.typepad.com
```

Click the big Start Free Trial button, and begin working your way through the sign-up forms. You do need to provide credit card information in these forms, but you'll be glad to know that — unlike some online services — it is easy to cancel the service before the trial period is over.

The one section of the sign-in forms that should give you pause is the part in which you choose a domain name (see Figure 7-4). At this point, you are not registering a new domain name that can be hosted at any Web hosting company (see Chapter 8). In fact, you are really choosing a *subdomain* name that gets attached to one of TypePad's domains.

Figure 7-4:
Choose a
subdomain
word, which
becomes
part of your
blog's Web
address,
or URL.

TypePad's two domains are

- ✔ typepad.com; your domain would be *yourdomain*.typepad.com
- ✔ blogs.com; your domain would be *yourdomain*.blogs.com

Use the drop-down menu to choose typepad.com or blogs.com, and then choose a subdomain name. This choice is irrevocable, so don't be capricious. The only way to change your subdomain is to cancel the account (discarding any blogging you had done) and start over.

The subdomain that you choose when signing up serves as an anchor name for all your blogs if you have two or more (see the service levels in the next section). Imagine that John and Alice Smith want to blog together and also blog individually. They start three TypePad blogs, called Our Family Blog, John Smith, and Alice Smith. The account holding these three blogs is assigned just one subdomain, selected by Alice. Each blog is located in a folder attached to the main domain that includes their subdomain. Here is what the three Web addresses look like:

```
subdomain.typepad.com/ourfamilyblog
subdomain.typepad.com/johnsmith
subdomain.typepad.com/alicesmith
```

As you can see, the subdomain is not yet chosen. When signing up for an account, Alice should keep in mind that the subdomain is part of the Web address for each of the three blogs, so it shouldn't be too individual or unique to her. If, for example, she were to choose *alicemom* as the subdomain, the Web address of John's blog would be:

```
alicemom.typepad.com/johnsmith
```

A better subdomain would be *smithfamily,* or some other choice that would apply well to each blog.

Although you cannot change your subdomain after signing up, you can change the names of the folders assigned to each new blog. When you start a second blog, the default folder-naming process makes the choice for you. What might escape your attention is that you can change the default folder name (identical to your subdomain name). Going back to Alice and John, let's imagine that Alice chose *smithfamily* as the subdomain during sign-up. Alice and John intend to call their joint blog Our Family Blog, but the default Web address of that blog would now be:

```
smithfamily.typepad.com/smithfamily
```

There's nothing terribly wrong with that, and the Smiths might even prefer to leave it for simplicity's sake. But if they want the folder name to match the blog name (Our Family Blog, which is displayed on the site's banner), that folder name should be changed to *ourfamilyblog*.

If you want to change the default folder name of the first blog (that's the default blog TypePad sets up immediately after sign-up), you should do so *before* you start blogging. If you change any folder name after posting entries to that blog, you mess up any existing links to archives and photo albums. You don't actually lose anything you've written, but the functionality of everything posted before the change is compromised. See the "Setting Up Your Blog" section, later in this chapter.

Choosing a service level

TypePad offers three service levels: Basic, Plus, and Pro. They are essentially the same product, with varying amounts of storage space on the server and certain features withheld from the Basic and Plus levels. You must choose a subscription level when signing up, but that doesn't prevent you from canceling during the free trial or changing your subscription level at any time.

Price is perhaps the most obvious differentiator among the plans, along with storage space, the number of permitted blogs, and the number of permitted authors. Currently, the plans break down as follows in these important categories:

- ✔ **Basic:** $4.95 per month for a single Weblog, 100 megabytes of space, and one author. No other name but yours can be associated with a blog post.
- ✔ **Plus:** $8.95 per month for three Weblogs, 500 megabytes of space, and three authors.
- ✔ **Pro:** $14.95 for an unlimited number of blogs and authors, squeezing into one gigabyte of space.

Note: These terms are fluid. By the time you read this, the storage limits might have been raised; they have been raised before.

On the face of it, the Basic plan would seem to be best for a single blogger whose family or friends don't want to participate. The Plus plan, with three permitted authors, is an effective family arrangement. Plus also works for an ambitious solo blogger with a lot to write about. Another application of the three blogs allowed by Plus would be a written blog for one, a photo blog for another, and a moblog (mobile blog) for the third. As long as I'm brainstorming, how about this: A couple makes one joint blog, and each also gets a solo blog. Or a family takes one blog for day-to-day entries and uses the other two as a vacation blog and a special events blog.

Believe it or not, the Pro package can be appropriate for single bloggers who care about Pro's design features. (I'll get to them in a bit.) When you consider that hosting a Web site can easily cost $12 to $20 a month, TypePad's cost is reasonable for a single blog allowance of blogs and authors in many ways.

Five features, that may or may not be important to you, are withheld from the Basic service:

- **Custom design:** TypePad is capable of three types of custom page design. At the most basic level, Plus and Pro users can choose from a selection of preset color themes and design templates. Changing from one to another is simple, and the entire blog is transformed after the change. At a higher level, Pro users can rewrite the HTML and CSS code that underlies the blog pages. This feature is for advanced page builders only; for them, it is perhaps essential.

- **Scheduled posts:** Plus and Pro customers can back-date and forward-date their entries. This might seem trivial, but forward-dating, in particular, enables the blogger to store up entries in advance during free time, and then let them fall into the blog in a measured fashion.

- **Domain mapping:** This technique enables users to blog at TypePad using a purchased domain (www.*yourdomain*.com). Chapter 8 discusses domains and hosting. If you have a domain and have parked it at a registrar that allows advanced DNS management, you can arrange for browsers seeking your domain to be taken directly to your TypePad blog. TypePad provides a sample e-mail for inquiring at your registrar about this service. Using Plus, you can map three domains to three blogs; Pro users can map an unlimited number of domains to an equal number of blogs.

- **Search and replace:** This feature enables Pro users to search through the entire blog for specified words or phrases, and automatically replace them with other text. Not, perhaps, the most essential feature. But if you misspelled your wife's name throughout your blog, you'd want to replace each instance with the correct spelling before checking the classifieds for bachelor apartments.

- **Text ads:** TypePad offers a packaged service of Google text ads, turning the blog into an AdSense publisher and perhaps making a few bucks. (See Chapter 15 for more on blogging revenue and Google AdSense.) TypePad doesn't advertise it too loudly, but Basic and Plus users can work Google ads into their blog sidebars, customizing the ad placement more than the packaged service allows; doing so is complicated and difficult.

This chapter is written in the viewpoint of a Plus user, partly because it's important to cover custom design available in Plus (and Pro) accounts. Additionally, TypePad handles shared elements among multiple Plus blogs in unexpected ways, and this chapter untangles those idiosyncrasies.

Setting Up Your Blog

After completing the sign-up process, you have a TypePad account, and for the remainder of the chapter I'm going to blithely assume it's a Plus account, and that you plan to operate two or three blogs. Immediately after signing up and starting your trial, TypePad shows you an overview of your blog's control panel. (See Figure 7-5.) This is the last time you'll see this particular page; from this point onward, you'll be working with a system of control pages within tabs. There, you do everything described in the remainder of this chapter.

The basic method of posting to a TypePad blog is through the TypePad site. (You can also use a bookmarklet, as described later in this chapter.) If you are surfing the Web and blogging at the same time, it's a good idea to keep one browser window or tab anchored at your TypePad control panel. That way, your administrative tools are always available to you, and you don't have to repeatedly visit the TypePad site to post entries.

Before posting any entries, tempting though it is to blast your way into the blogosphere, you should take the time to configure your blog. The settings described in this section can be revisited at any time, but these basic configurations are meant to be selected sooner rather than later.

Figure 7-5:
The first view of TypePad's author controls after signing up.

Three Tip icons in a row? I am nothing if not tipful. Or maybe tipsy. Anyway, I advise perseverance at this stage; you're going to need it. TypePad's administrative layout is not without logic, but the logic isn't immediately apparent. At first, it might seem as if you have to hunt through tabs within tabs for every little thing. This chapter directs you to the important functions, but the layout won't feel truly comfortable until you can toss me aside and work on your own. A few days of poking around are required before the layout of TypePad's features coheres in your mind.

As you can see in Figure 7-5, the TypePad administrative area has four main tabs: Weblogs, Photo Albums, TypeLists, and Control Panel. To configure your blog, follow these steps:

1. **Click the Weblogs tab.**

   Four tabs are revealed within the Weblogs tab.

2. **Click the Configure tab.**

   Five more tabs!

3. **Click the Weblog Basics tab.**

4. **Make your selections on this page (see Figure 7-6 and the description after this list), and click the Save Changes button.**

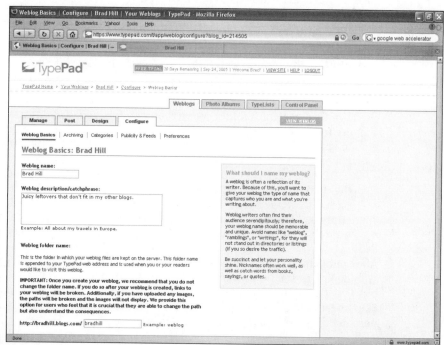

Figure 7-6: Weblog Basics is where you set the blog name and description.

   5. **When the page reloads, click the Publish My Site button.**

      This is your first encounter with an important distinction between saving changes and publishing changes. Publishing your saved changes re-creates every page of the blog affected by the changes. As your blog grows bigger, publishing changes takes longer. As I describe later, your blog entries don't have to go through this two-layered save/publish process, thank goodness. Likewise, you can change themes and layouts (also described later) with a single click.

   6. **In the pop-up window, click the Publish button.**

      This extra step is, by any measure, ridiculous.

   7. **When the pop-up window says your files have been published, click the Close button.**

      I like TypePad, but this unnecessary clicking is foolish.

Fortunately, TypePad keeps navigation pretty clear at all times, so you can always see where you are in the box-within-a-box system of nested tabs. I would prefer a list or drop-down menu so you could go directly to an inner tab, but for some reason the TypePad people are not calling me up for suggestions.

Anyway, let's look at the settings on the Weblogs, Configure, Weblog Basics page, which is also shown in Figure 7-6:

   ✔ **Weblog name:** Type the name that you want to appear in the banner atop your pages.

   ✔ **Weblog description/catchphrase:** This tagline goes below your Weblog name on the page. (See Figure 7-7.)

   ✔ **Weblog folder name:** I discussed blog folders earlier in this chapter. TypePad assigns a folder name that matches your subdomain, but you are free to change it. Your default blog (which starts out being the first blog you create but can be changed if you create more blogs) always appears to visitors who type the domain without a folder in the address: *yourdomain*.typepad.com. The site also appears to anyone who types the domain with the folder after a slash, like this: *yourdomain*.type pad.com/*yourdomain*. (Second and third blogs need the folder in the address.) There is no need to change the default folder name; but if you want to change it, do so now, before you start posting entries.

After publishing your changes, you might be tempted to click the <u>View Weblog</u> link to see how your newborn site is coming along. The link is there, but TypePad won't let you see anything until you write and post an entry. Skip ahead if you like, or follow me through the next short section about personalizing your profile.

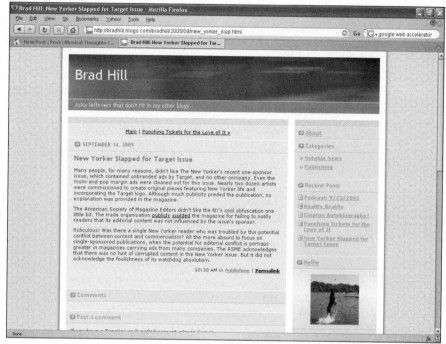

Figure 7-7:
The blog
title and
description
appear at
the top of
every page.

Personalizing Your Blog Profile

Your blog might divulge a lot about you, and you also might want to give visitors an easy way to quickly know who you are. Like many blog services, TypePad offers a Profile section for filling in personal information. A link to the Author Profile appears (if you want it to) in the blog's sidebar as an <u>About</u> link. You can provide a picture of yourself (or somebody else, if that gives you a kick) under the About header.

Create your profile like this:

1. **Click the Control Panel tab.**

2. **Click the Profile tab.**

3. **If you want to assign a photo to your profile, click the Browse button, select a photo, and then click the Open button.**

4. **Scroll down to fill in Your Interests, Your Extended Biography, and Your One-Line Biography.**

   All of these fields are optional. Fill in as complete or sketchy a profile as you want.

Figure 7-8 illustrates a profile page that displays when a visitor clicks the <u>About</u> link in a TypePad blog. This particular About page shows all the available information fields from the Profile page, but it's not unusual to see far sketchier information.

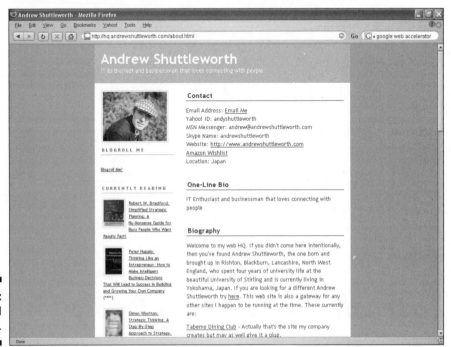

Figure 7-8: A TypePad profile page.

The profile information you enter is attached to your entire account, not to a specific blog. This means that Plus and Pro users who maintain two or more blogs should write a profile that applies equally to all the blogs — if you intend to use an <u>About</u> link in your sidebar. (See the section later in this chapter called "Filling Your Sidebars.")

Blogging Entries in TypePad

Having set up your blog with basic configuration settings, you're ready to post your first TypePad entry. Follow these steps:

1. **From anywhere in your TypePad account, click the Weblogs tab.**

2. **In the Weblogs tab, click the Post tab.**

   There are tabs in this tab, too, but the one you want — the New Post tab — is selected by default. Figure 7-9 shows this page.

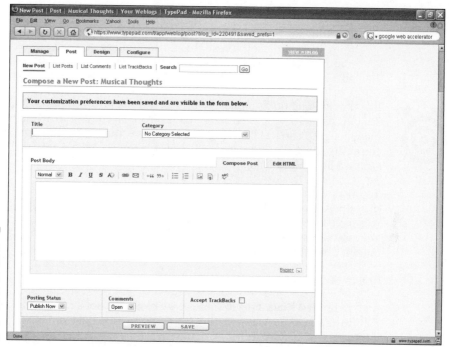

Figure 7-9:
This is
where you
post a
TypePad
entry.

3. In the Title field, type a title for your entry.

4. In the Category drop-down menu, select a category.

You can assign any entry to one or more categories. TypePad comes
loaded with about a dozen preset categories that are too broad to be
useful; effective categories are narrow subdivisions of broader subjects.
You can manage your blog categories (though you don't have to use
them at all) on the Weblogs, Configure, Categories page. For now, you
can get started with the Category drop-down menu on the New Post
page by either selecting a preset or choosing the Add a New Category
selection. Doing the latter displays a pop-up window in which you can
create a category for the current post; that category remains available
for future posts.

5. In the Post Body form, write your entry.

Like many e-mail services, TypePad gives you one-click control of basic
formatting such as bold, italic, underline, bullets, numbered lists, and
font colors. It's generally best to keep formatting to a minimum in blog
entries and remember that underlined words look like links. When you
want to embed a link, highlight a word or group of words, and then use
the Insert Link button (roll your mouse over the buttons to find it).

6. Click the Save button.

The Preview button shows what the entry will look like in the blog, but there is little reason to use this button unless you've inserted lots of formatting. As long as the Posting Status menu shows Publish Now, your entry appears in your live blog as soon as the New Post page reloads.

If you write long posts, consider breaking them into two parts. Many bloggers split up posts to keep their index pages from stretching to accommodate many lengthy entries. Breaking the post gives the reader the option of seeing the entire thing; TypePad makes it easy for the reader by automatically providing a link to the full entry.

To break your entry, you need two message-writing forms, called Post Introduction and Post Continuation. Click the <u>Customize the display of this page</u> link to place these two fields on your New Post page. A pop-up window appears (see Figure 7-10). Scroll down the window to the Post Screen Configuration section and click the Custom radio button.

You have several screen items available:

- ✓ **Extended Post:** This is the one we're after. Check Extended Post to place the second message-writing form on the New Post screen.

- ✓ **Excerpt:** This selection puts another text box on the New Post page, in which you can compose an excerpt for partial-entry RSS feed and TrackBack excerpts. If you do not use the Excerpt box, TypePad clips the first 40 words of the entry for both purposes.

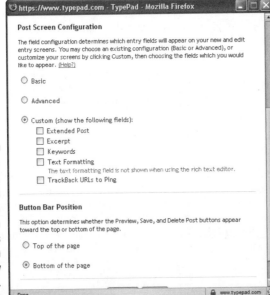

Figure 7-10:
Use this pop-up to determine which options appear on the New Post page.

✔ **Keywords:** The Keywords text box, when placed on the New Post page, gives you a chance to assign searchable words to your entries. Keywords are not visible in the blog, but they are associated with the entry to make it easier to find when searching. The search box is located at the upper-right of the New Post page.

✔ **Text Formatting:** A little-used feature, text formatting prevents the use of bold type, italics, colored fonts, bullets, and numbered lists. If you use text formatting, you must create links by writing out the HTML code.

✔ **TrackBack URLs to Ping:** You need this field on the New Post page if you want to place a TrackBack on another blog's entry page. (See Chapter 3 for more about TrackBacks.) Enter the TrackBack URL (not the other blog's entry-page URL) in this box.

Click the Save button after making your selections. The pop-up window disappears and the New Post reloads to show your selections.

Near the bottom of the New Post page is a drop-down Comments menu that enables you to turn comments on (Open) or off (None) on a per-entry basis. The Closed selection pertains to already posted entries and serves to prevent further commenting.

You can schedule a post for the future or even date it in the past. TypePad makes no judgments about the here and now; all dates are equal in its eyes. TypePad's job is to file entries in chronological order. Use the Posting Status drop-down menu and select Publish On to pop up a calendar and clock (see Figure 7-11). Set your time and date, and then click the Set Time button. You still must click the Save button on the New Post page to publish your entry.

Figure 7-11: Use this pop-up to post-date or pre-date a TypePad blog entry.

Posting to TypePad from any site

The default method of posting to a TypePad blog is through the TypePad site, which furnishes the extensive administrative area that this chapter describes. But the truth is, it's a hassle to log in to TypePad every time you want to post. You can keep a browser window or tab anchored at TypePad, as I suggested earlier in the chapter, but that, too, is an extra step and clutters your screen.

The solution to browser clutter is a bookmarklet. Bookmarklets are tiny programs that reside on your browser's toolbar. They are simple buttons with a little built-in functionality. The TypePad bookmarklet generates a pop-up posting window with a ready-made link to the site currently displayed in your browser. This function is handy when you want to key a blog entry to a page of news or another blog post. You can post an entry from any Web page, circumventing the TypePad site entirely.

Follow these steps to set up the bookmarklet, which TypePad calls QuickPost:

1. **In your TypePad administrative area, Click the Weblogs tab.**

2. **Click the <u>Set up QuickPost bookmarklet</u> link.**

3. **Select options that will appear in the QuickPost pop-up window.**

4. **Click the Create button.**

5. **Using your mouse, drag the <u>TypePad QuickPost</u> link to your browser's toolbar.** In Firefox, you must have the Bookmarks toolbar visible.

The bookmarklet is now active, living on the toolbar, as shown in the figure. Click it on it when visiting any page to write a blog entry that contains a link to that page. Note that pop-up blockers, which are built into many browser toolbars (such as Google Toolbar) and browsers themselves (such as Firefox), can prevent TypePad QuickPost from popping open its posting window. You might have to disable pop-up blocking on any page from which you want to write a blog entry.

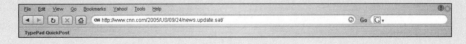

TypePad Themes and Layouts

Some people don't care a whit about site design; others obsess about the colors and layout of their blogs. I lean to the latter camp, but I recognize the time-wasting danger in spending too many hours playing with the design of every little page element. TypePad supports your need to tweak at whatever level.

After signing in, your default blog is set up with a default theme (colors) and default layout (number of sidebars and position of page elements). You don't need to do a thing; TypePad will present a decent looking blog. Many people use those defaults, and their blogs are instantly recognizable as TypePad blogs.

A little individuality can easily be gained by choosing among several preset themes and layouts, combining them to you heart's content. It's fun. You can change your site's appearance at any stage; all themes are compatible. Layouts come in two groups, and all the designs within each group are compatible. A great deal more individuality is obtained by creating your own theme, which is then imposed upon your chosen layout. Having built a custom theme, you can change layouts beneath that theme.

Creating a custom theme does not require any knowledge of HTML or CSS coding. TypePad supplies a fun and easy tool for altering all background colors, typefaces, borders, and border widths. If you want ultimate control, a Pro account is required to get your hands directly on the HTML.

Choosing TypePad themes and layouts

To be clear, TypePad's two basic design templates are

- **Themes:** Themes involve color more than structure. Minor structural elements such as the size of the top banner and the width of sidebar borders are part of themes. But mainly, when you choose a theme, you are choosing a color scheme.

- **Layouts:** Layouts involve structure, not color. Your layout choice determines whether you have one sidebar next to your blog entries or two sidebars surrounding your entries. Or no sidebars.

You can choose from two types of layout: classic layouts and mixed media layouts. Classic layouts are for text-oriented blogs where the main content is written. These blogs do take uploaded photos, but the layout puts photos around the edges. Mixed media layouts are more photocentric. Some of these layouts take standard written entries, but three of them do not feature an index page of recently posted entries.

To experiment with different preset themes and layouts, follow this path:

1. **Click the Weblogs tab.**

2. **Click the Design tab.**

   You are on the Edit Current page.

3. **Click the <u>Change Theme</u> link.**

   The next page defaults to Pre-defined Theme, not Custom Theme. Leave it that way. At this point, you can see five possible themes (see Figure 7-12). Use the pull-down menu to see categories of themes.

4. **In any theme category, select the radio button below a theme.**

Figure 7-12:
Choosing
a theme
applies
a color
scheme to
your site
elements.

5. Click the Save Changes button.

The newly selected theme is saved but not yet applied to your blog.

6. Click the Preview button or the Republish Weblog button.

The Preview button displays a pop-up window showing what your site will look like with the new theme. The Republish Weblog button applies the theme to the blog. You can change themes as often and frequently as you like. When testing many themes, save time by previewing before republishing.

Now move on to selecting a layout. Follow the same process as changing your theme, but start by selecting Change Layout on the Edit Current page. Again, use the Preview button to audition multiple layouts. (See Figure 7-13.)

Creating a TypePad template

A template is a theme/layout combination with additional content selections. These content selections determine what gets placed in your site's sidebars. In TypePad terminology, *content* does not mean blog entries; it means photos, lists, archive links, blogrolls, and other information modules that get placed on sidebars. You choose among the available content groups, and then determine the order in which they appear on your sidebar(s).

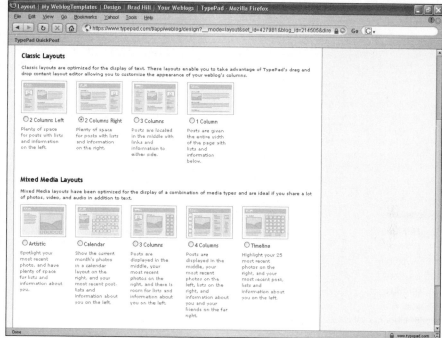

Figure 7-13:
Choosing a
layout
applies an
entry and
sidebar
structure to
your site.

Creating an entire template takes more time than merely changing the theme or layout. At some point, you probably want to take the time to make those content selections, and then create the actual content that goes in the modules. The following steps walk you through the basic process:

1. **Click the Weblogs tab.**

2. **Click the Design tab.**

3. **Click the Create New tab.**

4. **Select a layout, and then click the Step 2: Select the Content for Your Weblog button.**

   These layouts are identical to the selection in Change Layout.

5. **Select your content modules, and then click the Step 3: Order Your Weblog Content button.**

   This is an important page, one that I return to in the "Filling Your Sidebars" section. Keep reading after this walkthrough for notes about the content choices. Also, look at Figure 7-14 to see a portion of this page.

6. **Drag the content bars with your mouse to order them on your sidebar, and then click the Step 4: Customize Your Weblog's Style button.**

   Only the modules selected in Step 5 appear here. See Figure 7-15.

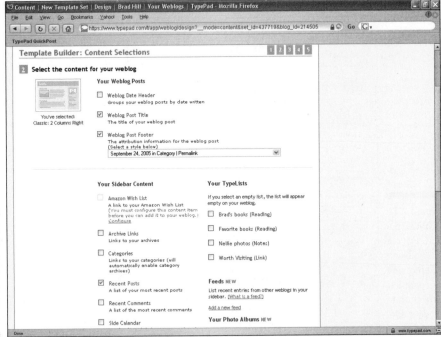

Figure 7-14:
Choose which information groups appear on your blog.

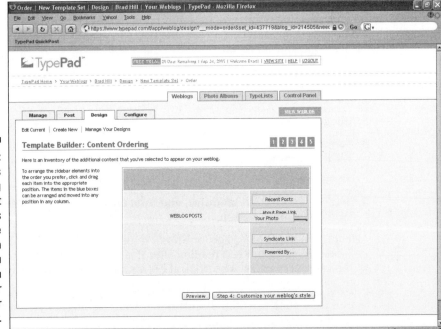

Figure 7-15:
Use this page to drag content modules into the order in which you want them to appear in your sidebar.

7. **Select a theme, and then click the Step 5: Save Your Template button.**

8. **Fill in the Name and Description fields for this template, and then click the Save This Design button or the Apply This Design button.**

   The second button republishes the blog with your new template.

Let's examine the screen in which you choose content for your sidebars. The Content Selections page is a long page. Some items are self-explanatory or well explained by the accompanying notes. Here are my suggestions:

- ✔ **Weblog Date Header:** For some reason, this box is deselected by default, even though most blogs use daily date headers on the index page. Even if you use the date in the footer (see that check box and pull-down menu to select a footer format for each entry), you might want to use the date header.

- ✔ **Categories:** When you get a couple dozen posts, I recommend displaying your categories in the sidebar. They appear as links, making it easy for visitors to read entries of particular interest.

- ✔ **Recent Comments:** If you are creating a discussion forum, you probably want to highlight recent comments. I have found those links quite useful when visiting TypePad blogs.

- ✔ **About Page Link:** This link displays your author profile, and its box is checked by default. That's why you see so many TypePad blogs with blank About pages; the bloggers haven't filled in their profile information and don't realize that the About link is turned on. Fill in your profile on the Profile tab (which you get to by clicking the Control Panel tab).

- ✔ **Online Status:** This feature also connects with the blogger's profile, in which you can identify the instant messaging system you use. If you list an IM program and if you select this box, TypePad alerts visitors when you are available through your chosen IM service.

- ✔ **Email Link:** I keep this turned off, preferring communication in the form of comments.

- ✔ **Subscribe Link:** This feature makes it easy for other bloggers to add your blog to their blogroll, which in TypePad lingo is a kind of TypeList. (I get to TypeLists later.)

- ✔ **Syndicate Link:** This link is for your RSS feed and should definitely be turned on.

- ✔ **Podcast Link:** If you are not creating podcasts, you should ignore this setting and leave it deselected.

- ✔ **Recent Updates:** Select this box if you want links to other people's blogs, as chosen by TypePad, appearing in your sidebar. That's a bit too communal for me; I like to choose my own sidebar content.

✔ **Powered by TypePad Link:** You are paying for this service, so you shouldn't feel that you must assist the advertising efforts of your service provider. The box is selected by default.

✔ **Feeds:** Great feature, this. If you want to include content from other sources in your sidebar, copy the RSS feed address here. Just click the <u>Add a new feed</u> link and paste the feed address into the pop-up window; entire blog entries from that feed appear in your sidebar. This feature works best with headline-only feeds, but I've seen blogs running full-entry feeds from other sources in their sidebars. (See Figure 7-16.) It gives the appearance of an info-packed site. (By the way, see Chapter 13 for a full discussion of feeds.)

✔ **Your Photo Albums:** When you create photo albums, this feature lists them, each with a check box for inclusion in your sidebar. Each album that you include displays the most recently added photo in the sidebar — not the entire album. See the "Putting Photos in Your TypePad Blog" section, later in this chapter.

Figure 7-16:
This site uses Type-Pad's Live Feeds feature in the right sidebar.

Creating a custom theme

If you want to get in up to your elbows with page design, use the Custom Theme tools. Here's how:

1. **Click the Weblogs tab.**

2. **Click the Design tab.**

3. **Click the <u>Change Theme</u> link.**

4. **Click the radio button next to Custom Theme.**

   Now you see four groups of page elements waiting to be customized, as shown in Figure 7-17.

5. **Click one of the four Edit This Element buttons.**

   A pop-up window displays your customization tools. Use the color selectors and drop-down menus to alter each page element. The thumbnail diagrams illustrate the changes you make as you go along.

Figure 7-17: TypePad allows customization of all major blog elements.

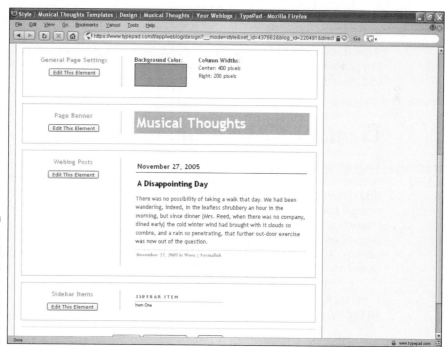

6. **Click the Save Changes button.**

7. **Click another Edit This Element button, as in Step 5, and repeat.**

8. **Click the Preview button each time you save your changes to see how your design is coming along.**

Creating a custom theme is trickier than it might appear, but it's a lot of fun. Your custom design is always saved as a work in progress, as long as you use the Save Changes button. Click the Manage Your Designs tab to switch from one saved design to another.

Putting Photos in Your TypePad Blog

TypePad is photo-friendly. You get photos into your blog in two ways:

- ✔ Create a photo album and upload photos into it.
- ✔ Insert a photo into a blog post.

Photo albums generate separate pages specially designed for viewing photos. Your normal blog design does not carry over to photo album pages. You can link from your sidebar to your photo albums, and you can put several photos in your sidebar in a couple of ways (neither of them particularly convenient, unfortunately).

Creating a photo album

You can create as many photo albums as you want and have an unlimited number of photos in each. Your TypePad account does have memory limitations, though, which might restrict voluminous photo uploading. If you are using a classic layout, you presumably want to leave room for blog posts. It's important to remember, though, that written posts take much less memory than photos, so you can safely use a healthy portion of your allotment on photos. You can see how much account space you are consuming in the Overview section of the Control Panel tab.

Creating a TypePad photo album with your digital photos requires several steps, but they are not difficult:

1. **Click the Photo Albums tab.**

2. **Under Create a New Photo Album, on the right (see Figure 7-18), fill in the album name and folder name, and select whether it will be public.**

   The folder name needn't be the same as the album name, but confusion will probably beset you if they are different.

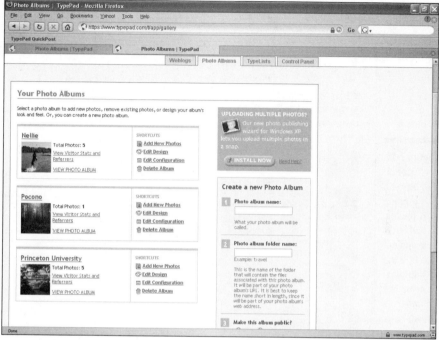

Figure 7-18:
This page
lists your
existing
photo
albums and
invites you
to create a
new one.

3. **Click the Create button.**

4. **Click the <u>Add photos to this album</u> link.**

5. **Click a Browse button.**

   This page assumes you want to upload more than one photo. It doesn't matter which Browse button you click first. Each Browse button locates a single photo on your hard drive.

6. **Select a photo from your hard drive, and click the Open button.**

7. **Click the Upload button.**

   Wait for a pop-up window to pop up, as pop-up windows are wont to do. Then wait a little longer as the photo is uploaded. Turns out, the only purpose of the pop-up window is to notify you of the uploading progress. The pop-up window closes (pops down?) when the upload is complete.

8. **Click a photo to name it and caption it.**

   TypePad displays the filename of each uploaded photo. When photos are transferred from a digital camera to a computer, the resulting file-names are often numbers (see Figure 7-19). Whatever the case, you can leave that original name or rename the picture. On the renaming page, use the Photo Cloning section to copy the picture to other, already exist-ing photo albums in your account. Unfortunately, cloning literally makes a copy of the photo, using more memory. Far better would be a tagging system whereby a single photo could virtually reside in multiple albums.

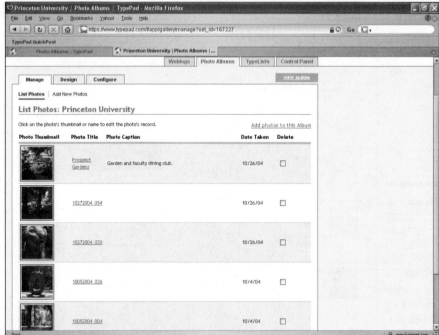

Figure 7-19:
TypePad
lets you
rename
photos,
which is
convenient
if the
original
name is a
number, as
shown here.

9. **Click the Save button.**

   You could click the Save and Publish button, but publishing takes time.
   You might as well wait until you've finished naming and captioning the
   last uploaded photo, and then use the Save and Publish button to publish the whole lot. Publishing makes your photo album live, online. If you
   made the photo album public, TypePad.com places the album on its
   recently updated album list for all to see.

10. **If you want to upload another photo, go back to Step 5.**

11. **When you've finished uploading photos, click the Save and Publish
    button.**

    Publishing makes your photo album live, online. If you made the photo
    album public, TypePad places the album on its recently updated album
    list for all to see.

Photos albums are directly accessible on the Web by using your domain and
album folder name. The following example illustrates how the direct address
works, using a fictional album folder called Vacation:

```
subdomain.typepad.com/photos/vacation
```

Shared photo albums

Your photo albums belong to your TypePad account and can be accessed by all the blogs in that (Plus or Pro) account. This arrangement has good points and bad. On the good side, your various blogs can share photos without having to upload them more than once, taking up valuable memory. That consideration is the major reason for arranging photo albums in this manner. On the bad side, the shared-album configuration prevents TypePad from allowing the automatic display of photos from albums in a blog's sidebar. TypePad does not have a command or setting that puts an uploaded album photo into the sidebar with no effort on your part. That's because TypePad wouldn't know which blog you wanted the photo in and which blog you didn't want the photo in.

I hope TypePad devises an easy way to correct this inconvenience. In the meantime, there is a somewhat awkward way to manually place album photos in the sidebar: You must create a TypeList of links to individual photos in your albums. I cover TypeLists in this chapter. An easier but not necessarily desirable way to automatically place a photo in the sidebar is to insert the photo in a blog entry. This strategy works if you choose a mixed media layout, not a classic layout. Recently posted photos appear in mixed media layouts with no effort on your part. In mixed media blogs, you often see entries with many photos embedded in them; it's the quickest way to get those photos in the sidebar of every page in the blog. At this writing, you can't automatically stream photos from a photo album or from blog posts into the sidebar of classic layouts.

Note that you must insert `/photos/`*`directory`* between the domain name and after your TypePad domain name. In the preceding example, *subdomain* would be replaced by the name of your subdomain.

You can adjust the presentation of each photo album. Click the Design tab within the Photo Albums tab to adjust the layout, style, and content of the album. Making these choices is not unlike choosing a layout and theme for your blog, as described earlier. Each album can have different design characteristics. Here's what goes into your three design sets:

- Click the Layout link. There, as you see in Figure 7-20, you select a structural layout for the album's cover page and another layout for the album's photo page. The cover page displays an overview of the album, showing either a collection of album thumbnails or one big picture used as a teaser. The photo pages result when a photo is clicked; a caption and descriptive material can be displayed with a large view of that photo — plus thumbnails of the other album photos, if you like. The layout of each photo page within an album is identical.

- Click the Style link. There, as shown in Figure 7-21, you select from a range of colorful themes. The structure of the photo album pages, determined by your layout choice, is not altered here. Use the pull-down menu to audition the styles; the sample screen shots change every time you click a style from the list.

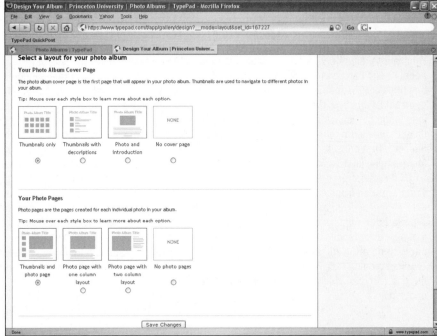

Figure 7-20:
Select the layout structure of your photo album's cover page and photo pages.

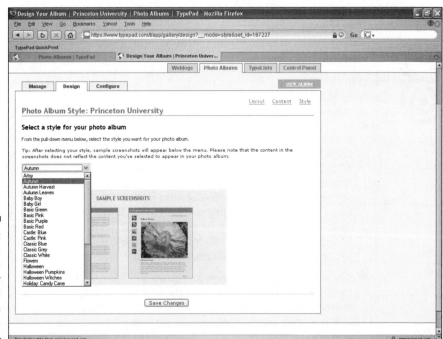

Figure 7-21:
Select the color style of the cover page and photo pages.

✔ Click the <u>Content</u> link. On this page you determine which types of content accompany the displays of your photos. For example, you might want to show photo captions but not photo descriptions. Or you might prefer captions and descriptions, but no locations (where the photos were taken). In each case, you should be prepared to fill in whatever information blocks you choose, whenever you upload new photos. Note that, on this page, you make one set of decisions for the album cover page and another set of overlapping decisions for the photo pages.

You might think, after all this design manipulation of your photo album, that no other configurations would be necessary. Indeed, none are . . . but more fine-tuning of how your album works is possible. Click the Configure tab (within the Photo Albums tab) to see what awaits finicky perfectionists:

✔ In Photo Album Basics, you have a chance to change the basic photo album settings that you created when first making the album: name, description, and whether the album is public. You can also upload a photo that isn't in your album to act as a cover-page image.

✔ In Advanced Configuration, you can set the size of your thumbnail displays, how many columns of thumbnails will be shown for large albums, and whether to square off rectangular images (most people do square them off). You can choose a date format for the cover and photo pages and decide on the size of large photo displays. (On that last point, surprisingly, TypePad does not offer a size larger than 640 pixels in width.)

When you save any photo album design or configuration settings, TypePad assumes you want the album republished and takes the initiative to republish it live on the Web. Unlike with many other blog changes, which require saving and then a separate republishing step, tinkering with your photo albums is a streamlined, change-and-publish process.

Figure 7-22 shows a designed photo page of an album.

Inserting a photo into a blog entry

Photo albums offer the most formal method of presenting pictures. You can share your albums by linking directly to them as destinations distinct from your blog. You can place album references and descriptions in your sidebar using the Content Selection page of the Weblogs, Design tab (see the following section, "Filling Your Sidebars").

A quicker, more down-and-dirty way of sharing photos is to simply toss them into a blog entry, as follows:

1. **Create a blog entry in the normal fashion.**

2. **Click the Insert Image button.**

Figure 7-22:
A photo
page of a
TypePad
photo
album.

Roll your mouse cursor over the buttons to find it. Wait for the pop-up window.

 3. **Click the Browse button, select a picture from your hard drive, and then click the Open button.**

 4. **Click the Use Custom Settings radio button and choose the custom settings. (See Figure 7-23.)**

 These settings allow you to determine how your entry text wraps around your photo, the size of the thumbnail displayed in the entry (full-size photos are likely to be bigger than the entry space in your blog), and whether you'd like a pop-up to display the full-sized image when visitors click the thumbnail. These settings do not persist; the next picture you insert will revert to the default settings unless you customize them again.

 5. **Click the Insert Image button.**

 The picture now appears in your post as you continue to write or edit it.

 6. **Repeat these steps to insert additional pictures.**

As I mentioned before, posted pictures automatically appear in the sidebar of mixed media layouts, under the Most Recent Photos banner.

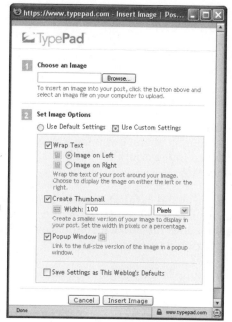

Figure 7-23:
This pop-up assists in inserting a photo into a blog entry.

Filling Your Sidebars

Aside from blog entries, your site's content is presented in sidebars. TypePad offers layout designs with one, two, or three sidebars. In those spaces, you can stuff photos, links, and lists that stretch vertically down the page alongside your entries. Sidebars replicate throughout the blog; they appear identically on all pages except photo album pages.

Choosing your sidebar content

In TypePad, the stuff that goes into sidebars is assigned using a modular system. That is to say, you select certain categories of content, and TypePad automatically puts that category into a sidebar with a header. In some cases, you must create special sidebar content before a module shows anything below its header. In other cases (such as Most Recent Photos, Recent Posts, and Recent Comments), TypePad takes the content from entry pages and spools it automatically in the sidebar.

We have seen the sidebar content selection page before (look back at Figure 7-16). But that was many pages ago, so here's a reminder:

1. **Click the Weblogs tab.**
2. **Click the Design tab.**
3. **Click the <u>Change Content Selections</u> link.**

On that page, scroll down to Your Sidebar Content, and select the boxes next to modules you want to see in your sidebars. If you have created photo albums, notice that they are listed under Your Photo Albums, and the album, too, can be placed in the sidebar.

When selected, an album is represented in the sidebar *by a single photo,* not by every photo in the album. It's important to really hear this because it can be confusing. Selecting an album does not spool its photos onto the sidebar (though I wish there were such a choice).

One curious content selection group is called Your TypeLists. Keep reading, dude.

Creating TypeLists

TypePad uses a flexible list system for adding a blogroll, favorite books, favorite music, and favorite links to your sidebar. Each one of these lists is called a *TypeList,* and the TypeList feature makes it easy to create them. Each TypeList that you create is available to your entire (Plus or Pro) account, just as photo albums are. This means that if you operate more than one TypePad blog, each TypeList you create can be used (or ignored) by each blog.

TypeLists are easy to create, and TypePad makes the process even easier by preconfiguring a few list types and pulling content from Amazon.com to add pictures of book covers and CD album covers. To illustrate, the following steps walk you through creating a reading TypeList:

1. **Click the TypeLists tab.**
2. **Under Create a New TypeList (see Figure 7-24), use the pull-down menu to select Reading.**
3. **In the List Name field, name your list.**
4. **Click the Create New List button.**
5. **Under Add a New Book, enter book information.**

    Notice that you can use an ISBN number, if you have one. Otherwise, enter the book title and author.

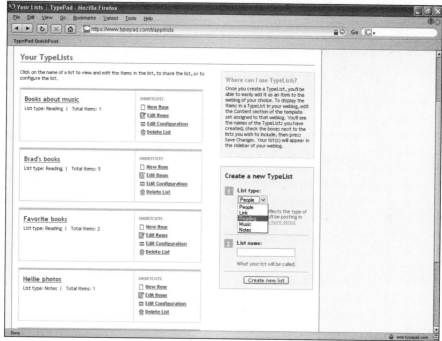

Figure 7-24:
This page
displays a
summary
of your
existing
TypeLists
and invites
you to
create a
new one.

6. Click the Add button.

TypePad finds the book at Amazon and pulls a thumbnail image of the book's cover. Figure 7-25 shows this process in midstream; one book has been added and the page awaits information about the second item of the list. Each time you click the Add button, the new item is displayed on the page. Use the drop-down menu to add a rating if you want; I always leave it set at "None," because the book wouldn't be in my list if it wasn't top-flight.

7. Repeat the previous two steps for each additional book in the list.

That's it; you don't need to save the TypeList after adding each item. The list is created. Go to the Change Content Selections page, where the list now appears, and select it for placement on your sidebar.

When you put books in a reading list, TypePad links from each book to its page at Amazon.com. Furthermore TypePad inserts the Amazon Associate code of TypePad's parent company, SixApart, in the link code. If visitors click these links and buy books during that visit to Amazon, SixApart receives a small commission. From your traffic! This unseemly tactic reflects badly on TypePad and SixApart. There is no simple way to strip out SixApart's associate code, but you can replace it with your own affiliate code. To do so, you first must be an Amazon Associate. If you don't know what that is, or you want to join Amazon's Associates program, visit this site:

```
associates.amazon.com
```

To insert your Amazon Associates name in place of the SixApart identifier, go to the Profile tab under the Control Panel tab. Scroll down to Miscellaneous Information and enter your Amazon Associates ID there.

To create a blogroll, which is traditionally found in blog sidebars, do this:

1. **Click the TypeLists tab.**

2. **Use the drop-down menu to select Link, and then name your list.**

   If you want your link list to be called "Blogroll" on the sidebar, name it such here.

3. **Enter a URL, and then click the Add button.**

4. **Add or edit the link title.**

   TypePad attempts to title your link based on the site name of the URL, but it doesn't always succeed. You can name each link as you see fit.

5. **Click the Save and Update button.**

Your blogroll is ready to be added to the sidebar.

Figure 7-25: Here is a book-oriented TypeList in progress. One book has been added so far.

Moblogging in TypePad

Mobile blogging (moblogging) is handily accomplished in TypePad. You can post an entry from e-mail or from a portable device equipped with e-mail, such as a cell phone or PDA (personal digital assistant). Chapter 17 explains the basics of moblogging.

In TypePad, a moblogged entry is assumed to be either text or a photo, and you can send each type to a different blog (in Plus and Pro accounts). You need to specify between one and five addresses you will be using to send messages. These addresses can be standard e-mail addresses or cell-phone e-mail addresses. A secret, cryptic address is provided to your account — this is the address to which you send moblogged posts. If you don't like the secret address, you may use a generic TypePad address, and then specify your account using confirmation messages (this process takes longer).

All the settings described in the previous paragraph are located on the Control Panel, Profile, Mobile Settings page. Use that page to route your text messages and photo posts to one blog, or each to a separate blog in your account. Enter the e-mail address(es) from which you will moblog. Scroll down to see your account's secret e-mail address. For cell-phone moblogging, you need to get that address into your phone.

The exact procedure for posting a moblog entry through a cell phone depends on the phone and its carrier (your cell-phone company), but the basic procedure for posting a photo is simple:

1. **Take a picture with your cell phone.**

2. **Using your phone's e-mail function, send the photo to your TypePad's secret address.**

   You must have previously listed your phone's e-mail address on the Mobile Settings page.

That's it. If you elected to receive a confirmation e-mail on the Mobile Settings page, you will soon get one affirming that your photo was posted to the blog you specified for photo entries. That entry contains no text.

Moblogging photos is a more common use of mobile blogging than sending text entries, mainly because it is so difficult to compose a text message of any length on a cell phone. Snapping a picture, however, is (I hesitate to type this) a snap (darn, I actually typed it). So, the more crucial of your two desti-nation choices is where to send photos. TypePad lists all your blogs and photo albums as potential destinations on the Mobile Settings page (in the

Control Panel, Profiles tab). If you select a blog, your moblogged photos are posted as regular entries, without any accompanying text. If you choose a photo album, moblogged photos are simply added to that album. Remember that if you use a mixed media blog layout, photos inserted in entries are automatically placed in the sidebar. This system is great for moblogging. Your mobile photo appears simultaneously in a blog entry and in a sidebar. In most cases, it's a better choice than aiming moblogged photos at a photo album.

Your mobile settings apply to the entire TypePad account, not to a single blog.

A Final Note

I can't cover every TypePad feature in this chapter. It's not much of an exaggeration to say that TypePad could fill a book. A small book, but a book nonetheless. Fortunately, TypePad provides a fairly complete reference of its features, which you can access with the small <u>Help</u> link atop every page of your account area. There you can find customer support contact information (personal help is provided through e-mail), but you might never have to use it. The User Manual is searchable, and the Frequently Asked Questions area is helpful. When you want to take time out from actually blogging, I recommend poking around this documentation to discover features you'd never find otherwise.

Part III
Installing Your Own Blog Program

The 5th Wave   By Rich Tennant

"Hi all. Turns out that the rash I posted about last night is contagious..."

In this part . . .

This part contains the book's most ambitious chapters. In these pages, you can explore three of the most powerful and flexible blog programs: Movable Type, WordPress, and Radio UserLand. These programs are not for everyone, not least because they require more installation than the hosted blog services described in Part II. That's where Chapter 8 comes in — it's a rundown of how to install a blog program on a server. Reading that chapter can give you an idea of whether or not such an installation is something you'd like to try.

Chapters 9, 10, and 11 illustrate and explain details of three blog programs and can also play into your decision. Finally, Chapter 12 offers a compromise; in that chapter you'll find pointers to Web-hosting services that install Movable Type or WordPress for you. It's the best of both worlds, power and ease . . . for a price.

Chapter 8

The Ins and Outs of DIY Blogging

In This Chapter

▶ Buying your blog's domain and starting a Web hosting account

▶ Understanding the basics of installing a blog program

▶ Initializing a newly installed blog

*T*his is the most challenging chapter in the book and certainly the most technical. These pages are also pure gold for anyone contemplating running a self-installed blog program. For those readers going down the do-it-yourself path, this must-read chapter helps get you over the installation hump of using Movable Type (see Chapter 9) or WordPress (see Chapter 10). For more cautious readers who are uncertain of what self-installed blogging entails, this chapter pins down the basics common to all such installations. If you are undecided about your blogging platform, this chapter will help you make a choice.

The decision at hand is not between Movable Type and WordPress, the two blog programs I cover in this book that the user installs on a server. Reading through Chapters 9 and 10, and viewing the screen shots, will help you clarify that personal decision. The choice faced by this chapter is whether to install your own blog program or use a hosted service such as Blogger, TypePad, or a social network.

I want to be clear about two phrases that I'm throwing around: *self-installed blogging* and *hosting your own blog.* It might sound as if these phrases refer to installing blog software on your personal computer and allowing readers to access your PC to view the blog entries. Not true. Self-installed blogging refers to putting the blog software on a remote computer, called a *server.* It is your blog, and it is called *hosting* your own blog because you lease space on that remote server and operate the files in that space as if they were on your computer.

Hosting your own blog is a much larger project than starting a blog on a ready-to-go platform, and it implies a long-term commitment. Most DIYers own their Web domains (`www.yourdomain.com`) and have shopped for and selected a generic Web host. (When I say *generic Web host,* I mean one that doesn't specialize in Weblogs or offer preinstalled Weblogs.) In the context of Internet real estate, hosting a blog yourself at your domain is like owning your house instead of renting a virtual home in a blog service.

There is great satisfaction to be had in hosting your own blog. Doing so is not necessarily less expensive than the hybrid solutions described in Chapter 12, but it needn't be more expensive. Like someone who repairs his or her own car, you have the pleasure of knowing that the blog would not be on the road at all if it weren't for your efforts. Finally, working with the elements of blog and hosting software gives you a better understanding of how the Internet works.

This chapter blazes the general path to self-installed blogging from step one. I say "general" path because the details of installing blog programs differ among the programs. Even so, the major points are similar, and it's those major points that confound most people. From registering a domain to writing your first self-hosted blog entry, this chapter provides the reference map.

Master of Your Domain

Owning your site has two major aspects:

- ✔ Owning your domain
- ✔ Leasing server space from a Web hosting company

Owning the domain name of your site is like owning a brand name, and buying the server space on which the site is hosted is like owning virtual real estate. Traditionally, owning a catchy or memorable domain helps attract visitors and keeps them coming back — a truism that loses a little traction in an RSS world. I do nearly all my blog reading by calling up feeds in my newsreader (see Chapter 13), like a lot of people. I don't know about, care about, or ever see the domain names of blogs I read every day. But I still believe in the power of a good domain name, which can help the site get a high ranking in search engines (see Chapter 15 for more on search engine marketing).

Buying a domain

Domains are administered and sold by *domain registrars,* which are companies certified by the Internet Corporation for Assigned Names and Numbers (ICANN). The first domain registrar was Network Solutions (www.network solutions.com), and that company is still doing business. Another popular one is Register.com (www.register.com), which benefits from a great domain name. I have used both those registrars as well as Go Daddy (www.godaddy. com). Dozens of others exist.

A domain is just a name paired with a *top-level domain extension* (such as *.com, .net, .biz,* or *.org,* or one of many other approved extensions). When a name is available (not owned by anyone), it never costs more than $35 a year to own it. Ownership must be renewed every year or less frequently if you buy a longer term. Unrenewed domain names fall into the public market. Many registrars sell domains at a lower annual cost and offer discounts for long-term purchases or bulk purchases of multiple domains. Domains may be purchased in the private market and transferred from one owner to another at a negotiated price.

When you buy a domain, you own only the specific Web address, not the name generally. For example, if your domain is `www.greatdomain.com`, you own `greatdomain.com`, but do not own `greatdomain.net` or the term `greatdomain` paired with any other extension. If you want to lock down the domain term to prevent copycat site names, you must buy all the extensions individually (if they are available).

You don't need a Web host to buy a domain name, but you may get your Web hosting deal in place before shopping for a domain if you want. In other words, it doesn't matter which you get first.

When it comes to buying the domain, here's the drill:

1. **Select a name.**

   This first step might take some brainstorming. Take the time to think of a domain you really like, because changing a blog-in-progress from one domain to another is a headache.

2. **Check the domain's availability.**

   Obvious domain names are not generally available in their *.com* versions. I always check availability as I brainstorm; you can do so at any registrar. Many registrars allow multiple simultaneous checks, which saves time. (See Figure 8-1.)

3. **Buy the domain.**

   Have a credit card at the ready. Most registrars attempt to sell you additional domain-related products and services, such as Web hosting and e-mail service. The checkout process for a domain name can be among the most obnoxious on the Web.

If you do not yet have a hosting account, that's your next step. In the meantime, you need do nothing with your domain. It's yours, even though you're not yet using it.

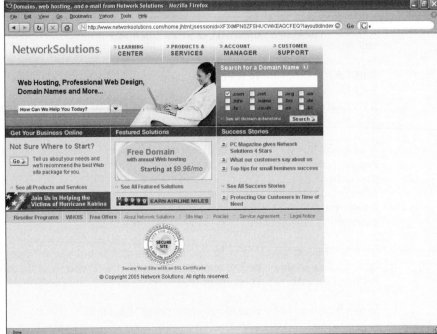

Figure 8-1:
At Network
Solutions,
you can
check the
availability
of multiple
domain
names. You
may buy a
domain at
any official
registrar.

Starting a hosting account

Web sites of all sorts, including independently hosted Weblogs, exist on
Internet computers called *servers*. When you visit a Web site, your computer
communicates over the Internet with that site's server. The server sends
pages to your computer for viewing. Servers are specialized for this kind of
activity in volume; various types of servers can serve hundreds, thousands,
or even millions of simultaneous users.

Internet servers are available for public use through leasing arrangements.
Customers rent portions of the server by the month or by the year. The portion
is defined by storage capacity, which is to say, amount of memory. Capacity
is measured in megabytes (MB) in most cases. Typical hosting limits are
100MB, 500MB, or 1000MB (a thousand megabytes is one gigabyte, or 1GB).
A text-only blog can run for a long time in 100MB, but a larger space is necessary if you plan to add many pictures or a little audio or video.

In addition to capacity limits, hosting companies put a ceiling on transfers,
sometimes called bandwidth. Allowable monthly transfer is always measured in
gigabytes; count on getting between 10GB and 50GB. Again, the more pictures,
audio, and video you have on your site that visitors can download (transfer),
the more bandwidth you need.

Most hosting accounts suitable for blogging cost between $4 and $15 a month. When shopping for a host, five considerations apply specifically to self-hosting a Weblog, and particularly to hosting Movable Type or WordPress, the two self-hosted blogs covered in this book:

- **Unix server:** Unix servers are easier to deal with than Windows servers. Both Movable Type and WordPress have created installation documents geared to Unix. Most hosting accounts state up front whether they are Unix or Windows, or both (your choice). Among Unix hosts, the Apache operating system is not uncommon, but you might have to write or call the hosting company to determine whether it is in use.

- **Perl:** Perl (Practical Extraction and Report Language) is a programming language developed to process text. Perl is often used in blog programs to write *CGI scripts,* which are automated functions commonly found in Weblogs. CGI scripts written in Perl process the creation of entries, comments, archives, and other blog elements. Different blog programs require more or less current versions of Perl. Movable Type requires version 5.004_04 and recommends version 5.6. WordPress does not require Perl.

- **MySQL:** MySQL is a type of server database. A *database* organizes blocks of information — in this case, blog entries, comments, and other elements. MySQL is not the only database type that works with some programs (Movable Type works with several others), but it is the most common database used by Web hosts. Good Web hosts offer one MySQL database per customer as a standard feature. You activate the database in the host's control panel by assigning it a name and giving yourself a username and password for that database. When blogging, you don't directly access the database; the blog software uses it behind the scenes.

- **FTP access:** This feature is almost a given with a Unix host, but make sure you have FTP access to your server space and the files in it. *FTP* (file transfer protocol) is the native method of moving files around the Internet, and good, easy-to-use, programs are available that make uploading files to your server almost as easy as moving files around your own computer with Windows Explorer. One of these programs is WS_FTP (see Figure 8-2); another is CuteFTP.

- **CGI control:** Finally, your Web host should give you control over your own CGI installations. Most Web hosts offer an assortment of *CGI scripts* — little programs such as newsletter sign-up forms. Blog programs are far more complex and require uploading component files into a CGI directory (usually called the *cgi-bin* by default). You need a Web host that provides you with a CGI directory in your server space.

When you've selected your hosting account, proceed through the sign-up and payment process provided at the site. You will be given a username and password, plus an FTP address that you plug into your FTP program when you're ready to upload the files of your blog program (see later sections of this chapter).

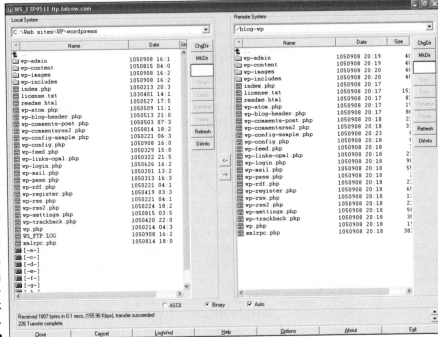

Figure 8-2:
A popular
FTP
program,
WS_FTP
makes
uploading
files a point-
and-click
operation.

Basic Blog Installation

Here we go. It's time to get hard core. This section details the elements of a typical blog installation on a server, after you've acquired a domain and established an FTP path through which files get uploaded. At this point, you should own your domain (www.*yourdomain*.com), own an account with a company that is hosting your domain (a Web host), and have gained some experience uploading files through FTP to the host's server — all described in the previous sections. If you haven't done these things, imagine that you have and read along.

Acquiring and installing blog software is accomplished in three basic steps. Many smaller steps transpire along the way, and I'll get to those soon. The three basic steps are

✔ **Downloading:** Blogging programs such as Movable Type and WordPress are usually acquired by download, not by store purchase.

✔ **Configuring:** After the program is in your computer and unpacked, you usually need to tweak a few component files.

✔ **Uploading:** After making whatever configuration changes are necessary, you upload the files to your server. Doing so installs the blog program on your server.

The following sections expand these three basic steps.

Downloading the blog program

In all likelihood, you will download your blog software, not take it home from a store. For download locations of Movable Type and WordPress, see Chapters 9 and 10, respectively. If the software you choose is commercial, you pay for the download with an online payment.

Like other large software packages, blog programs are compressed for faster downloading and must be uncompressed, or unpacked, in your computer. The compression not only makes the delivery quicker, but also bundles the many component files of blog programs so you can download just one file. Unpacking that compressed file spills out the component files so you can see them and configure them (in the next step). Two types of compression are in common use: Zip and Tar.gz. Both Movable Type and WordPress (and others as well) offer a choice; most readers should select the Zip file, which unpacks easily on Windows computers.

At this stage, downloading the program does not differ from any other download-and-unpack process you've followed with other types of software. You might download the Zipped package to your computer desktop (or to a download folder you have specified). On most Windows XP computers, double-clicking the Zipped file brings up the default decompressing utility program. In this program, select the Extract feature and choose a location for the unpacked files.

Immediately after unpacking the program, things diverge from the standard install-and-use routine you're accustomed to with new software. Your hard drive is not the final destination of your blog program; the software is resting there temporarily. You will always retain the files in your computer, but the program will run on your server, not on your PC. Before you upload the program to the server, you need to alter at least one (in most cases) and sometimes several of the component files. So, when unpacking the files, put them in a location on your hard drive that is easy to find and access. You might need to find the files several times during the configuration stage and possibly later when troubleshooting any problems that arise. But I advise against unpacking the program directly to the desktop, as the dozens of resulting files would clutter it terribly.

After extracting the program files, look them over. In most cases (certainly with Movable Type and WordPress), the program uncompresses into a structure of folders within folders. Such a structure is called a *folder hierarchy* consisting of *nested folders*. You don't need to do anything just yet, but acquaint yourself briefly with the folders holding the component files and especially with the files in the *root folder* — that's the outermost folder that holds other folders as well as a group of individual files. Figure 8-3 shows the directory structure of Movable Type. Note that in this case (and the structure is typical), the root folder is nested within another folder (called *MT*). The *MT* folder exists only to hold all the folders nested within it; I created the *MT* folder when I extracted the program files from the Zip package. It is not necessary to upload such container folders to your server, although you might create a container folder there to hold nested folders. I'll get to that later. In this directory structure, the *MT* folder is the root folder, because it is the top folder that contains program files outside folders.

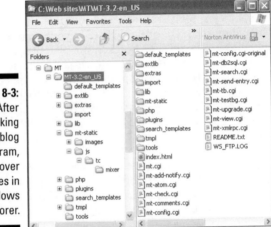

Figure 8-3:
After unpacking your blog program, look over the files in Windows Explorer.

Configuring the files

At this point you've downloaded and unpacked the blog program, and glanced over the directory structure and component files in the root folder. In nearly all cases (and certainly with Movable Type and WordPress), at least one file must be altered before you can proceed. This alteration inserts a few details of your personal Web host and domain setup.

The installation instructions of your blog program explain exactly what must be changed in each file. In most programs, two kinds of alterations are necessary:

✔ Some information must be plugged into a configuration file.

✔ An address path to your server's Perl location must be specified in several program files.

The first of these two is almost always required. The necessity of the second round of alterations depends on whether there is a default match of your server's path to Perl and the path specified in the program files. If there is a match, no alteration is necessary. Some blog programs don't use Perl, in which case an address path is unnecessary. WordPress does not require a Perl address path.

The following sections examine these two configurations more closely.

Altering the config file

Most blog programs contain a component file known as the *configuration,* or *config,* file. In many cases, the original config file that gets unpacked after downloading also contains the word *sample* or *original* in its name, to distinguish it from the altered config file that you will create. The original config file serves as a reference original that you can always go back to.

✔ In Movable Type, the original configuration file is called *mt-config.cgi-original.* Note that the word *original* is appended to the file extension (*.cgi*), which prevents the file from operating when uploaded — the server's CGI functionality cannot recognize the file as a *.cgi* file. The file extension is sabotaged in this manner to prevent you from accidentally attempting to use the original config file as the working config file. You must alter the file and rename it with an unencumbered file extension; more on that later. It doesn't matter whether you upload the original config file, but you must upload a correctly altered and renamed file.

✔ In WordPress, the original configuration file is called *wp-config-sample.php.* The file extension in this case (*.php*) is not sabotaged, but the word *sample* alerts you that this is the original file and you should rename it after you alter it.

Configuration files are text files readable in any text editor (such as Notepad in Windows computers), despite the use of non-*.txt* file extensions. For the remainder of this chapter and in later chapters, I assume that Notepad is the chosen program; it is what I use. Heaven forbid anyone do things differently from me. You edit the original config files the same way you'd edit any other piece of text. Save and rename the file using the Save As selection on the File menu.

When saving and renaming the original config file, do not change the default location presented to you by Notepad! I put an exclamation point there to emphasize how important this is! There's another one! I can't stop! If you change the location, saving the file outside the root directory from which you opened it, it won't be included in the big server upload that you do later and you'll never find the darn thing again. You will gnash your teeth, rend your garments, and scare the kids. Just rename the file by getting rid of the *sample* or *original* portion of the filename, and save it.

So, what gets plugged into the config file? Each program has its own requirements. Some original config files contain multiple settings, at least one of which must be altered and some of which are optional. The role of the config file is to provide basic operational settings to the blog program. In a typical installation, two of those settings are crucial:

- ✔ **Program path:** This is the server address that locates the main blog program file. This setting is sometimes called the *cgi path* because it is often located in a server folder dedicated to holding CGI scripts. Not every blog program requires this setting in the config file; WordPress, for example, does not. WordPress uses a simpler server folder structure than Movable Type and some other programs, so it doesn't need this particular direction.

- ✔ **Database configuration:** This setting is required in the config file by Movable Type, WordPress, and most other blog programs. Your database (MySQL in most cases) is located on your server and is protected by a username and password. Additionally, the database has a name and an address path. You must plug all this information into the config file so the blog program can get its hands on the database, which contains all your entries and archives.

I imagine you're plenty sick of the config file by now, but I'm not going to stop talking about it until you're actually in bed with a fever.

Figure 8-4 shows an original config file (the one that comes with Movable Type). Notice all the pound signs (#)? They (and sometimes other ASCII symbols) are used to provide instructions; any line of text preceded by a pound sign is ineffectual as program code — the blog program ignores that line. Because these disabled lines are used for comments, such lines are called *comment lines*. Removing the pound sign is called *uncommenting* the line. You must know this because uncommenting is part of altering most config files. Not only do you need to plug in correct information, you must also uncomment the lines holding that information if they are comment lines in the original config file. (Configurable lines are not always commented in the original file; those lines do not need to be uncommented.)

Let's zoom in on an example of plugging in database information. Remember, as I described earlier in this chapter, you created a MySQL database on your server using your Web host's control panel, and you established three pieces of information: the database name, your username, and a password. A fourth piece of information is now required: the address path of the database. This address is called the *database host*. Typically, the database host is your Web hosting company, and that address is `mysql.webhostname.com`. You must be certain of the address, an annoying bit of crucial information for which you might have to dig around. Check your control panel settings and your Web host's help files; if necessary, call the hosting company and ask for the address.

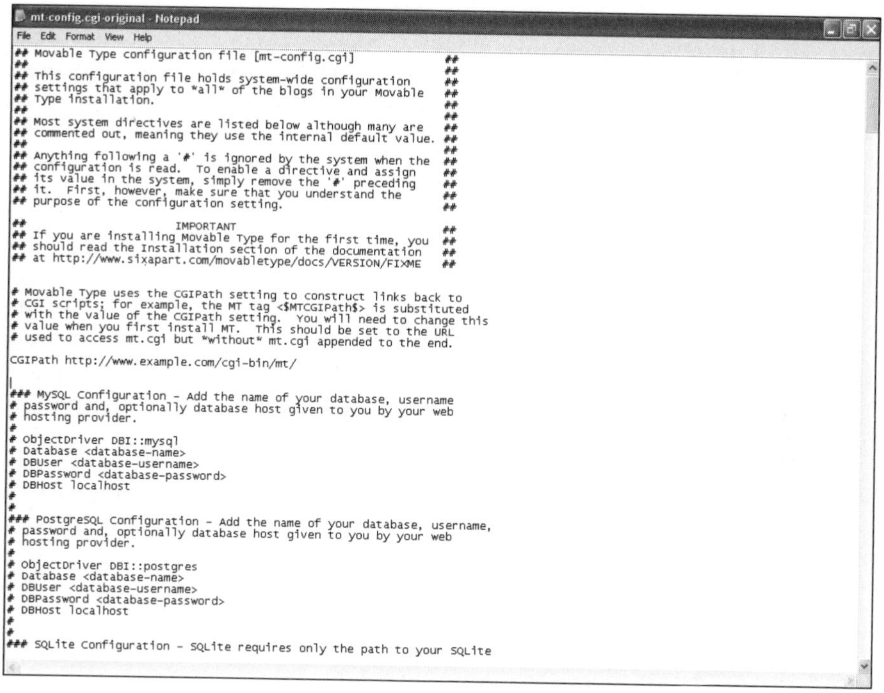

Figure 8-4:
An original configuration file before alterations. Remove the pound sign to activate (uncomment) any line.

Armed with the four pieces of information, you are ready to alter the original config file. Here is an example portion of an original config file; this example mimics the Movable Type file:

```
### MySQL Configuration - Add the name of your database,
# username, password, and, optionally, database host given
# to you by your web hosting provider.
#
# Database <database-name>
# DBUser <database-username>
# DBPassword <database-password>
# DBHost localhost
```

All these lines are commented, so you would need to fill in the information *and* uncomment the information lines. But you would leave the first three lines commented, because they contain instructions to you, not to the blog program. Note that the instructions claim that the database host address is optional. That is because `localhost` is a command that works with many database host addresses. I always plug in the exact address, but you can try uploading the altered config file with `localhost` in place and see whether it works.

Here is an altered version of the preceding file portion:

```
### MySQL Configuration - Add the name of your database,
# username, password, and, optionally, database host given
# to you by your web hosting provider.
#
Database blog
DBUser myusername
DBPassword mypassword
DBHost mysql.webhost.com
```

The information is plugged in and the lines are uncommented. I italicized the information that I added to make it distinct, but do not italicize anything in your config file. Note, also, that I removed the caret brackets surrounding the information portions of the original file. Installation documents generally neglect to tell you that part.

For comparison's sake, here is the same portion of the original config file in WordPress:

```
// ** MySQL settings ** //
define('DB_NAME', 'wordpress');      // The name of the
             database
define('DB_USER', 'username');       // Your MySQL username
define('DB_PASSWORD', 'password');   // ...and password
define('DB_HOST', 'localhost');      // 99% chance you
             won't need to change this value
```

As you can see, WordPress uses double slashes (//) to create comment lines, and this config file puts comments and working code on the same line. When you plug in your information, you can leave the comments as they are, because the double slashes do not begin any line. In this program, you do not need to remove the single quotation marks around the information pieces, whereas in Movable Type you must remove the caret brackets. Both providers fail to address this point — so, as you can see, some trial and error is involved in self-installed blogs.

Setting the Perl location

I spent so much time discussing the config file that you might have forgotten the second part of the configuration process: plugging in your server's directory path to its Perl program. A directory path is a server address that specifies where in the server's directory structure the Perl program is located. Your Web host provides Perl; you must find where it's located in your server space. This information gets plugged into several blog program files, as indicated in the installation instructions.

If you're lucky, you won't have to do this step. That's because many blog programs (such as Movable Type) assume that Perl is located in the most common directory path, which is this:

```
/user/bin/perl
```

The `user` is you — or, more accurately, your server space on the host company's computer. But you really don't need to know that or any other technical details of the directory path.

You do need to know what that directory path is, and you probably need to dig your hands into your hosting company's help files to find it. If you run into a wall, send an e-mail to customer service or make a phone call. Ask this: "What is my directory path to Perl?" or "Where is Perl located in my account?" Make them spell it out for you slowly. To ensure that your blog files are correctly configured, you need two pieces of information:

✔ Your Web host's directory path to Perl.

✔ Your blog program's default directory path to Perl, as spelled out in one or more program files. Usually, the directory path is the first line of those files.

The two directory paths must match in every file listed by your program's installation documents.

If alteration is necessary, edit the files using Notepad and save them *with the same name to the same location*. Notice how I italicized that instruction. That's because if you change the name or saved location, I will personally come to your house and eat your muffins. I'm not sure what that means, but it won't be pleasant. If you move the files or rename them, your blog program is screwed. A great wailing would be heard across the land, and that would be you, regretting your error. The undead would rise and converge upon you, seeking to enjoin you to their unholy mob. Sweet nectars would turn bitter on your tongue and life's joy would sour. I hope I've made myself clear.

Uploading the program

After making whatever configuration changes are necessary to match the component files with your domain and hosting setup, you must upload the files to your server. Doing so installs the blog program on your server.

You should, of course, refer to your installation instructions before uploading the files. Your program might require that the unpacked directory structure remain intact (as with WordPress); conversely, the program might require that you separate certain folders or files from their companions (as with Movable Type). Some programs (Movable Type) need to be installed in a CGI directory, most commonly the *cgi-bin* directory. Other programs (WordPress) do not require *cgi-bin* placement.

ASCII and binary uploading

When uploading files, always remember that they can be transferred as ASCII files or binary files. Your FTP program probably provides a radio button for each selection. The difference is important. If just one component file of your blog program is uploaded in the wrong way, it will foul up your blog at some point; usually sooner than later. Many are the cases of installed blog programs that seem absolutely broken: They simply don't work at all, and the hidden problem is that a binary file was uploaded in ASCII, or an ASCII file as binary. Unaccountably, online installation manuals are often murky on this point, failing to clarify exactly which files need to be uploaded in each mode.

Some FTP programs can discern how a file should be uploaded — in ASCII or binary mode. This automatic setting is valuable, and takes the pressure off of you, who would otherwise have to constantly keep the setting in mind while uploading many dozens of files. In those FTP programs that offer this automatic feature, the Auto setting must be manually enabled. Remember that if you close the FTP program and reopen it, you have to reset the Auto feature if it defaults to the unselected state. If your FTP program has the Auto feature, *use it!*

A final note about the ASCII/binary uploading issue. If your FTP program does not offer an Auto selection, or if you prefer making the correct uploads manually, or if you don't trust your FTP program because it once insulted your sister, or if for some other reason beyond my imagination you must make the ASCII/binary distinction yourself, then Table 8-1 covers most file types in blog programs. When deciding whether to upload a file as ASCII or binary, note the file extension (the part after the dot, such as *.cgi* in *filename.cgi*) and then look at this table.

Table 8-1	ASCII and Binary Uploads
Upload as ASCII	*Upload as Binary*
cgi	gif
php	jpg
txt	png
html	bmp
tmpl	
pm	
pl	
js	
css	

Setting permissions

After uploading your program files, you must complete an obscure but crucial task that trips up people. That task is setting the permission level of the uploaded files. The permission level determines what the file is allowed to do, and for whom, on Unix servers. Three functions are involved here: read, write, and execute. And three levels of access are available: owner, group, and other. You are the owner. Groups are defined by a server command that you will probably never need to know. Other refers to any visitor to your blog. The intersection of these three types of users and the three functions creates a matrix that looks like this:

	Owner	Group	Other
Read	x	x	x
Write	x		
Execute	x	x	x

Notice that I have checked off some but not others. These settings give full privileges to the owner, while Group and Other users cannot use the Write function of any file. That means other people cannot, for example, alter your pages or configuration files (only a hacker would be able to get into your server space in the first place). However, the pages of your blog can be seen (Read) by everyone, and the scripts on those pages (such as leaving a comment or searching the archive) can be set in motion by any visitor (that's the Execute function). The particular setting makes the blog fully functional for all users and reserves executive control of its files for you.

The settings in Table 8-1 are typical for blog program files and represent the required file permission setup for Movable Type and WordPress. It is called the 755 setting, or *chmod 755* — I kid you not. Each different permutation of the preceding matrix is given a different number, based on a bizarre assignment of values to the rows and columns. *Chmod* is the Unix command for changing file permissions. It is absolutely unimportant for you to know any of the other matrix numbers when dealing with Movable Type or WordPress.

Most FTP programs make it pretty easy to make chmod changes. Figure 8-5 shows the setting panel in one such program. If your Web host offers a file management utility in your control panel, you might also be able to change the permission settings there. You can alter the chmod of an individual file, or a group of files at once, or an entire folder.

This is how you change a chmod setting in the WS_FTP program:

1. **Select (highlight) the file, files, or folder whose permissions you want to set.**

2. **Right-click the highlighted file and choose the chmod (UNIX) selection.**

3. **In the chmod panel, assign permissions for chmod 755.**

4. **Click the OK button.**

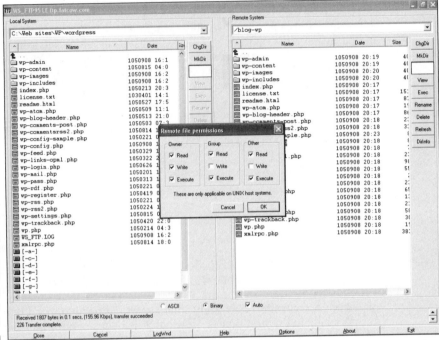

Figure 8-5:
Setting
permissions
with the
Unix chmod
command is
simple in
WS_FTP.

Initializing the Blog

After everything I've described — downloading, configuring, and uploading your blog software — another step is required before you start blogging. This step can be considered the final step of installation or the first step after installation. The blog software needs to undergo a brief initialization process to ready the server database to receive entries. Each blog program behaves a little differently at this point, so follow your installation instructions.

Another part of initialization happens within your blog's administrative control area, in which you set the blog's name, the blog's descriptive tagline (if you want one), your public name as author, and your customized username and password.

When these final chores are finished, you're ready to actually write your first blog entry, and believe me, it's a thrill to see your self-installed blog start to unfold. You can still make plenty of design and function changes as you go along, including changing the entire template (design theme) of the site. Different programs make such changes variously easy or hard. Basically, though, you are off and running. See Chapters 9 and 10, which pick up from here in Movable Type and WordPress, respectively.

Chapter 9

Running a Movable Type Blog

Movable Type is possibly the most powerful blogging option and personal Web publishing program you can find. Created by SixApart, the same company that operates TypePad (see Chapter 7), Movable Type and TypePad resemble each other. If you've read Chapter 7, or if you use TypePad now, you'll notice that this chapter illustrates and describe controls and screens that look strikingly similar to TypePad.

Movable Type could be considered a premium version of TypePad. Or, if you prefer, call TypePad a light version of Movable Type. The two products are distinct, though, and are being developed independently, so it would be a mistake to call TypePad a dumbed-down version of Movable Type. The truth is that TypePad offers certain power features (such as custom template design, photo albums, and mobile blogging) that Movable Type lacks. On the other side of the coin, Movable Type provides greater flexibility and configurability in the fine points of blog publishing.

Some people agonize over the choice between Movable Type and TypePad, but I don't think they should be compared that way. More realistically, I would group TypePad with Blogger.com (see Chapter 6), and compare Movable Type with WordPress (Chapter 10). Movable Type and WordPress are both standalone programs that require server installation. (If you don't know what that means, prowl through Chapter 8.) Those two programs demand more of you, and return more in blogging power. But Movable Type and WordPress don't make you more creative, so if your focus is determinedly on writing the blog, TypePad and other hosted services might be your best bet.

If you want the power of Movable Type (or WordPress) without the installation difficulties (and believe me, installing Movable Type can be difficult), look in Chapter 12, which spotlights Web host companies that preinstall Movable Type (or WordPress) for you. This chapter does not detail how to install Movable Type. Chapter 8 gives you the basic understanding needed to install any blog program on a server, and the Movable Type site (`www.movabletype.org`) provides detailed instructions. Here, I pick up the story immediately after the program has been installed.

This chapter cannot possibly deliver a complete tutorial on all Movable Type features. Whole books have been written about how to blog with this sophisticated program. One such book, *Movable Type 3 Bible* (Wiley), is 438 pages long. That book, and others in bookstores at the time of this writing, are not up to speed with version 3.2 of Movable Type, although they might be by the time you read this. Version 3.2 is covered here, and the purpose of this chapter is to give you a general feeling for Movable Type. Reading the descriptions and looking at the screen shots should convey a sense of the program and whether it's for you.

Getting an Overview of Movable Type

I have said that Movable Type is powerful, and it is, but its power is skewed. Movable Type is not a well-rounded blogging environment, and some functions that are standard in other services are difficult to accomplish without either advanced technical knowledge or a willingness to install additions to the basic program.

Because of these difficulties, Movable Type can easily be considered a clunky, obstinate program, and even a slightly obsolete one for modern bloggers who expect click-and-publish photos, blogrolls, and new templates. Movable Type was developed in a simpler blogging era (the fall of 2001), and it hasn't caught up with newer systems in certain ways. For all its publishing prowess, Movable Type lags behind free services such as MSN Spaces and Yahoo! 360 in certain ways that might be important to you.

To be specific, Movable Type's strong points are these:

- **Writing:** The entry-writing interface is simple, without a lot of formatting options to distract from the basic text presentation of the blog. The basics are there — you can use bold, italic, and underlined text, embed links, and put photos in the entries. Post-dating and pre-dating entries are no problem. Editing is easy, as is bulk deletion of entries. Movable Type blogs are primarily written blogs, as opposed to photo blogs, podcast containers, or video blogs.

- **Organizing:** Multiple archive options allow past entries to be grouped by month or by category. You can display a calendar in the sidebar or rely on text links to archived groups.

✔ **Networking:** Movable Type is particularly strong in comment and TrackBack options, letting you choose the level of authentication needed for a visitor to leave feedback on your site.

On the down side, Movable Type should not be a newcomer's first choice in these departments:

✔ **Designing:** Changing templates is harder to accomplish in Movable Type than in TypePad, Blogger, WordPress, MSN Spaces, Yahoo! 360 . . . shall I go on? Movable Type bloggers must use a *plugin* to change the site design — plugins are add-on software modules that fill in Movable Type's missing functionality. Without a template-changing plugin, you would have to be capable of working in HTML and CSS, the two primary coding languages underlying Movable Type pages, to change the page design.

✔ **Personalizing:** Not to be found is any sort of built-in profile, such as users of other services have become accustomed to. You can create your own profile page using traditional Web-page creation tools, but blogging is supposed to free you from all that. The lack of a profile page is a perfect example of functionality that has become standard in the years since Movable Type was first launched.

✔ **Photoblogging:** There are ways to create a photo album on a Movable Type site (and plugins that assist you), and I explain how to put photos in the sidebar later in this chapter. But you'll see that my explanation is complex (if doable), and the other options might seem impossibly intimidating compared to standard click-and-display photo features in other services.

Given these important negatives, you might be wondering how anybody (like me, for example) can promote Movable Type as a powerful modern blogging solution. Part of the answer lies in those plugins I just mentioned. People have developed innumerable Movable Type plugins that add all kinds of great features, and it is this expandable quality of Movable Type that makes it so powerful and liberating. The happiest Movable Type users are inquisitive, adventurous, experimental, willing to download and install many little programs, and insatiable tweakers. Those people are unhappy with the many restrictions that constrain their blogs in the services offering contemporary preset features.

You also might simply prefer Movable Type's administrative look and feel — the way the software handles on your screen — better than other options. Nobody says you must install plugins and build a Movable Type palace. It is a beautiful program when used conservatively.

The Learning Movable Type site offers a wealth of tips and how-to's for Movable Type users of all levels. It's located here:

```
www.learningmovabletype.com/
```

Naming Your Blog

Immediately after installation, Movable Type is a blank slate, ready to receive your blog settings and entries. A template is provided, but no others are offered to start. Movable Type, unlike many services, does not preset entry categories. Your blog comes out of the box (so to speak) with the title First Weblog. Figure 9-1 illustrates what your nascent blog looks like, and Figure 9-2 shows the first thing you see after logging into your Movable Type controls, immediately after installation. That view in Figure 9-2 is of the Main Menu.

Help when you need it

Movable Type weaves Help files through the program, so you can get assistance with features when you need it most — while stumbling over settings you don't understand. Notice the tiny question marks in Figure 9-3. If you can't see them clearly on the page, trust me that they are sprinkled all over the place on all the control pages. (The question marks do not appear in your published blog.) Click any question mark to pop up an explanatory window. This type of Help system is called *context-sensitive help*. But who cares what it's called? Forget I mentioned that. It is danged useful. Forget that I used the word *danged*.

The figure illustrates one of the Help pop-ups looming over the control page from which it sprang.

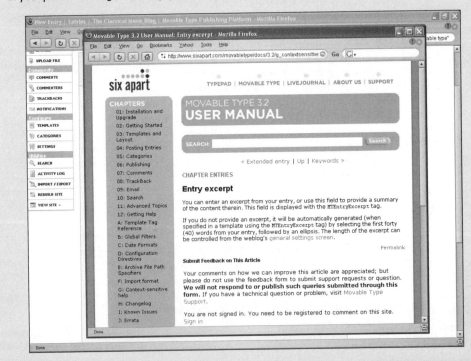

Figure 9-1:
A Movable Type blog immediately after installing the program, before any entries are posted.

Figure 9-2:
The Main Menu immediately after installation. The blog has not yet been renamed.

Your first task should probably be to rename the blog. Along with renaming, you can add a description that appears as a tagline below the blog's title. Here's how:

1. **On the Main Menu, click the <u>First Weblog</u> link.**

   If your installation calls your blog something else, click that. You are navigating to the control page for the blog, as opposed to the System Shortcuts you see on the Main Menu in Figure 9-2.

2. **On your blog's control page, click Settings in the sidebar.**

   The sidebar contains shortcuts to the groups of controls that create your blog. That sidebar remains in place as you navigate through the controls.

3. **On the General Settings page (see Figure 9-3), change the Weblog Name and Description.**

   The description is optional.

4. **Scroll down and click the Save Changes button.**

   Along the way, you can alter any other setting on this page, but none of them is important before posting your first entry. The page reloads after you click the Save Changes button.

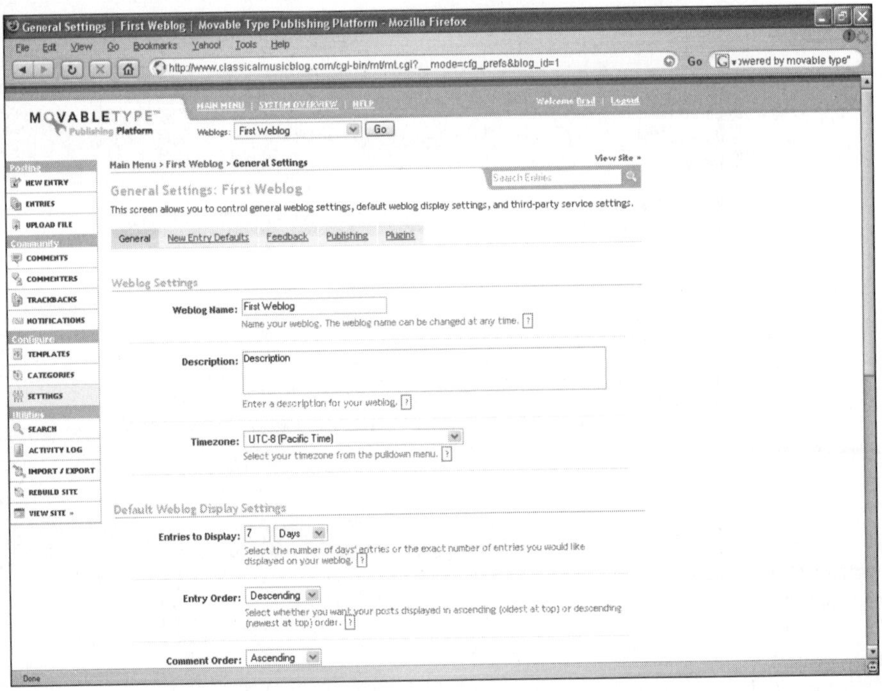

Figure 9-3:
The General Settings page for your Movable Type blog.

5. **Click the Rebuild My Site button.**

6. **In the pop-up window, click the Rebuild button.**

   This extra step allows you to use the drop-down menu to select the extent of rebuilding you want. The choice seems unnecessary now and the extra step is annoying. But when the blog gets big, rebuilding takes longer and you might sometimes want to limit the job to certain portions of the site affected by the saved setting changes.

7. **Close the pop-up window.**

   That's right — Movable Type makes *you* close the window. Who knew software could be so lazy?

8. **Back on the General Settings page, click View Site in the sidebar.**

   This command brings up your blog, and you can see the renamed banner and added description. (See Figure 9-4.) If you viewed your blog before, you might have to replace your browser's cache of the earlier version by clicking the Reload (or Refresh) button on your browser's toolbar.

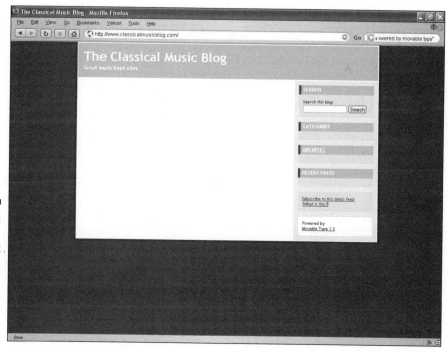

Figure 9-4:
A still-nascent blog with renamed title and a descriptive tagline.

Writing and Posting Entries

Posting an entry in Movable Type is straightforward. Figure 9-5 shows the New Entry page.

Starting from scratch, follow these steps to write and post your first Movable Type entry:

1. **On any of your blog's control pages, click New Entry in the sidebar.**

   If you start from the Main Menu shown in Figure 9-2, click your blog's title to reach its controls, and then click New Entry.

2. **On the New Entry page, enter a title and write your entry.**

   Note that long entries can be broken into two parts by using the Extended Entry box to hold the second part. In the published blog, only the first part (typed in the Entry Body box) appears on the index page (the blog's home page). Movable Type automatically provides a link to the entry's unique page, which displays the complete, unbroken entry.

3. **Select a category from the Primary Category drop-down menu.**

   This step is optional. At this point, you might not have created any categories. Not a problem. Pull down the menu and click the Add New Category selection. A pop-up appears (see Figure 9-6); type a category and click the Add button. After you have at least one category, the Parent Category menu in that pop-up lists your categories, enabling you to create categories within categories.

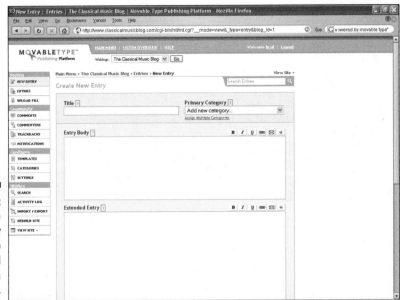

Figure 9-5:
Use the
New Entry
page to
write and
publish a
blog post.

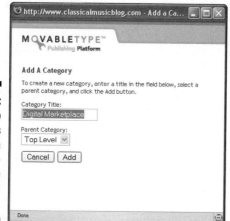

Figure 9-6:
This pop-up window lets you create a new category while writing a new entry.

4. **Scroll down the page and click the Save button.**

Your entry is automatically published to the blog if the Post Status menu is selected as Published (which it is by default). Choose Unpublished in that menu to save the entry without making it appear on the blog. You can also select Scheduled in that menu, and then create a date and time at which the entry will automatically appear on the blog. Figure 9-7 shows these controls. Notice that you can also choose to allow comments and TrackBacks for individual entries, and you can plant TrackBacks on another site with the Outbound TrackBack URLs box. (Please see Chapter 3 for a complete explanation of TrackBacks.)

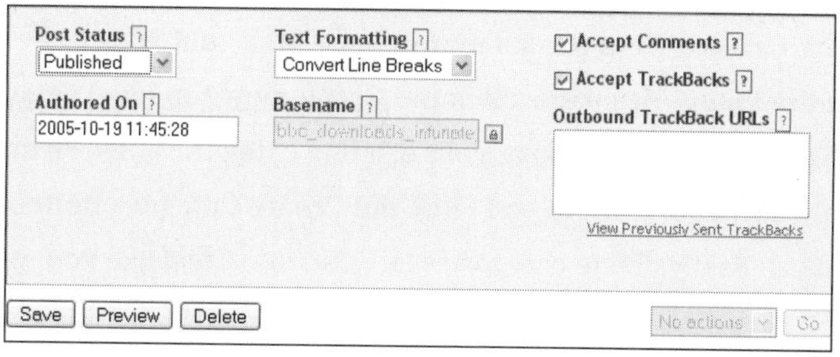

Figure 9-7:
Use these controls to publish an entry, save it for later, and select comments and Track-Backs for that entry.

Figure 9-8 illustrates our blog-in-progress with its first post. Notice that the Recent Posts and Archives sidebar modules now have something in them, and the two categories I created along with this first entry are showing.

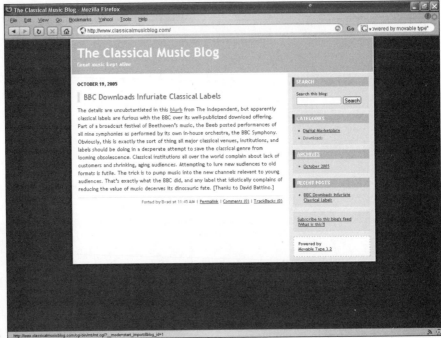

Figure 9-8:
A Movable
Type blog
after posting
the first
entry.

Creating categories and subcategories

Speaking of categories, it's a good idea to plan your blog's topic areas before posting many entries and setting up your main categories. Movable Type makes it easy to create categories and subcategories. Follow these steps:

1. **Click Categories in the sidebar of your blog controls.**

2. **On the Categories page, click the <u>Create new top level category</u> link.**

   A fill-in box appears above your existing categories (see Figure 9-9).

3. **Type a category name and click the Create Category button.**

   You can easily delete categories later, so don't feel like you're etching categories in stone. As you create each category, it is saved but not published to the blog. The Rebuild My Site button is available, but continue creating categories until you're out of ideas, and then click that button to make all the categories appear on the blog at once.

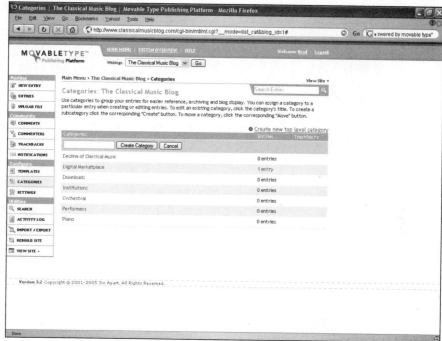

Figure 9-9:
Creating
a new
category.

4. **Next to any category, click Create to establish a subcategory within the selected category.**

5. **Type the subcategory name and click the Create Subcategory button.**

6. **When you have finished creating categories and subcategories, click the Rebuild My Site button.**

7. **In the pop-up window, click the Rebuild button.**

Figure 9-10 shows the blog with a list of categories and subcategories in the sidebar.

You can create subcategories of subcategories. Click Create next to any sub-category to bundle finely tuned categories within it.

You can delete any category or subcategory — or several at a time — by selecting check boxes next to categories and then clicking the Delete button. There is no verification box asking if you're certain . . . so be certain.

Figure 9-10:
Categories
and sub-
categories
in a new
blog's
sidebar.

Posting with a Movable Type bookmarklet

As I discuss in other chapters, a *bookmarklet* is a clickable item that resides on your browser's toolbar. Blogging bookmarklets enable you to post an entry without going to your program's control panel. The bookmarklet is like a portable control panel that travels around the Web with you. In this way, when you get an urge to post something — perhaps inspired by another blog or an article — you can do so without disrupting your surfing.

Follow these steps to place a Movable Type bookmarklet on your browser:

1. **Click the <u>Main Menu</u> link at the top of any blog control page.**

2. **On the Main Menu page, click <u>Set Up a Quick Post Bookmarklet</u> link.**

3. **On the QuickPost page, configure the bookmarklet.**

   Figure 9-11 shows this page; as you can see, the check boxes allow you to add or remove features from the bookmarklet. Leave all options selected (as they are by default) for the most flexible bookmarklet.

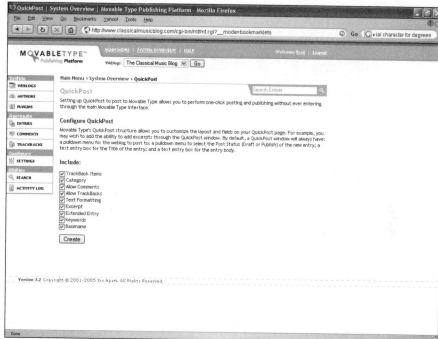

Figure 9-11:
Configure
the Movable
Type book-
marklet on
this page.

4. **Click the Create button.**

5. **On the next page, use your mouse to drag the QuickPost link to your browser's menu bar or toolbar.**

   Click the link and, while holding down the left-click button, drag the link up to the toolbar. Note that in the Firefox browser you must use the Bookmarks toolbar; the bookmarklet does not stick to the menu toolbar.

Simply click the QuickPost bookmarklet that now resides on your browser toolbar whenever you want to write an entry. Figure 9-12 shows the QuickPost pop-up window overlaid on the site that inspired a new post entry. You can also see the QuickPost bookmarklet itself in the browser's toolbar. The full-featured version of the bookmarklet pop-up stretches down the screen; you might have to scroll down to see the Post button.

The QuickPost pop-up is automatically configured with a link to the page currently displayed by your browser. If you're not posting about that page, simply highlight the text in the Entry Body box and press the Delete key on your keyboard to get rid of that link.

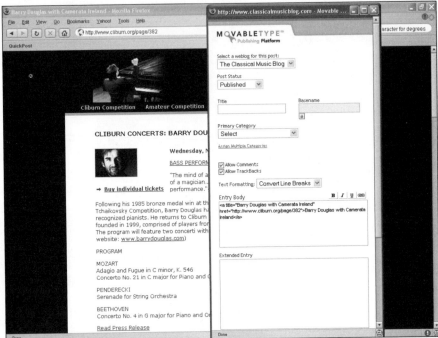

Figure 9-12:
The
QuickPost
bookmarklet
pop-up in
action.

Note: Some browsers and toolbars attached to them implement pop-up blockers that prevent the QuickPost bookmarklet from working. In Firefox, for example, you have to enable pop-ups for any site you happen to be parked at when the urge to post an entry overcomes you — otherwise the bookmarklet is thwarted.

Installing One Essential Plugin: StyleCatcher

If you ever want to change blog templates — and who wants to be stuck with a single default template? — you need a key Movable Type plugin that makes switching styles reasonably easy. I'm not saying that Movable Type is especially template friendly; it is not. Immediately after installation, there is not an alternate template to be found within the program. However, a suite of official Movable Type template designs exist, and with StyleCatcher — that's the plugin — you can switch among them with aplomb. If you can't muster aplomb, please keep your cursing in French.

What follows here is a fairly long series of steps that takes you outside the program control pages. You must do the following:

1. Go to the StyleCatcher download page.

2. Download the plugin.

3. Unpack the plugin on your computer.

4. Upload the plugin files to your Web server.

5. Enable the plugin within the Movable Type control pages.

6. Use the plugin to switch templates.

Take it one step at a time and you'll be fine. The plugin is worth the hassle of getting and installing it. Here we go:

1. **Go to the StyleCatcher download page here:**

   ```
   www.sixapart.com/pronet/plugins/plugin/stylecatcher.html
   ```

2. **Click the Download button.**

3. **On the next page, click the** <u>StyleCatcher 1.01</u> **link to start the download.**

   What happens next depends on your browser settings. I assume that your browser downloads the compressed StyleCatcher file to your computer desktop. Continue these steps from wherever the file lands. The version of the plugin, and therefore the appearance of the download link, might have advanced by the time you see it.

4. **Unpack the compressed file on your computer.**

   Chapter 8 discusses downloading compressed files and decompressing them; if you installed Movable Type yourself, this is old hat to you. You need to select a destination on your hard drive for the unpacked files; I always put unpacked plugins in the *plugins* folder of my Movable Type installation directory. Again, see Chapter 8 for more about this. Sorry to jerk you around from chapter to chapter; it does work out for the best this way.

5. **Upload the unpacked files from your computer to the server installation of Movable Type.**

   On the server, as on the computer, the files go in the *plugins* folder. Whereas I *suggested* you put them there on your computer, I must insist you put them there on the server. Otherwise the plugin won't work.

6. **In Movable Type, click Settings in any blog control page (not the Main Menu).**

7. **On the General Settings page, click the <u>Plugins</u> link.**

   On the Plugin Settings page, StyleCatcher should appear as enabled. (See Figure 9-13.)

8. **Click the <u>StyleCatcher</u> link.**

9. **In the Theme or Repository URL box, enter the following address:**

   `www.sixapart.com/movabletype/styles/library`

10. **Click the Find Style button.**

    The official Movable Type templates appear in the Movable Type — Style Library box. (See Figure 9-14.)

11. **Click any style.**

12. **Use the drop-down menu below the style library to select the blog whose style you want to change.**

    If you're following along with the examples in this chapter, there is only one blog.

13. **Click the Choose This Design button.**

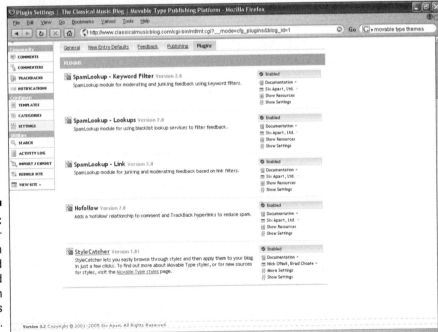

Figure 9-13: StyleCatcher has been installed and is enabled on the Plugin Settings page.

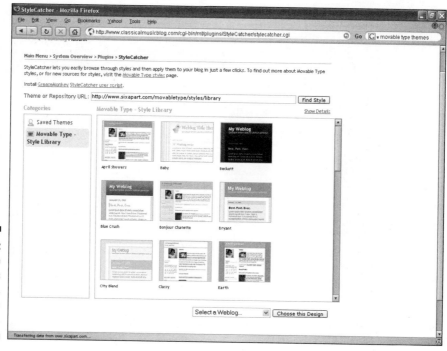

Figure 9-14:
Movable
Type styles
on display,
ready to be
selected.

14. In the pop-up verification box, click the OK button.

Visit your blog now to see the style change. (Figure 9-15 shows a transformed blog.)

Every time you select a theme in StyleCatcher, it is saved in the Saved Themes section (refer to Figure 9-14). You can put your favorites in there and switch among them whenever you like.

All plugins are installed in the same basic fashion as just described. The company that owns Movable Type, SixApart, maintains a plugin resource page here:

```
www.sixapart.com/pronet/plugins/
```

I suggest you look at it if your interest in Movable Type is wavering. The plugins reveal Movable Type as a muscular program, and browsing through the extensive selection of functions that you can add to Movable Type is inspiring.

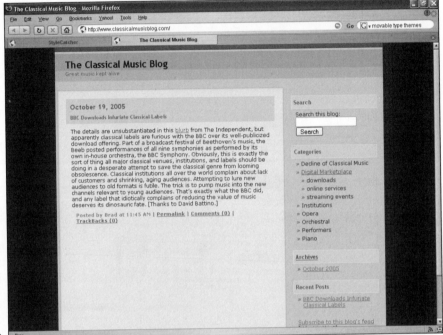

Figure 9-15:
After
selecting
and applying
a new blog
style, the
site is
transformed.

Adding Links and Photos to the Movable Type Sidebar

One significant advantage of TypePad (and some other services) over Movable Type is the ease with which you can add sidebar content: a blogroll, other lists, and photos. You can do these things in Movable Type, but you have to get your hands into the template code. By that I mean you have to alter the code that underlies the pages of your blog. This is not pushbutton publishing, it's more like using . . . well, like using *real* movable type, which was invented in 1436.

You can use the plugin resource page listed a few paragraphs back to find expansion plugins that give you sidebar support. Here, I show a down-and-dirty way of creating a list in a sidebar and a nearly identical way of placing a photo in the sidebar. In exchange for avoiding the plugin installation routine, you must explore Movable Type's template code. It is easier than you probably think. You can do this. Take each step carefully, and it'll happen.

Adding a sidebar blogroll

A *blogroll* is a list of links to favorite blogs, and it traditionally resides in the sidebar of the index page. To accomplish the steps in this section, you need one or more (let's say three) links. Think of three sites you like; they don't have to be blogs. Go to each and write down its URL (the site address that appears near the top of your browser; it begins with `http://`). You have three URLs written on a sheet of paper next to you. Follow these steps:

1. **Click Templates in the sidebar.**

   You are delivered to the Templates page, which lists eight (more or less, depending on the style in use) templates, each with a check box next to it.

2. **On the Templates page, click Main Index.**

   The list of templates is replaced by a large text box called Template Body, displaying the page code of your index page. (See Figure 9-16.) Note that the text box has a right scroll bar; the page's code is lengthy.

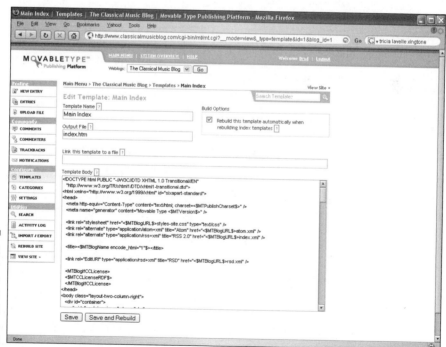

Figure 9-16: The template code of the blog's main index page.

3. Scroll down the Template Body box until you see this line of code:

```
<div id="beta">
```

That line indicates the start of the index page's sidebar. Below it are code descriptions of sidebar modules such as Archives and Recent Posts. You are almost where you want to be; scroll slowly from here.

4. Scroll down until you see this line:

```
<div class="module-syndicate module">
```

That is the first line of code that describes the blog's syndication feed link. In this example, we will put your blogroll in a module immediately above that link. You are about to add some code above that line. After you get the hang of this, you'll be confident enough to arrange the modules differently in the sidebar.

5. Above that line, copy the following lines:

```
<div class="module">
<h2 class="module-header">Links</h2>
<div class="module-content">
First link<br>
Second link<br>
Third link<br>
</div>
</div>
```

That's a lot to type. I have placed this code online; you can copy and paste it from this Web page:

```
www.bradhill.com/mt-sidebar.txt
```

6. Replace the `First link` line with an HTML hyperlink to your first Web site.

An HTML hyperlink is specially coded and looks like this:

```
<a href="http://www.yourfirstlink.com">Web Site</a>
```

Place the URL within the quotation marks, and leave the quotation marks there. Instead of *Web Site* type the name of the Web site. Also replace the *yourfirstlink* domain name with the actual address of the linked site. When you perform this step, be sure to leave the <br> in place on each line, immediately after the </a>.

7. Repeat Step 6 for the next two lines.

This is what your finished code might look like:

```
<div class="module">
<h2 class="module-header">Links</h2>
<div class="module-content">
<a href="http://www.nytimes.com">NY Times</a><br>
<a href="http://www.cnn.com">CNN</a><br>
<a href="http://news.yahoo.com">Yahoo! News</a><br>
</div>
</div>
```

In this example, I used the NY Times, CNN, and Yahoo! News as my three sites, with links to their home pages. Figure 9-17 shows the Template Body box with the added code.

8. Click the Save and Rebuild button.

Figure 9-17:
The main index code with an added code that will translate to a Links sidebar module.

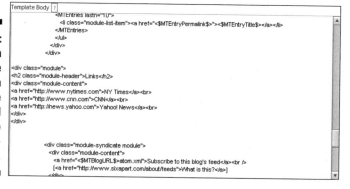

Visit your blog to see the blogroll (see Figure 9-18).

You can add as many links to your list as you want; simply repeat Step 6.

Figure 9-18:
The blog-in-progress with a small blogroll under the sidebar's Links heading.

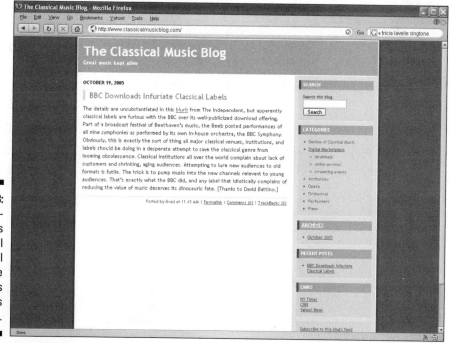

Adding a photo to the sidebar

You can add photos to your sidebar in its own module by replicating the preceding steps, but with the following variations:

- ✔ In Step 5, replace Links with another header, perhaps Photos.

- ✔ You need to upload the photos to your server.

- ✔ In place of the site URLs, type the URL of your uploaded photos in Step 6. Use this HTML tag:

  ```
  <img src="http://www.yourdomain.com/photo-1.jpg">
  ```

- ✔ The final added code should look like this:

  ```
  <div class="module">
  <h2 class="module-header">Photos</h2>
  <div class="module-content">
  <img src="http://www.yourdomain.com/photo-1.jpg">
  <img src="http://www.yourdomain.com/photo-2.jpg">
  <img src="http://www.yourdomain.com/photo-3.jpg">
  </div>
  </div>
  ```

Many digital photos are larger (wider, to be precise) than your blog's sidebar. You can make the photo display in smaller dimensions by specifying a number of pixels in width. The other dimension — height — scales down proportionally. An easy width to remember, and one that works with most Movable Type sidebars, is 100 pixels. You add that constraining fact to your tag like this:

```
width=100px
```

So, the entire photo tag would look like this:

```
<img src="http://www.yourdomain.com/photo-1.jpg"
          width=100px>
```

Add that pixel constraint to each photo tag; they will all display with the same dimensions in the sidebar.

Chapter 10

Blogging with WordPress

*W*ordPress has taken blogging geeks by storm. Both underrated and overrated, WordPress should be better known by the hordes of Blogger and TypePad users, but it needs important improvements before it's ready for primetime in the mass-market blogging arena. At the time of this writing, I see many Movable Type users migrating their work to WordPress — though I don't know of any usage statistics to substantiate that apparent trend.

Bloggers who are abandoning Movable Type for WordPress are attracted by the latter's general ease. WordPress friendliness starts with a relatively simple and trouble-free installation; WordPress is the first big-name, self-installed, blog program to come anywhere near the ease of setting up a blog on a hosted service. You still have to deal with downloading, unpacking, configuring, and uploading to a server, the four basic steps fleshed out in Chapter 8. But as a veteran of many such installations, I can say for certain that WordPress is the most painless blog installation program I've encountered.

Understanding the Ups and Downs of WordPress

Ease of use extends to the daily blogging grind in WordPress, whose administrative panels are models of clutter-free, intuitive navigation. Operating a written blog in the WordPress environment is a breeze. Not least of its refreshing attributes is the speed of blog updates, contrary to the cumbersome save-then-publish system that acts like a ball and chain in nearly every other blog program, including the popular hosted services TypePad and Blogger. WordPress feels like a swift and streamlined sports car compared to those sedans. Movable Type, in this analogy, is more like a luxury SUV: lots of power and space but poor mileage.

WordPress is open-source software, and that fact is an important determinant in its user experience. Open-source software is not owned by any person or company in a traditional sense. Any programmer can add to its features and functionality. Successful open-source projects are not as anarchic as you might think; though not incorporated, they are highly organized. In this case, the organizational hub is located at this Web site:

```
www.wordpress.org
```

WordPress.org (see Figure 10-1) furnishes user manuals, discussion boards offering user support, and links to the work of developers all over the place. The most visible products published by those developers are of two types:

- ✔ **WordPress themes:** WordPress themes are prebuilt site designs available to all users. Hundreds of themes exist, and they are fairly easy to apply. WordPress themes differ from themes and templates provided by hosting services TypePad and Blogger, in that each theme also carries a certain set of features; in other words, different themes provide different functions to the blog. This characteristic is unlike TypePad and Blogger templates, designs, and layouts, all of which replicate an identical set of blog features in varying design packages.

- ✔ **WordPress plugins:** WordPress plugins are all about functionality; they add features to the program. The world of plugins is distinct from the world of themes. For the most part, themes do not come with bundled plugins. By the same token, plugins are independent of themes and work equally well (or badly!) in all themes.

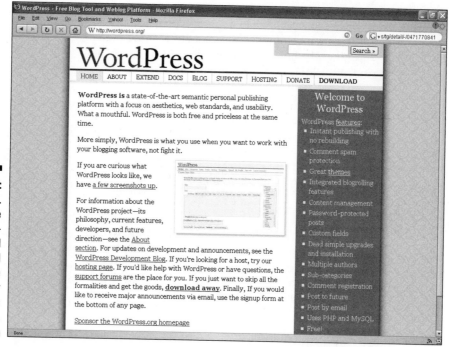

Figure 10-1:
WordPress.
org is the
organiza-
tional
hub and
resource
center for
WordPress
blogging.

WordPress plugins provide a range of extensibility that hosted blog services cannot match. The universe of plugins, matched by the global WordPress community of development and support, is one crucial reason the program is so popular with bloggers inclined toward technical experimentation. Installing themes and plugins is not particularly difficult (I step you through each process in this chapter), but in each case a process of downloading, unpacking, and uploading is required — a miniature version of WordPress installation. Many casual bloggers would rather pull their eyebrows out than spend time tinkering with their blog software.

Now for the downsides. In the first sentence of this chapter, I refer to the popularity of WordPress among "blogging geeks." And later I say that WordPress is a breeze for "a written blog." (I like quoting myself. Makes me feel important. Then my dog throws up on the carpet and my true place in the universe is reinforced.) These are WordPress's two big problems:

✔ **The program is geekish.** The interface lacks WYSIWYG (What You See Is What You Get) niceties that are commonplace elsewhere. The posting screen, for example, does not show embedded links as links — instead, it shows the link code. (See Figure 10-2.) Same thing with simple formatting commands such as bold type and italics. You don't see **bold** or *italic;* you see bold and italic. Yech.

✔ **WordPress is unfriendly to photo bloggers.** The program is hostile to photos generally, although it does not forbid them or prevent the insertion of photos in a blog entry. But WordPress makes it damnably hard to accomplish that insertion. See the section in this chapter called "Uploading and Posting Photos in WordPress" for the grisly details. Many users fall back on photo-related plugins, but that's like buying a car whose steering wheel is optional equipment.

The upshot of these pros and cons is this: WordPress is a beautiful environment in which to operate a fast-moving text blog with plenty of add-on power and a minimum of technical hassle. You probably shouldn't consider WordPress for a photo-heavy blog or if you prefer your administrative controls to be as consumer-friendly as an e-mail service. WordPress rewards technical acuity and inquisitiveness.

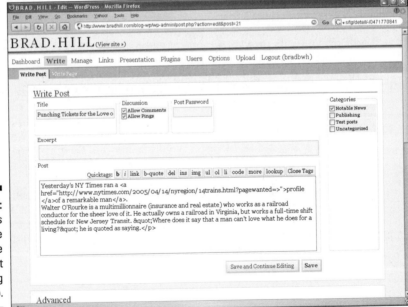

Figure 10-2: WordPress doesn't hide link code as most blogging services do.

The Look and Feel of WordPress

Before committing to the download and installation process, I recommend looking through this chapter — and the chapters on Movable Type, TypePad, Radio UserLand, and Blogger — to get a sense of the WordPress design. When I refer to program *design,* I mean both ends of it: the administrative controls on the back end and the live blog on the front end. You have to live with both ends. The administrative screens create the environment in which you write and post; the live blog provides the environment for your visitors.

This chapter shows many screen shots of the administrative panels. Before getting started with the administrative features, I want to highlight a few live blogs powered by WordPress. To a degree unmatched by many blog services, WordPress offers a diversity of design thanks to its many theme developers. But a lot of bloggers don't care to spend much time exploring alternative designs, and if you're among that number, your blog will probably display the open, clutter-free template characteristic of WordPress.

These examples show off the stunning range of theme designs offered by WordPress:

✔ **SystemFundraiser:** This no-nonsense site (see Figure 10-3) is devoted to fundraising relief funds for hurricane Katrina, and it appropriately refuses to gunk up its core mission with fancy designs. This theme is the default WordPress theme bundled with the program.

Figure 10-3: This site uses the default WordPress theme, which is unglamorous and functional.

✔ **San Diego Zoo Weblog:** The San Diego Zoo (see Figure 10-4) uses WordPress to create a straightforward, yet original and attractive, site design for its Weblog.

✔ **Beccary:** The Beccary site is run by a young woman who sometimes develops WordPress themes, and her gorgeous site bespeaks her skill. This design (see Figure 10-5), and her others, are available to anyone. They illustrate how individual a WordPress site can appear.

Figure 10-4: The San Diego Zoo uses this WordPress theme.

Getting WordPress

Down to business! Get WordPress here:

```
www.wordpress.org/download
```

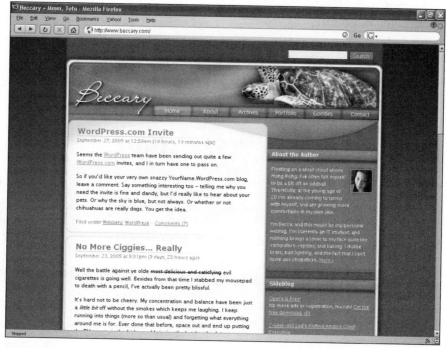

Figure 10-5:
The owner of Beccary. com designs WordPress themes, such as this one.

You have a choice of compression formats: Zip and Tar.gz. Windows users should take the Zip file.

Click the <u>Installation</u> link on the download page to see specific instructions on configuring the program files and uploading them. Just as important, read Chapter 8 of this book carefully. That chapter tells you everything you need to know to *understand* the installation instructions. Chapter 8 is essential to any WordPress (or Movable Type) user who has never installed a blog program on a server.

If I were to fully step through the installation process in WordPress and Movable Type, this book would contain many pages of repeated material, because the installation routines are similar. So, Chapter 8 gives you essential understanding of blog installation, and the on-site manual at the WordPress site provides specific instructions. This chapter is mostly about how to use WordPress after it is installed.

One point not covered in the WordPress installation documents is whether to upload the program files in ASCII or binary mode. (Chapter 8 explains this distinction and its importance, plus how to accomplish the right setting in FTP programs.) So here's the deal: All program files and folders should be uploaded in ASCII mode except the *wp-images* folder. If your FTP program has an Auto feature, it will probably work correctly during the WordPress upload.

Essential WordPress Setup

The WordPress administrative controls are beautifully laid out. In the parlance used by WordPress support documents, each main administrative area is called a *panel,* and each section within a panel is called a *subpanel.* That's a bit confusing, I think, so in this chapter I call the subpanels *tabs.* Tabs are grouped within panels. In Figure 10-6, you see the Categories tab within the Manage panel.

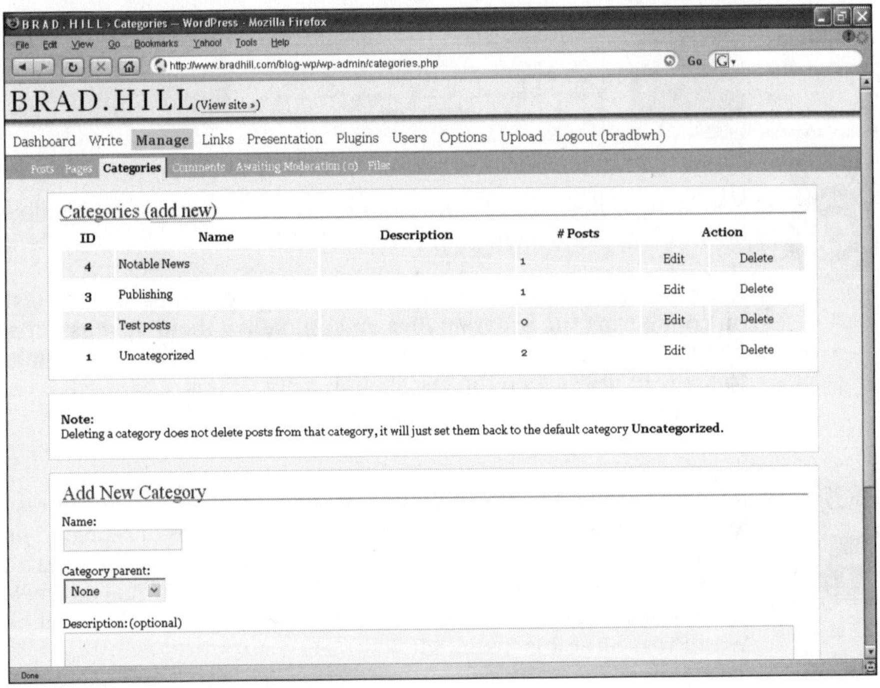

Figure 10-6:
WordPress administrative controls are laid out using tabs within panels.

Several tabs relate to setting up the blog to receive entries and comments. It's not essential to complete every possible bit of setup before posting. In fact, it's not essential to complete any of it. Skip down to the "Finally — Writing a WordPress Entry" section if you're irrepressibly eager to get started. This section covers the setup functions that I consider essential to a young blog. The next section covers less important blog setup.

Establishing your identity

The first piece of business is to establish your own identity in WordPress and in your blog. If you skip this step, your entries will be "signed" by the blog's default identity: Administrator. Sounds like a bureaucratic version of a Schwarzenegger character. ("I'll be back . . . with office supplies.") Follow these steps to escape from your WordPress identity crisis:

1. **Click Users.**

   The Your Profile tab opens by default. (See Figure 10-7.)

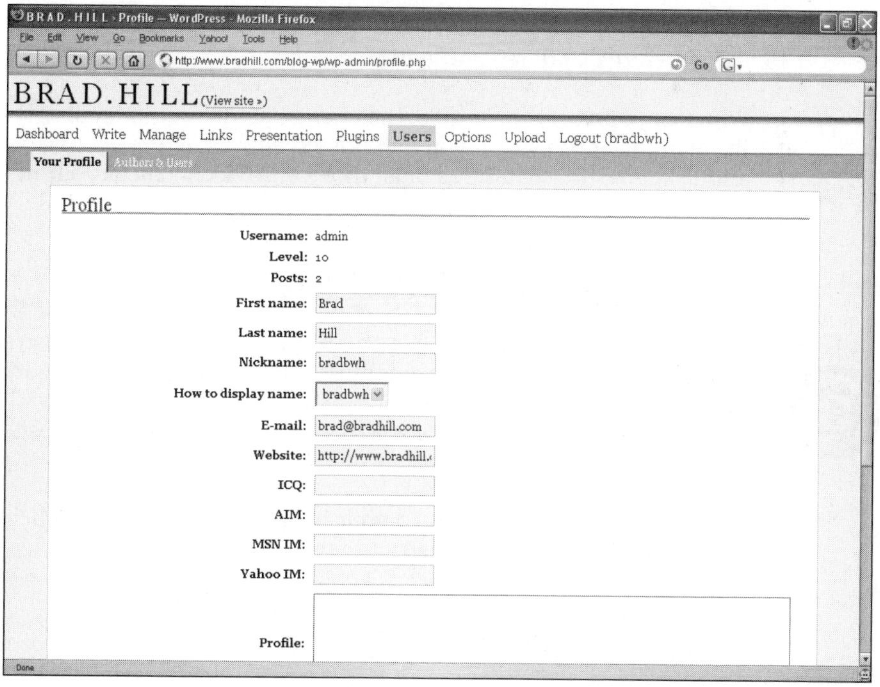

Figure 10-7: Use this page to establish your identity as author of the blog.

2. **Fill in your first name, last name, and a nickname.**

3. **Use the drop-down menu to choose how your entries will be signed.**

   WordPress mixes up your first name, last name, and nicknames in various combinations. You can stop here if you like; the remaining steps fill in details that don't normally appear on your blog.

4. **Fill in your contact information.**

   Contact information consists of e-mail, Web site, and instant message screen names. None of these fields is particularly important. The e-mail address is used for administrative purposes, for example, to notify you of a new comment.

5. **Fill in your profile.**

   Your profile information does not appear by default in your blog, and you cannot make it appear using basic WordPress tools. Some plugins use popups to display your profile information.

6. **Change your password.**

   This step is optional, but most people want to change their password from the random characters assigned by WordPress to something they can remember.

7. **Click the Update Profile button.**

When you update your profile, the change of identity immediately ripples through the entire site. If you had posted entries before establishing your author name, the signatures of all those entries change to your new name.

Adding a registered user

You can add authors to your blog with varying levels of administrative control. These added individuals might post entries or perform other administrative chores. I am an added author in one WordPress blog; though I can write entries, I cannot edit the entries written by the blog owner. These levels of control are determined on a scale of 0 to 10.

The process of adding a user to your blog is a little more complicated than it should be. Follow these steps:

1. **Click the Users panel.**

2. **Click the Authors & Users tab.**

3. **In the Add New User section, fill in the boxes.**

   You are filling in the user's nickname, first name, and last name at least. You must type an e-mail address; the Web site box is optional. Give the user a password for accessing the administrative panels of your blog. At this stage, perplexingly, you can't set the user's control level.

4. **Click the Add User button.**

   The tab reloads with the new user added to the list of registered users.

5. **Click the <u>Promote</u> link corresponding to the new user.**

6. **Click the plus and minus signs to raise or lower the user's control level.**

   New users start off at level 1. You can drop a user to level 0, which withdraws all posting privileges. Astoundingly, WordPress does not offer a drop-down selection menu for assigning the control level, so you must laboriously click your way upward, with the tab reloading after each click. (See Figure 10-8.) If you're lifting somebody up to level 9 (only the site owner can be a 10), you might want to put on some good music. You do not need to save level changes; they are saved the moment you make them.

Click the <u>Edit</u> link corresponding to any registered user, at any time, to adjust that user's properties. But use the plus and minus signs to adjust the user's control level.

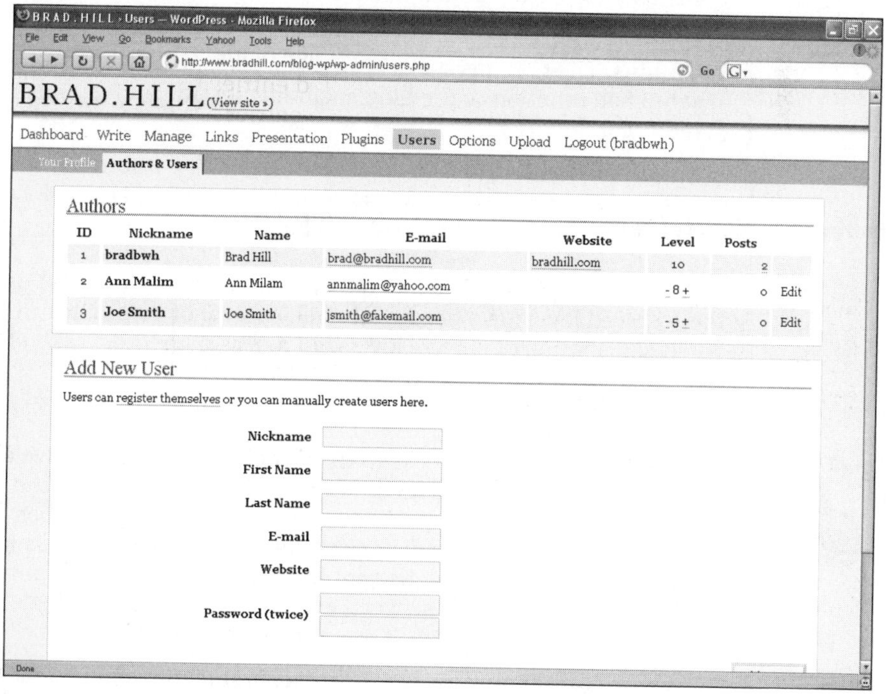

Figure 10-8: Click plus and minus signs to adjust a user's control level. Sorry, no drop-down menu.

So, what powers do the control levels confer? It would take a few pages to fully describe each level. Following is a brief rundown of the administrative panels and the lowest level required to control them. Some of these administrative features are covered later in this chapter, and you might not be familiar with them now:

- **Write:** All users above level 0 can write entries, but level 1 users cannot publish their entries. Writing pages (which exist outside the blog chronology) requires a level 5 or higher.

- **Manage:** The Manage panel provides editing tools for posts, pages, comments, and categories. Level 2 users can use these tools for editing everything except pages, which requires level 6.

- **Links:** The Links panel creates and edits sidebar content such as the blogroll. Level 5 is required.

- **Presentation:** This panel is where alternate themes are stored and activated, changing the appearance of the site. Level 8 is required.

- **Plugins:** This panel stores available plugins that have been downloaded and added to the WordPress server space. Level 8 users can activate and deactivate plugins.

- **Users:** Here, users modify their profiles and add new users. Any user, even a level 0, can modify his or her own profile. Level 5 is required to add a new user.

- **Options:** The Options panel is a power-packed set of tools that affect the setup and function of the blog, including its title and tagline. Level 6 is required.

- **Upload:** Uploading files to a specified directory within the WordPress folder system on your server is accomplished in this panel. Level 1 is required.

This rundown is general. In some tabs within the administrative panels, users at the required level have partial, not full, control of certain features. For a detailed explanation of control levels, go to this page:

```
codex.wordpress.org/User_Levels#User_Level_Capabilities
```

Control levels affect user access to the WordPress administrative controls and have nothing to do with access to your Web server where the WordPress program is stored. Conferring a high level to another person does not give that person FTP access to your server files. The one exception is in the Upload panel, where files can be sent from the computer to a specified WordPress directory on the server. Level 1 control enables a registered user to upload files.

Choosing a title and other basic settings

Before too many people see your new blog, you probably want to give it a title and make a few other basic setting choices. You can revisit these settings at any time, change them, and have those changes propagate throughout the blog:

1. **Click the Options panel.**

   The General tab (see Figure 10-9) displays by default.

2. **In the Weblog Title box, type a blog name.**

   Your blog name can be your name or any other general title that represents the site.

3. **In the Tagline box, type a short description of the blog.**

   The tagline appears either under the blog title of each page-top banner or in the sidebar under the About header, depending on the theme.

4. **In the E-mail Address box, enter your e-mail address.**

   WordPress uses this address to communicate with you; the address is not displayed in the blog.

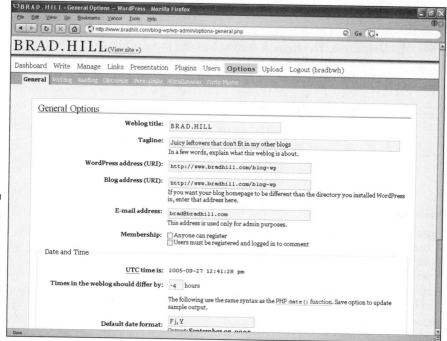

Figure 10-9: On the General Options page, set your blog's title and tagline.

5. **Leave the Membership check boxes deselected.**

   Selecting the Anyone Can Register check box opens the door to visitors gaining level-1 administrative control of your site. This setting should be chosen only in the most open sort of group blogging effort. The second box forces users to register before posting a comment, which is unusually strict.

6. **Set your local time by entering the number of hours local time differs from UTC time.**

   UTC time is accurately displayed whenever you view this tab; reload the page to get an up-to-the-second reading.

7. **Set your default date format.**

   This format determines how the date appears below each blog entry. See the next section, "Setting the date format," for details.

8. **Set your default time format.**

   This format determines how the time appears below each blog entry. See the "Setting the time format" section for more.

9. **Set a starting week day for your archive calendar.**

   Note that only some themes use an archive calendar.

Note that in the preceding steps, I omitted mention of the WordPress Address (URI) and Blog Address (URI) boxes. In most cases, those settings should be left alone. The default setting has the same address (the Web address of your blog's index page) in both boxes. That setup changes only in specialized installations where the blog is an embedded portion of a larger site.

Setting the date format

In Step 7, you are asked to set a format that determines how the date is displayed below blog entries. In the Default Date Format box (shown in Figure 10-10), a cryptic string of letters appears. These letters are part of a date code used by WordPress and other programs.

Figure 10-10:
Use code
letters to
set a date
format and
time format.

Default date format:	F j, Y
	Output: **September 27, 2005**
Default time format:	g:i a
	Output: **8:41 am**

Here is the cracked code:

```
l = full name of the day
F = full name of the month
M = Three-letter abbreviation of the month
j = numerical day of the month (01 to 31)
Y = full numerical year (2005)
y = two-digit year (05)
m = numerical month (01 to 12)
```

Note that uppercase and lowercase affect the meaning.

Use these letters with commas and spaces to generate a display of the date below your blog entries. For example:

```
l, M j, Y = Saturday, Feb 26, 2005
```

Of course, the actual day and date depend on the time of posting. The letters just affect the format. Here's another:

```
j F y = 14 July 05
```

Setting the time format

You set the format for displaying the time below your blog entries in the same way you set the date format. Naturally, a different code applies:

```
g = hour in 12-hour format (1 to 12)
H = hour in 24-hour format (00 to 23)
i = minutes (00 to 59)
s = seconds (00 to 59)
e = time zone identifier
a = lowercase am and pm
A = uppercase AM and PM
```

Use the letters with commas, colons, and spaces to create a time format. For example:

```
H:i e = 18:23 EST
```

Here's another:

```
g:i:sa = 3:15:44pm
```

Don't use AM and PM with the 24-hour format.

TIP

For a complete list of the date and time commands, which are part of the PHP programming language, visit this PHP help page:

```
us3.php.net/date
```

Setting your categories

Because WordPress doesn't allow you to create new categories on the fly, it makes sense while writing an entry to set up your categories in advance. You can't anticipate every category you will ever want to have available for a blog entry. At this point, just come up with a few categories with which to tag entries.

1. **Click the Manage panel.**

2. **Click the Categories tab (see Figure 10-11).**

3. **In the Add New Category section, type a category name in the Name box.**

   Whatever you type will appear in your blog's sidebar (in most cases) in the category list. The category will also appear with a check box on the Write Post page.

Figure 10-11:
Add new categories with which your entries can be tagged.

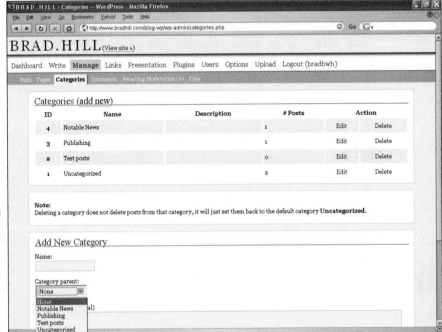

Posts or articles?

WordPress can't seem to make up its mind about what blog entries are called. Most people call entries, well, *entries* or *posts*. WordPress uses those words, but in the administrative pages, it also sometimes refers to entries as *articles*. (Look at the Discussion tab under Options.) Calling an entry an article is a curious usage, reminiscent of Usenet newsgroups (the native bulletin board system of the Internet), in which posts are historically called articles. There is a reason for that example, which is that Usenet has been around for decades and in its early days was mostly used for posting academic articles. With blogs, though, it's a stretch to think of most entries as articles by any reasonable standard. So don't be confused: In WordPress, when you see *article,* it just means a blog post.

4. Use the drop-down menu to assign a category parent.

The Category Parent list is populated with categories you've already created. Before creating your first, the list is empty. A parent category is like a top-level folder that holds other folders on your hard drive. Use a parent category such as Trips to hold categories such as Pocono, Shore, and The Big Apple. Actually, few people use parent categories, and I don't think they're useful to visitors. I would simply create independent categories such as Pocono trips, Shore trips, and New York trips.

5. In the Description box, type a description.

As indicated on the page, this field is optional. I suggest leaving it blank. Categories are neither novels nor rocket science. The category name should convey the gist of the category.

6. Click the Add Category button.

Finally — Writing a WordPress Entry

At last, we get to writing. If you skipped ahead to this section, your eagerness to create is admirable. If you are reading carefully through this chapter's sections in order, your patience is admirable.

In WordPress, simple writing is easy. Formatted writing is not difficult, but it is also not presented in a way that is instantly understood by all users. You don't see what a formatted post will look like until you publish it.

Composing and publishing a post

Follow these simple steps to create a blog entry:

1. **Click the Write panel.**

   The Write Post tab appears by default. (See Figure 10-12.)

2. **In the Title box, type an entry title.**

3. **In the Post box, type your entry.**

4. **Click the Publish button.**

Posting is as easy as that. Your entry is posted and archived on the blog speedily. You can also opt to Save as Draft (which doesn't publish the entry), or Save as Private (other registered users cannot see the saved entry, and it is not published).

If you leave the Write Post page before saving or publishing the entry, WordPress saves that entry as a draft and shows you a link to that draft when you return to the Write Post page. Figure 10-12 shows two drafts available for editing.

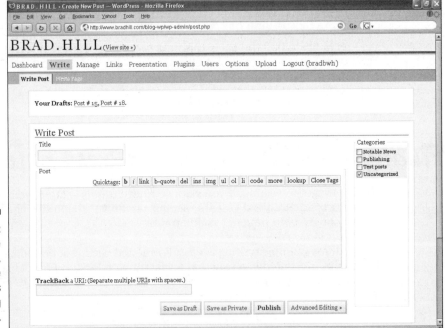

Figure 10-12:
The Write Post page, where WordPress blogging takes place.

Notice the Quicktags — little buttons above the Post box. Quicktags are for-matting buttons. Use Quicktags by selecting text in the Post box, and then clicking a Quicktag button. Tags are inserted around the selected text; those tags get translated to formatting in the published entry.

Here is what the fourteen Quicktags in version 1.5.2 of WordPress do:

- **b:** This tag creates bold text.

- **i:** This tag creates italic text.

- **link:** Use this tag to embed a link in your entry. The selected text becomes the link.

- **b-quote:** This tag stands for blockquote, which is a format style that jus-tifies text on the left (and usually on the right also), and indents the blockquoted portion of the entry. Blockquoting is an attractive way to set off quoted text. Each WordPress theme displays blockquoted text uniquely. (Figure 10-13 illustrates a blockquote. Note that the WordPress theme used in that figure uses left justification instead of right justifica-tion for its blockquotes.)

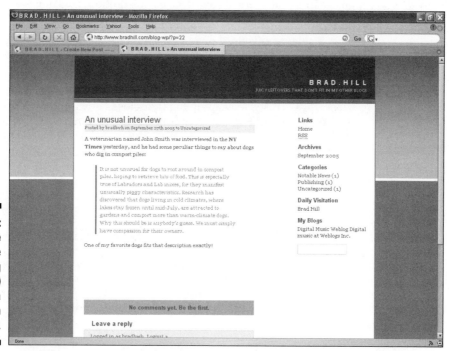

Figure 10-13: Use the blockquote Quicktag (b-quote) to set off a quotation in an entry.

✔ **del:** This tag looks like delete, but it actually puts a strikethrough line through selected text. Bloggers traditionally use strikethroughs to retract words and sentences while leaving them visible.

✔ **ins:** Rarely used, this tag underlines text but does not hyperlink it.

✔ **img:** Use this tag to include a digital photo in your entry.

✔ **ul:** This tag creates an indented, unnumbered list when a series of items is selected. Keep each item on a separate line (press the Enter key after typing each item), and then select all items and click the ul Quicktag.

✔ **ol:** This tag operates identically to the ul Quicktag, but it creates a numbered list.

✔ **li:** Use this tag on individual items in a list; it places a bullet next to each tagged item without indenting it.

✔ **code:** This tag turns highlighted text into Courier font.

✔ **more:** This important tag splits a post into two parts. The index page displays the first part, and a link is provided to read the entire post on the entry page. When composing a long entry, click this Quicktag at the point where you want the post to be divided. Some bloggers never divide posts; some bloggers always do. I use discretion, splitting long posts.

✔ **lookup:** This interesting tag functions on the Write Post page, not on the blog. It selects any word of an entry-in-progress, and a browser window pops open at the Answers.com dictionary page that defines your selected word. Using the lookup tag does not change the appearance of your entry.

✔ **Close Tags:** This is a clean-up tag that closes any open tags that resulted from manually adding tags (without using Quicktags). All Quicktags follow the HTML syntax of one open and one closed tag, like this: `<strong>bold</strong>`. If the closing tag is left out when tagging manually, the tag's function doesn't work. Use Close Tags to ensure good closure of any hand-typed tags.

Configuring the Write Post page

Oh, brother. More configuring. Well, this set of options can be disregarded as long as you want because the default appearance of the Write Post page is perfectly adequate. But if you'd like to tinker with the page's appearance, click the Options panel, then the Writing tab. These are the options at your command:

✔ **Simple controls or Advanced controls:** By default, WordPress shows simple controls on the Write Post page — nothing more than the average blogger needs. The most important advanced control is an Edit Time feature that allows post-dating and pre-dating entries. (See Figure 10-14.)

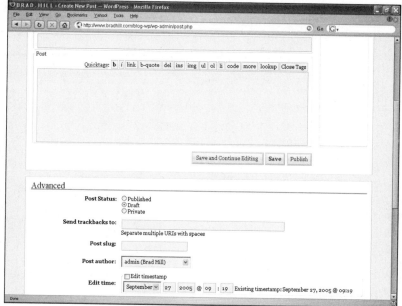

Figure 10-14:
A view of
advanced
writing
controls,
including
the time-
editing
feature.

✔ **Size of the writing box:** The default size is nine lines; set this to any size you want.

✔ **Formatting:** Two formatting controls are available. The first translates an emoticon into a symbol — for example, a :) into a smiley. The second and more obscure formatting option corrects any mistaken XHTML code you include in the post.

✔ **Default post category:** This drop-down list contains your existing categories and allows you to assign one as a default posting category. You can always change the category when composing the entry on the Write Post screen.

✔ **Newly registered members:** This option sets the posting power of blog visitors who register themselves. Obviously, this setting is valid only when you allow visitors to become registered users of the blog, which is an unusual setting.

Editing Entries

Posted entries can be edited. Just do this:

1. Click the Manage panel.

The Posts tab is displayed by default. (See Figure 10-15.) Your fifteen most recent posts are summarized on this page.

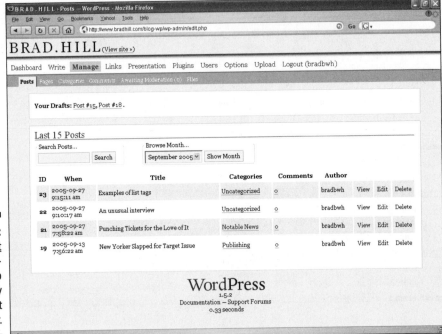

Figure 10-15:
Use the <u>Edit</u> link corresponding to an entry you want to alter.

2. **If the entry you want to edit is not on the list, use the pull-down menu to select the month in which the entry was posted.**

   Click the Show Month button to see that month's posts.

3. **Click the <u>Edit</u> link corresponding to the entry you want to edit.**

   The entry appears on the Write Post page.

4. **Edit the entry and then click the Save button.**

   Clicking the Save button saves and republishes the entry.

You can also use the Save and Continue Editing button, which locks down changes you've made but doesn't republish the entry. Keep making changes and use the Save button when you're ready to publish all your changes. Updates to a factual post are often marked as such, with the word *UPDATE* (sometimes in attention-getting caps) in the body of the entry or the entry title or both.

Using the WordPress sidebar and bookmarklet

Some blog services use a bookmarklet, which attaches to the browser and makes it easy to post an entry from any Web site. WordPress offers such a quick-post gadget, aptly named the WordPress bookmarklet. Look at the bottom of the Write Post page. There, you see a <u>Press It — *Your Name*</u> link. (*Your Name* should actually display your name.) Drag that link to your browser's toolbar. When you click the bookmarklet, a browser window pops open to a small version of the Write Post screen, and a link to the current page awaits in the Post box. (See the figure in this sidebar.)

WordPress also has something called the WordPress Sidebar, and it fills the same purpose. The name is a bit confusing because the sidebar of a blog, or any Web site, is the vertical panel that typically contains navigational links. In a blog, the sidebar contains the blog roll, links to archived posts, links to recent comments, photos, and all kinds of other blog elements.

The WordPress Sidebar is a browser feature that attaches to the Bookmark list in Firefox and the Favorites list in Internet Explorer. When the bookmark is clicked, a browser sidebar opens with an abbreviated posting form. Unlike most bookmarklets, the posting form does not place a link to the currently displayed Web page in the entry. Nor does it include any Quicktags, so links must be hand-coded. The form is so spartan, in fact, that it's nearly useless for most productive blogging.

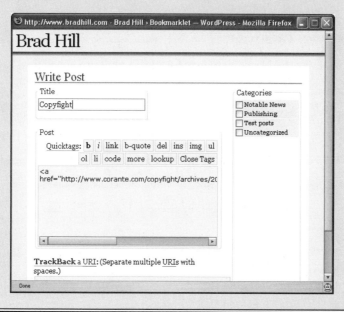

Uploading and Posting Photos in WordPress

As I mentioned at the top of this chapter, WordPress does not handle photos with impressive fluency. That's being gracious; it has no fluency at all compared to many hosted blog services. There is no such thing as a photo gallery created with native WordPress tools. (By *native*, I mean the administrative pages built into the WordPress program.) Inserting a photo in a blog entry? It's not easy, but it can be done. This section explains how.

WordPress is not a good program choice for casual or low-effort photo blogging. Because of the program's deficiencies in this regard, several developers have written plugins that supposedly make selecting and including photos a little easier. (See the preceding section for information about plugins.) Alas, all the plugins I have tried require specialized knowledge, demand too much work to configure, or simply don't function well. I could not find one that merited inclusion in this chapter. If you want to try them yourself, go to the following, which is one of the best directories of WordPress plugins of all kinds, not just photo plugins:

```
www.wp-plugins.net
```

Look under the Media category for photo plugins (see Figure 10-16).

Figure 10-16: If you are adventurous, try the WordPress Plugin DB for plugins of all types.

In any blog program, putting a photo on a blog must be preceded by putting the photo on the same server as the blog. The server is the Internet computer where your blog resides as well as all the blog components and pieces of content. In hosted blog services, the blog program, the blog itself, and the blog components all reside on the service's computer. If you use a self-installed program such as WordPress or Movable Type, the program, the blog, and the components reside on the computer of your Web host.

In all these scenarios, putting a photo on a blog requires two basic steps:

- ✔ Upload the photo to the server
- ✔ Assign the photo from the server to the blog

The exact process differs among programs, but the result is the same: A photo residing on a server is displayed in a blog residing on the same server. (Actually, it is possible to display a photo residing on a different server from the blog, but disregard that fact for now.)

In WordPress, you can upload files of all sorts, including photos, to a directory on your server that is preset to receive files, and then assign those photos to blog entries. It is possible to make uploads go to a different directory from the preset one, but because this entire photo process is so complicated, we'll avoid the extra complexity of changing the directory.

This first set of steps examines how to upload photos. The next set of steps describes how to display them in a blog entry. Follow these steps to upload a photo:

1. **Click Options.**

2. **Click the Miscellaneous tab.**

3. **Select the Allow File Uploads check box.**

   Clicking this option adds a new panel to WordPress called Uploads. While you're on the Options, Miscellaneous page, note the default upload directory in the box marked URI of This Directory. Below that box is a recommended Web address. The address in the box might be abbreviated.

4. **Place the entire recommended Web address inside the URI of This Directory box.**

   You may copy and paste it using the Ctrl+C and Ctrl+V keyboard commands. This step might seem finicky, but it is crucial. The address in the box must match the recommended address (as shown in Figure 10-17), or this entire process will result in frustration and a sudden desire to blame me for all your troubles, including those of your childhood. I don't need that, so match the addresses.

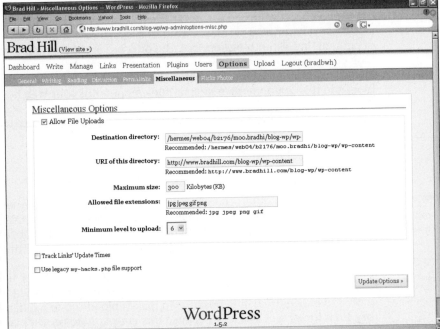

Figure 10-17:
On the Miscellaneous Options page, the recommended URI of the upload directory must match the directory in the box.

5. **Click the Update Options button.**

6. **Click Upload (see Figure 10-18).**

7. **Click the Browse button.**

8. **In the File Upload window, select a photo from your computer's hard drive and then click the Open button.**

9. **Enter a description in the Description box.**

   This step is optional.

10. **Click the radio button next to your desired thumbnail size.**

    WordPress can make a thumbnail version of your uploaded photo. If you do select a thumbnail size, WordPress creates two files: the original photo and the smaller, thumbnail version. Many digital photos are too large to effectively fit in a blog entry, so I recommend creating the thumbnail.

11. **Click the Upload File button.**

    When the file has completed uploading, the page reloads saying *File uploaded!* The page presents a single line of code below "Here's the code to display it." (See Figure 10-19.) Note that if you created a thumbnail in addition to uploading the full-sized file, only one line of code is presented, and that code represents the full-sized file. WordPress does not (as of this writing) give you display code for the thumbnail, even though that is quite likely the file you want to insert in a blog entry.

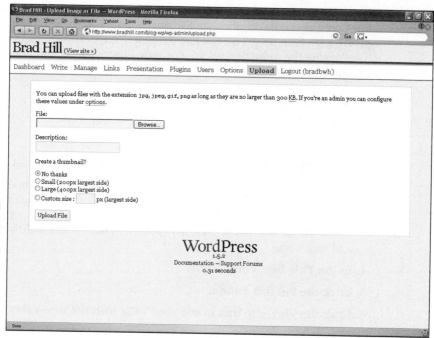

Figure 10-18:
The Upload panel appears after uploading is enabled.

Figure 10-19:
After your photo has uploaded, WordPress displays the code for displaying the picture.

Take a breather. Uploading a photo is the first part of getting it into your blog. The second part is inserting the photo in an entry.

The first three steps in the preceding list apply only to the first time you upload a file. WordPress installs with uploading capability disabled, and those three steps enable it. Once enabled, uploading stays enabled unless you disable it. So, starting with your second photo upload, begin the process with the fourth step.

All right, enough sitting around. Let's move on to inserting a photo in a blog entry. The problem with WordPress in this department is that it doesn't provide a photo-browsing tool on the Write Post page. You need to manually place the address of the uploaded photo in the post, surrounded by the proper display tags. We left off on Step 9 on the File uploaded! page, showing a line of code for displaying the uploaded photo. For now, ignore the lack of code for the thumbnail; we'll work with the full-sized file.

1. **Select and copy the display code.**

   Use Ctrl+C to copy the line to the Windows clipboard.

2. **Click Write.**

3. **On the Write Post page, paste the line of code into the Post box.**

   Figure 10-20 shows text preceding the line of code in a composed entry, but you needn't add any text for this example. In real blogging life, if you want the photo to be accompanied by some words, you would type the words above the line of code if you wanted the picture below the text, and vice versa.

4. **In the Title box, enter a title.**

5. **Click the Publish button.**

6. **Click the <u>View site</u> link to see your blog with the new entry displaying your photo.**

Figure 10-20:
Paste the photo display code into the Post box, with or without accompanying text.

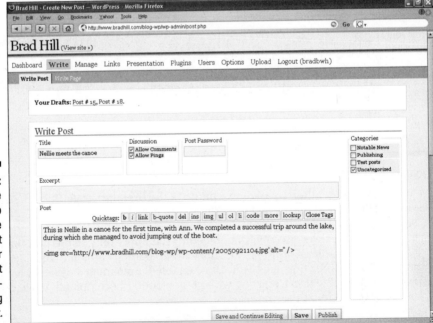

That's it. It took *only* seventeen steps to jam a photo into a WordPress blog entry, and it was carefree fun from start to finish. (Figure 10-21 shows the result. In this entry I used the thumbnail version of an uploaded photo, as explained next.) If you have several hundred photos you'd like to share, you have a lot of work ahead of you. However, if you post photos rarely, the WordPress process isn't much of a hindrance. WordPress doesn't invite photo blogging, but neither does it prevent you from showing images.

If you want to insert the thumbnail instead of the full-sized file in your entry, simply adhere to the file-naming routine used by WordPress. The program places the word `thumb` and a hyphen in front of the filename in the Web address of the uploaded photo. Here's how it breaks down. When you see your display code on the File uploaded! page, it looks something like this:

```
<img src='http://www.yoursite.com/wp/wp-content/
        20050921097.jpg' alt='Pocono' />
```

Your domain is different, of course, and the directory in which your blog resides (`wp` in this example) might also be different. The directory holding your uploads (`wp-content`) is the WordPress default directory for uploads. The `alt` part contains your description of the photo, and appears when visitors hover the mouse over the photo in your blog. Disregard that part. It is the following part that concerns us:

```
20050921097.jpg
```

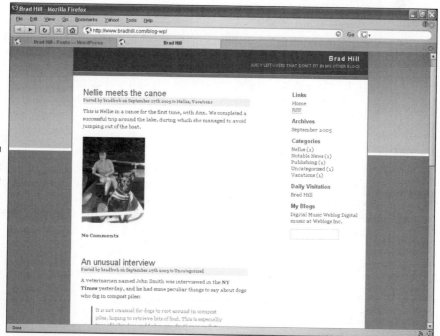

Figure 10-21: A blog entry with a photo. This one uses a thumbnail created by the WordPress upload process.

That is the filename of your uploaded photo. From that name, you can derive the filename of the thumbnail:

```
thumb-20050921097.jpg
```

The entire display code for the thumbnail picture is this:

```
<img src='http://www.yoursite.com/wp/wp-content/
          thumb-20050921097.jpg' alt='Pocono' />
```

To put a thumbnail in your blog entry, you must type that addition (thumb-) after pasting the original display code in your post.

Finding and Changing Themes

WordPress themes are powerful packages that do two things:

- ✔ Change the color scheme of your blog
- ✔ Change some of the features of your blog

That second point is unusual among blog programs. Themes (or templates or styles or whatever the program calls them) usually change only the graphic design, leaving features the same. In WordPress, one theme might implement a calendar interface to archived posts, for example, while another theme does not.

Hundreds of WordPress themes exist, most of them stored off the WordPress site. WordPress officially endorses all compatible themes and helps users find them to some extent. Locating themes is an informal business. You can search for them in Google, Yahoo!, or any other Web engine. One of the best repositories of themes, and one of the most effective galleries, is Alex King's WordPress Theme Browser, located here:

```
www.alexking.org/software/wordpress/theme_browser.php
```

This excellent interface (shown in Figure 10-22) displays any of dozens of themes listed in a drop-down menu and provides one-click downloading of most themes. In the next two sections, I walk you through visiting Alex King's gallery, auditioning the themes, and downloading, unpacking, uploading, and activating one theme in WordPress.

Figure 10-22:
Alex King's
WordPress
Theme
Browser in
action.

Downloading a WordPress theme

It doesn't matter where you find a theme or from where you download it. This example uses Alex King's WordPress Theme Browser.

1. **Go to Alex King's site.**

   In your browser, enter the Web address listed in the preceding section.

2. **At the WordPress Theme Browser, use the drop-down menu to select a theme.**

   Selecting a theme displays it in your browser; you might have to wait a few seconds.

3. **Click the <u>Download</u> link next to the drop-down menu.**

   Find a theme you like before downloading it, but also be aware that no theme change is necessarily forever. Part of the fun is acquiring many themes, and then applying them all to your blog (one at a time) before deciding on the best. Follow your browser's normal download process. In most cases, you will acquire a file in Zip compression format, which needs to be unpacked on your computer.

4. **Double-click the downloaded file to open your computer's default decompression program.**

   Computers using Windows XP should have no trouble with this. If your computer doesn't have a default decompression program, open WinZip or whatever program you used to unpack the WordPress program.

5. **Save the extracted files where your FTP program can easily find them; you'll be using the FTP program to upload the theme.**

   I place unpacked themes in the WordPress directory, which mimics the directory structure on my server. That means they go into the *Themes* folder, which lies within the *wp-content* folder. But where you put them in your computer isn't important, as long as you can find them.

The unpacked files are usually nested in a folder named for the theme. For example, the Flex theme unpacks to a *Flex* folder, within which are the theme files and another folder with a few necessary image files.

Next, you must upload the theme to your server into a certain WordPress folder, and then activate the theme in WordPress.

Uploading and activating a theme

Picking up where we left off in the preceding section, you have downloaded and unpacked a theme. Continue:

1. **Open your FTP program.**

2. **In your FTP program, locate your unpacked folder.**

3. **Upload the theme files to the *Themes* folder, which is nested in the *wp-content* folder on your server.**

   Upload the container folder holding the theme files. Include any nested folders located with the theme files. Throw the whole mess into that *Themes* folder.

4. **In WordPress, click the Presentation panel.**

   The Themes tab appears by default (see Figure 10-23).

5. **Click the <u>Select</u> link corresponding to your newly uploaded theme.**

   Wait for the tab to reload before checking your blog.

When the theme is activated, every page of your blog changes over to it.

Themes often contain an image folder that should be uploaded in binary mode. The other theme files should be uploaded in ASCII mode. If your FTP program has an Auto feature that selects the correct mode, use it. See Chapter 8 for more about file uploading.

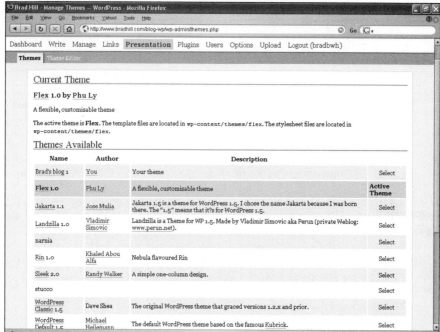

Side Content

The sidebar in WordPress is used mostly to list things. The most common list contains links and functions as a blogroll. However, you don't have to call such a list a blogroll, and it can be more descriptive to call it exactly what it is, such as My friends, or Sites of interest, or News sites. WordPress encourages users to create so-called link categories, which are distinct lists.

The following steps walk you through the process of creating a sidebar list. The list category will be called Daily Visitation, and it will contain the core sites of your daily routine.

1. **Click the Links panel.**

2. **Click the Link Categories tab.**

3. **In the Name box under Add a Link Category (see Figure 10-24), type** Daily Visitation.

   Leave all the other settings unchanged — which is to say, blank.

4. **Click the Add Category button.**

   The Link Categories tab reloads showing the Daily Visitation category along with the default Blogroll category.

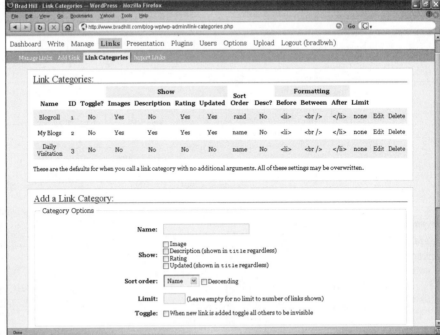

Figure 10-24:
The Link
Categories
tab is where
you add and
manage
lists.

5. **Click the Add Link tab.**

6. **In the Basics section, type the URI (Web address) of your first list destination.**

   You might want to copy and paste it from the Destination bar of your browser, when the browser is viewing that page.

7. **In the Link Name box, type the item name.**

   This is the name that will appear in the blog sidebar. Typically, it is the name of the destination site. I always leave the Short description box empty because I don't want the list gunked up with extra words.

8. **Use the pull-down Category menu to select Daily Visitation.**

9. **Click the Add Link button.**

10. **Repeat Steps 6 through 9 for each new item.**

After you add the first item of a new list, the list appears in your blog with that one item. Each added item republishes the entire blog (fast!) with the newly augmented list in the sidebar of every page.

Use the Manage Links tab in the Links panel to organize displays of your various link categories and to edit any item on any list.

WordPress comes with a default blogroll consisting of links to WordPress-related destinations. The preset list is an inconvenience because you will almost certainly want to get rid of it. The quickest way would be to delete the Blogroll category and start fresh if you want to use that category name. Unfortunately, WordPress doesn't let you do that, because Blogroll is the default category. I don't know why that should make it inviolable, but there you have it.

Unable to delete the Blogroll link category, the next best step is to make it invisible. WordPress magnanimously allows this operation. Here's how:

1. **In the Links panel, click the Manage Links tab.**

2. **In the pull-down Show Links in Category menu, select Blogroll.**

3. **Click the Show button.**

4. **Select the boxes corresponding to each Blogroll item (as shown in Figure 10-25).**

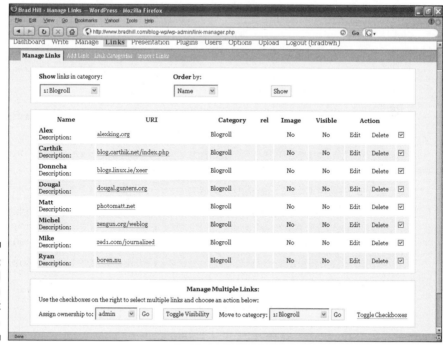

Figure 10-25: Select all items in the default Blogroll.

5. Under Manage Multiple Links, click the Toggle Visibility button.

This action turns off the Blogroll list, and it disappears from your sidebar.

If you want to use the Blogroll category for your own blogroll destinations in the future, use the <u>Edit</u> link next to each item in the original list and change its destination link.

Chapter 11

Power Plus Ease in Radio UserLand

*R*adio UserLand is an old-school blogging program that remains relevant. Back in the day (about six years ago), Radio UserLand made big waves by providing what might have been the easiest way to start blogging — and power-blogging, at that. Now, you don't hear people talking about launching Radio UserLand blogs as much as you hear about TypePad, Blogger, WordPress, and the social networks.

But Radio UserLand is still unique among the top blogging platforms; it offers power without the hassle of a server installation. The program gets installed on your computer like any other program (a new version of a browser, for example, or a downloaded music player such as iTunes). That program connects with the Radio UserLand online server and feeds what you create up to that server.

Radio UserLand started in 2000 as a program for building and sharing music playlists. The program did not share actual music, as the original Napster did — just lists of favorite music drawn from music-file collections in the users' computers. There was nothing illegal about Radio UserLand in those days, but lawsuits were banging away on other companies (such as the original Napster), and its owners grew weary of paying lawyers to keep the program on the right side of the law. So Radio UserLand kept its name and switched to blogging.

This chapter works with version 8.2 of Radio UserLand. Version 8.0 was introduced in 2001, so it might not be a surprise to learn that the program has a rather old look and feel. Like LiveJournal (see Chapter 5), which also hosts a community several years old, Radio UserLand has not kept pace with the pushbutton advances of hosted blogging. The program is on the clunky side of the elegance divide, its design themes are not inspiring, and the people who get the most out of it are technically oriented folks who can get their hands into the page code.

At the same time, Radio UserLand explains itself better than most advanced blog programs and does have that tantalizing advantage of power without the installation hassle. Read on to see whether Radio UserLand is right for you.

Understanding Radio UserLand's Unique Operation

Radio UserLand operates differently from every other blog service and program in this book. Here are a few clarifying points:

- ✔ Radio UserLand is a program that resides on your computer, just like Word or iTunes.

- ✔ Radio UserLand does not operate in its own window, like Word or iTunes. Instead, the program operates through your Web browser.

- ✔ Although Radio UserLand remains on your computer, your blog is stored on an Internet server.

- ✔ Radio UserLand uploads your entries to the server. At the same time, the program keeps copies of all your entries on your computer.

- ✔ *Upstreaming* (the process of updating your live blog on the Internet) occurs automatically according to preset time intervals. You can also force upstreaming to occur.

From these main points, you can see how Radio UserLand operates. You work on your blog in your browser, creating entries that are placed on your computer's hard drive. Radio UserLand upstreams everything you create to your blog, published live on the Internet. The program is a liaison between your computer and the server storing your blog. After you download and install Radio UserLand, it operates similarly to the other programs in this book: You make changes to your blog in a browser window. The difference is that you are keeping a copy of your entire blog on your computer.

Note: Radio UserLand's upstreaming process replaces the *publish* and *republish* functions in other programs such as TypePad, Movable Type, and Blogger. Publishing and republishing a blog, which push changes through the entire site, add an extra step to the blogging process that is unwelcome and sometimes accidentally neglected. The advantage of Radio UserLand's system is that the program looks for changes and pushes them through to the site behind the scenes, with no effort from you. New entries are detected and published within ten seconds, which is certainly fast enough for any blog. This auto-maintenance leaves you free to write and adjust settings without worrying about forgetting to click a Publish button.

Downloading and Installing Radio UserLand

Like WordPress and Movable Type, Radio UserLand is a program that must be acquired and installed on your computer. Unlike WordPress and Movable Type, a boxed version of Radio UserLand is available, so you can install from a CD if that's your preference. The faster route is to download a trial version of the program, which remains full-featured for 30 days, after which period you must buy a one-year subscription to continue using the program. That subscription pays for the server space in which your blog is stored and served to online visitors. Radio UserLand is a hosted blog platform like TypePad and Blogger, but differs from those two platforms by the fact that you must install a program on your computer to access the server space.

Go here to download the version of Radio UserLand made for your computer type:

```
radio.userland.com/download
```

When the downloaded file is on your computer, install the program as you would any other application. At the end of the installation process, a page called It Worked! appears in your browser (see Figure 11-1). If your default browser is not already open, Radio UserLand asks for your browser and opens it.

On the It Worked! page, fill in your name, e-mail address, and a password. All the other forms on the page are unnecessary in most cases. Click the Submit button and you're on your way to blogging in Radio UserLand.

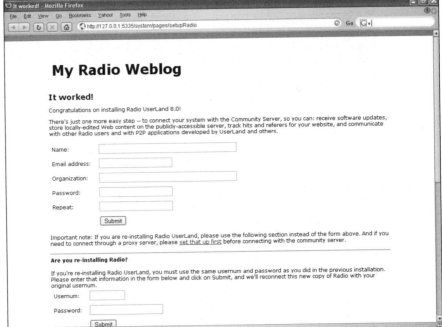

Figure 11-1:
After instal-
lation of
Radio
UserLand,
fill in your
name,
e-mail
address,
and a
password.

Now, about that browser. With most blogging services (a notable exception being MSN Spaces, profiled in Chapter 4), your choice of browser doesn't matter to the appearance and functions of the blog service and your blog controls. But Radio UserLand is tailored for Internet Explorer (IE). The differences are important. So again, as I did when describing MSN Spaces, I must depart from this book's default browser choice, Firefox, and write from an IE perspective. When Radio UserLand asks for your default browser during installation, I suggest naming Internet Explorer even if you normally use Firefox. Your default setting for all browser uses except Radio UserLand will not be changed.

To start Radio UserLand and work on your blog, simply double-click the Radio UserLand desktop icon as with any other program. (You can open the program also in the All Programs menu from the Windows Start button.) When Radio UserLand opens, it displays your blog's control panel in Internet Explorer. Figure 11-2 shows the Home screen of the control panel — that's the default screen where you write entries.

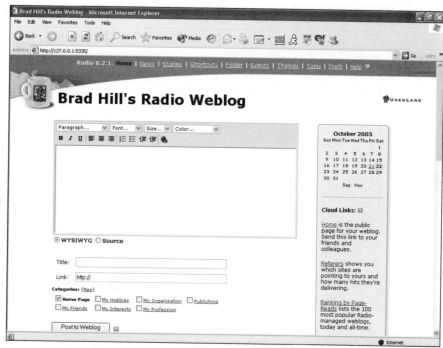

Figure 11-2:
The Home
screen in
Radio
UserLand,
where you
compose
blog entries.

Setting Up Your Blog

Radio UserLand is a powerful, highly configurable blog program containing more settings and options than this chapter can describe. A few of these settings are crucial and should be visited before posting entries. All settings are selected on the Prefs page, the link to which is in the menu bar atop every control panel page (refer to Figure 11-2). Figure 11-3 shows just a portion of the Prefs page.

To get these few important settings out of the way, follow these steps:

1. **On the Home page, click the <u>Prefs</u> link.**

2. **On the Prefs page, click the <u>Title and Description</u> link.**

    This link is the first one in the Weblog group.

Figure 11-3:
The Prefs page lists all possible settings and options in Radio UserLand.

3. **On the Title and Description page (see Figure 11-4), type a blog title and tagline in the boxes.**

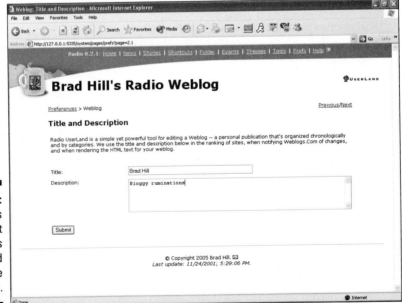

Figure 11-4:
Use this page to set your blog's title and descriptive tagline.

4. **Click the Submit button.**

5. **Still on the Title and Description page, click the <u>Prefs</u> link in the menu bar.**

   For some reason, the program fails to return you to the Prefs page after you have submitted a title and description. Programs can be so dumb.

6. **On the Prefs page, click the <u>Enable the WYSIWYG editing tool</u> link, and select the check box on the next page.**

   This is an important feature that should be set by default, but isn't. The setting makes it easy to include pictures in blog entries. You can activate this feature only when using the Internet Explorer browser.

7. **Click the Submit button, and then return to the Prefs page.**

   Dumb program.

8. **On the Prefs page, click the <u>Upstreaming</u> link in the Basic Preferences group.**

   This setting enables automatic publishing of your settings and blog entries.

9. **Select the check box next to Check This Box to Enable Upstreaming.**

   This page informs you of the upstream schedule for different parts of the blog. Don't worry if you don't understand all the scheduled items. Radio UserLand upstreams timely items, such as entries, every ten seconds. Less immediate changes, such as to monthly archive lists, get upstreamed less frequently.

10. **Scroll down and click the Submit button.**

These settings prepare your blog for writing and posting entries. So . . . let's start doing that!

Writing and Posting Entries

Composing an entry in Radio UserLand, as in many programs, is about as easy as writing an e-mail message. Figure 11-5 illustrates the process, showing an entry in progress.

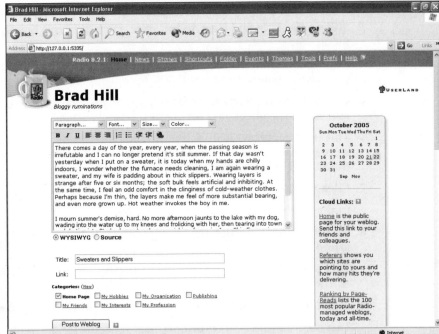

Figure 11-5:
Composing
an entry
in Radio
UserLand.

A few things about this page to note:

- The title entry box is below the text entry box. Don't forget to type a title for your blog entry.

- In most cases, you want to select the WYSIWYG radio button below the text box. That acronym stands for What You See Is What You Get, and clicking that choice shows everything in the text box (such as an embedded link) as it will appear in your published entry. Use the Source radio button for writing HTML tags.

- Use the drop-down menus to select paragraph choices (such as bold headers), font type, font size, and font color. Using multiple font colors is usually a poor stylistic choice in a blog.

- The Link box turns your entry title into a link, and the URL (Web address) you type in that box determines the link destination. If you leave the box empty, the title link leads to the permalink, or unique entry page, for that entry. I always prefer the permalink option, because I think it's natural for an entry title to connect the reader with the entry page. So I leave the Link box blank.

✔ Categories must be enabled to appear on the Home page. Click the <u>Prefs</u> link, and on the Prefs page click the <u>Categories</u> link. On the Categories page, select the box enabling categories — and don't forget to click the Submit button. Click the <u>New Category page</u> link on the Categories page to create your own categories; there is no need to use Radio UserLand's dorky presets.

✔ Click the Post to Weblog button to save your entry and prepare it for upstreaming, which will occur within ten seconds.

✔ In the right sidebar, click the <u>Home</u> link to see your published blog. (See Figure 11-6.) This is a bit confusing, because you are already on the Home page of the Radio UserLand controls. You just have to get your mind around the fact that Radio UserLand uses the same word for two very different things.

✔ Scroll down the Home page to see the ten most recently posted entries (Figure 11-7). Click the Edit icon next to any entry to alter it. Select the check box next to any entry or entries and then click the Delete button to wipe them off your blog.

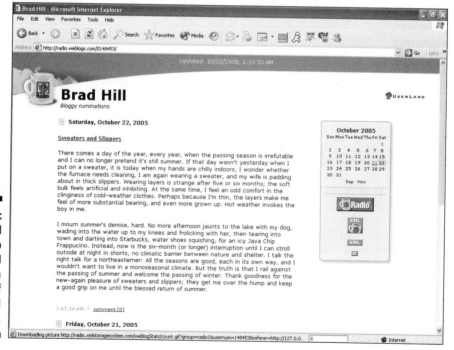

Figure 11-6: A published Radio UserLand blog with a couple of posted entries.

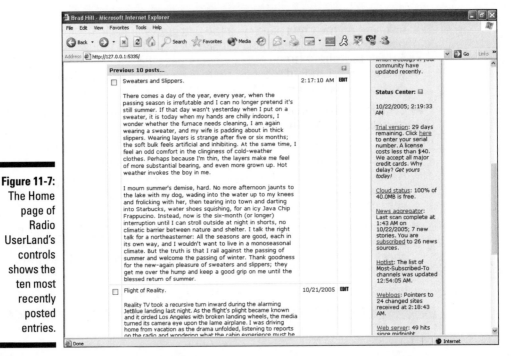

When you have finished composing your entry, click the Post to Weblog button.

Including a Photo in a Blog Entry

Posting a photo in Radio UserLand is so arcane as to be nearly Gothic. This is not the program to use if you seek point-and-click photo publishing. Still, there are systems in Radio UserLand for getting it done. I am going to step you through one of those systems in detail. Before I do, I want to describe more generally how the program deals with images, upstreams them, and makes them available to you for including in an entry.

Radio UserLand maintains a duplicate of your blog site on your computer. The duplicate site is housed in a series of folders on your computer. From those folders, the program upstreams everything you create (such as a blog entry) or copy into a folder (such as a digital photo). To include a photo in a post, that photo must reside online — that means, in Radio UserLand lingo, it must be upstreamed. To get upstreamed, a photo must be placed into a folder that Radio UserLand routinely checks for upstreamable material.

Given all that, here are the general steps that must happen to post a picture (I'll get to the specific steps next):

✔ You copy a photo from its spot on your hard drive to the *Images* folder in Radio UserLand's directories, which are also on your hard drive. You can view the *Images* folder by clicking it on the Folders page. (See Figure 11-8.)

✔ Radio UserLand upstreams that photo (or photos) to your space on Radio UserLand's online server.

✔ You determine the exact address on Radio UserLand's server to which your photo was upstreamed.

✔ You copy that address into an HTML tag when composing the entry in which the photo will be embedded.

✔ You publish the entry and your photo appears in it.

A far cry from clicking a button on the entry-writing page and choosing a photo, eh? If this exercise puts you off of Radio UserLand as a photo-friendly blogging tool, I understand. The program (version 8.2) includes a tool called My Pictures, which you can read about on the Tools page (click the Tools link in the menu bar). If you activate My Pictures, you can use it by copying your pictures to a special folder set up by Radio UserLand; the program then copies them again to the *Images* folder; from there the pics get upstreamed and are available for entries as in the method just shown.

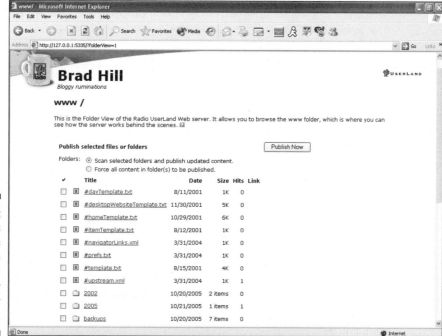

Figure 11-8:
The Folders page shows the Radio UserLand directory on your hard drive.

The idea behind My Pictures is that you routinely put digital photos in that special folder, and they all get upstreamed to their available spots online. That part of it is slightly easier than manually copying pictures to the *Images* folder, but you still have to code the photo's location into an entry box in Source mode, which is unfriendly no matter how you get there.

Radio UserLand is primarily about blogging information, presented as text. The next section describes one of its strongest features: the built-in newsreader.

Using the Built-In Newsreader

Many bloggers, especially those writing topical blogs about current events, rely on newsreaders to provide a full range of articles and commentary from around the Web. If you don't use a newsreader or don't understand how newsreaders fit into blogging, Chapter 13 can help. Radio UserLand was founded by the same person who helped invent RSS (again, see Chapter 13), so it's natural that the program includes some kind of RSS functionality. Indeed, Radio UserLand shows off one of the most powerful combinations of newsreading functions and blogging features.

Blending news with a blog platform isn't unique to Radio UserLand. Sites such as Bloglines, Technorati, and Digg encourage some level of blog creation, but the blogging features are sometimes rudimentary at sites whose primary function is searching for or displaying news. Radio UserLand reverses that formula by matching strong blogging with a newsreader that is, to be frank, a little primitive compared to dedicated newsreaders.

The newsreader in Radio UserLand has three basic functions:

- Subscribe to any RSS feed
- Display a list of stories from your subscribed feeds
- Create an entry directly from a news story

Manipulating your feeds, mixing them to create unique news feeds, and auto-tracking what you've read — these basic features of dedicated newsreaders are lacking in Radio UserLand. But I find the built-in newsreader convenient for tracking a few important feeds — especially feeds whose items often form the basis of a blog post — while another newsreader performs the heavy lifting of handling dozens or hundreds of feeds.

The newsreader is located on the News page; click the <u>News</u> link in the menu bar to see it. (See Figure 11-9.) Radio UserLand starts you off with a bunch of feed subscriptions, which can be kept, deleted, or added to.

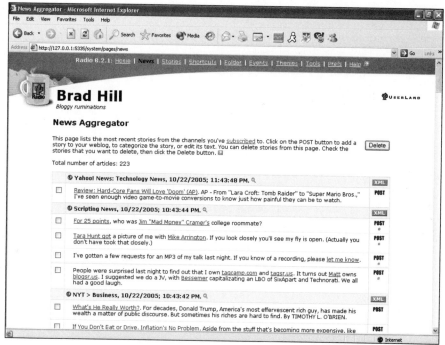

Figure 11-9:
The Radio
UserLand
newsreader
has no
frills, and
connects
directly to
blog entries.

On the News page, click the <u>Subscribed</u> link to manage your feeds. Subscribing to a feed requires knowing the URL of a page containing an RSS feed — you don't need to type the actual feed address. (See Figure 11-10.) For example, typing `www.nytimes.com` results in subscribing to the RSS feed for the front page of the Web edition of *The New York Times*. You can get that address on any Web page that offers a feed. Look for the orange XML chicklet (once again, look in Chapter 13 for a good deal of elevating literature about XML chicklets) on a page.

On the News page, click the Post button corresponding to any news story to create a blog post based on that story. The Home page immediately appears, with the entry box containing a link to the story and whatever text is included in the feed. (See Figure 11-11.) You can post the story as is or link to it as part of your own commentary on the story.

When composing an entry based on a news story, Radio UserLand does not fill in the Title field. Be sure to add a title to your blog post.

Figure 11-10:
Add feeds
to your
newsreader
by entering
the URL of
any Web
page
offering a
feed.

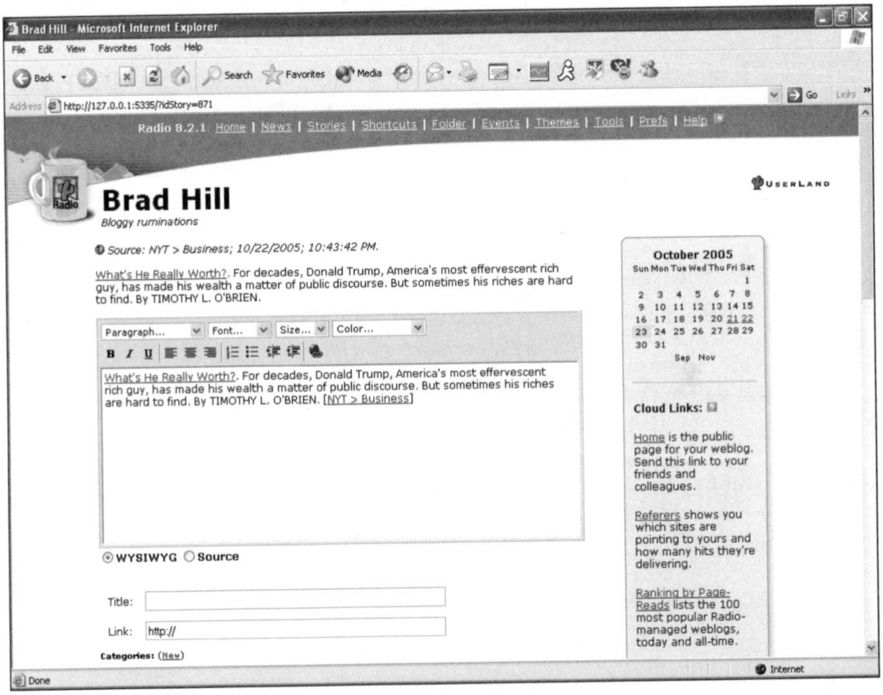

Figure 11-11:
Radio
UserLand
creates a
blog entry
around a
story link;
add your
own com-
mentary or
post as is.

Changing Themes

In Radio UserLand, a *theme* is a site design. The figures in this chapter show off Radio UserLand's default theme. Several other themes are available. Switching among them is easy enough, but auditioning them is hard. No graphics are provided on the Themes page, neither is a Preview button, so the only way to find a theme you like is to switch and then load your site to check what it looks like. The control pages in your browser also switch to the new theme, so you get some idea of its color scheme right away. Follow these steps:

1. **Click the <u>Themes</u> link in the menu bar.**
2. **Select the radio button next to any theme.**
3. **Scroll down and click the Apply Theme button.**
4. **On the confirmation page, click the Apply Theme button.**

   The Themes page reappears, displayed in the new theme.

Radio UserLand: The Upshot

Throughout this chapter I both praise and damn Radio UserLand: It's powerful but primitive around the edges. You can produce an impressive text-oriented blog with it, especially a newsy blog. But photos are a nightmare and the whole presentation could use more buttons to accomplish things faster. Radio UserLand is getting upstaged by new blog services that cater to newcomers and nontechnical bloggers of experience.

That's one key to success with Radio UserLand — how technical you are. The program doesn't provide many themes but is highly configurable if you know your way around template code. Look at Sexy Magick (see Figure 11-12), a personal site built with Radio UserLand that looks strikingly different from the basic templates. Crooks and Liars, a well-known political and current events blog, bears traces of its Radio UserLand foundation (see Figure 11-13) but has been seriously tweaked.

If you want a personal blog with occasional or frequent photos, I would turn away from Radio UserLand and head for MSN Spaces or TypePad. If you want a newsy blog integrated with unlimited news sources, and are adventurous enough to configure your site from the code up, Radio UserLand could be a lot of fun and can produce a terrific site.

Figure 11-12:
The Sexy
Magick site
was created
by a pro-
fessional
Web
designer
using Radio
UserLand.

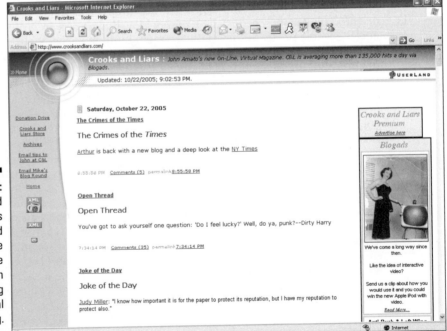

Figure 11-13:
Crooks and
Liars uses
an altered
template
to produce
a clean
looking
political
blog.

Chapter 12

Hybrid Blog Hosts: Power Without the Pain

In This Chapter

▶ Understanding the benefits of Web hosts with preinstalled blog programs

▶ Surveying Movable Type hosts

▶ Previewing WordPress hosts

C hapters 9 and 10 might give you a hankering to get your hands on the power-blogging tools Movable Type and WordPress. At the same time, Chapter 8 might give you serious pause. For those who like tons of features, heavy blog programs are fun to grapple with, but hoisting those programs to a server and installing them correctly can be far removed from anything resembling fun. Not every painter wants to construct his own canvas, and not every blogger wants to install his or her own program.

Recognizing a need for installation services, some Web hosts offer domain-hosting accounts with Movable Type and WordPress preinstalled. Chapter 8 covers domain ownership and Web hosts in detail. For this chapter, here's what you need to know:

✔ A *domain* is the last part of a Web address: www.*domain*.com. The most popular domain type is .com, but others are available, such as .net, .org, and .biz.

✔ Domains are bought and sold like virtual real estate. Most people buy unclaimed domains at *domain registrars,* companies sanctioned by ICANN (Internet Corporation for Assigned Names and Numbers).

✔ A domain name is the address of a Web site, which may or may not be a blog.

✔ Domains are *hosted* by Web hosting companies. If you own a domain name, you can lease space on a Web host's server and build your blog on that server.

✔ Many Web hosts are also sanctioned registrars, or work with an official registrar. In both cases, users can register their domains at the Web host's site, which streamlines the process of assigning the domain to the Web host's server.

This chapter highlights several Web hosts that offer preinstalled Movable Type or WordPress programs.

The Unique Power of Hybrid Hosts

Great features combined with ease of use make a powerful mix. The services profiled in this chapter offer easy startup with one of the most powerful and popular blogging programs around — Movable Type (which I describe in Chapter 9) or WordPress (see Chapter 10).

If you're considering opening an account at one of these Web hosts, you should definitely look through those chapters first to get a feel for which program, if either, you prefer. This suggestion is more than the usual "Read my words!" plea, though I am not above such pathetic bleating. At issue here is time and money. Assigning a domain name to a Web host is a bit of a hassle, and you can wait up to 48 hours for the assignment to take effect. Most of the companies in these pages make smooth sailing of the domain registration and first assignment. But yanking your domain out of one host and assigning it to another is not a task you want to perform capriciously. So my point is this: Don't open one of these hosting accounts to get a first look at Movable Type or WordPress. Make an educated choice the first time, and enjoy a stable relationship with your Web host.

The price of hybrid hosting

Now for an economic reality: Web hosting with preinstalled blog software costs more than most other options described in this book. The cost is not unreasonable, when you think about it — especially for Movable Type affiliates, which tend to cost more than hosts working with WordPress. First, the preinstalled blog software is an added feature, and added features tend to have charges associated with them. Second, in the case of Movable Type, some hosts provide the Personal Basic or Personal Unlimited version of the program, each of which charges a license fee to users — and to Web hosts that supply the program to users.

The result of this economic reality is that hybrid hosting accounts can be a bit pricey compared to standard Web hosting accounts without built-in blog software. In some cases, the hosting plans break down the monthly charge into two parts: regular hosting plus the blog software as an added feature.

However it is broken down, Movable Type hosting plans cost in the neighborhood of $10 to $16 a month. WordPress plans tend to be cheaper — WordPress itself is free software to all users and providers.

How does that price range compare to nonblog Web hosting? It is not difficult to find traditional hosting plans in the range of $5 to $10 a month. So, with blog hosting, you are paying each month for the convenience of not installing the program at the start, plus customer service whenever you need it. Some companies reduce the monthly rate for customers who pay in advance — three months, six months, a year, or two years.

Part of the deal with blog-oriented Web hosting is the nonblog part of your plan, which is substantial and adds to the cost. You get all the perks of traditional hosting, such as multiple e-mail addresses, FTP access to the account for uploading nonblog material, scripts for adding functions to Web pages, e-commerce features such as an online shopping cart, and sophisticated traffic measurement statistics. If your eyes are glazing over, that might be an indication that you would be paying for a lot of stuff you don't want and would never use.

Evaluating hybrid hosts

The short profiles in this chapter provide a sketch of basic features and values, as of the writing of this book. Naturally, you should check the sites listed for current details. My evaluations of the services are based on published specifications such as cost, storage, and added features — not necessarily on personal experience or any appraisal of customer service. Web hosts of all sorts also differ on reliability, which is reflected in your site's continuous *uptime,* or availability to visitors. That factor does not play into these snapshots and, admittedly, is hard to determine in advance. All Web hosts proclaim superb reliability.

Here's the upshot. Web hosting accounts with preinstalled blog software are great for enthusiastic domain owners, either new or experienced. There is unique pleasure in owning a piece of Internet real estate. If you want to dive into that rarified realm, go for it. And if you've hosted domains before, one of these hybrid hosts might tempt you to switch or to start a blog with a new domain.

Movable Type Hosts

Movable Type arguably has the most powerful set of blogging tools you can find and is certainly a complex beast to install. The hosts spotlighted in this section offer preinstalled Movable Type and, in some cases, interesting additions.

AQHost

www.aqhost.com

AQHost offers two blogging accounts: Blogger and Blogger Plus, the latter providing more storage for the prolific blogger. Don't confuse this Movable Type account with Blogger.com! (Read about Blogger.com in Chapter 6.) Monthly rates are $10 and $16 for Blogger and Blogger Plus, respectively. Discounts apply for a quarterly or annual payment.

AQHost is seriously dedicated to top-flight Movable Type service. The Unlimited Personal edition of the program is offered in both plans, allowing a limitless number of blogs and authors. Future upgrades are included, and video tutorials are provided.

Storage capacity is moderate: 350 megabytes and 600 megabytes for the two plans. The smaller plan includes plenty of room for an ongoing text blog and plenty of pictures. High-volume photobloggers can start with Blogger and move up to Blogger Plus as needed.

LivingDot

www.livingdot.com

LivingDot covers many bases; the service offers preinstallations of both Movable Type and WordPress. Plans start at $10.95 a month, which gets you a substantial 750 megabytes of space. LivingDot owns about a dozen beautiful, straightforward Movable Type templates (site designs) and makes them available to customers. (See Figure 12-1.)

LivingDot offers two interesting features, the first of which is unique to my knowledge:

- ✔ **TypePad Booster:** TypePad is a hosted blogging service I describe in Chapter 7, and it uses special software based on, but different from, Movable Type. TypePad and Movable Type were created by the same company, SixApart. LivingDot has fashioned a special account that merges TypePad blog hosting with LivingDot Web hosting, so you can get multiple e-mail boxes and other Web-host perks while running a TypePad blog.

- ✔ **Photoblogging:** LivingDot provides software (neither Movable Type nor WordPress, but usable with either) dedicated to photoblogging. This service empowers you to create photo albums and automatically makes thumbnails of your full-size photos.

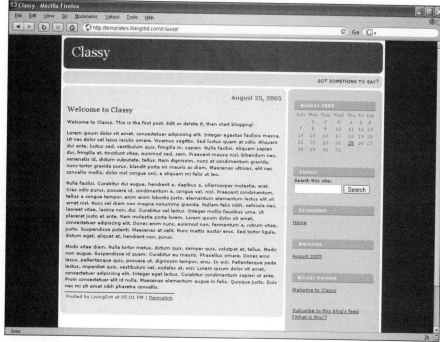

Figure 12-1:
LivingDot
provides
exclusive
Movable
Type
templates
such as
this one.

MediaTemple

www.mediatemple.net

MediaTemple advertises exceptional value in the storage department: $7.95 per month for 2 gigabytes (2000 megabytes) of memory, which should be enough to keep you blogging with photos for the next 37 years. Maybe 38. You can also put more than one Web site (in other words, more than one registered domain name) in all that space. However, Movable Type installation adds $5.95 a month to the account. Even so, at about $14 a month, it's a better deal than TypePad Pro, which costs $1 more and offers only half the storage.

Nexcess.net

www.nexcess.net

The default Movable Type edition installed in Nexcess.net accounts is Unlimited Personal, which places no limitation on the number of blogs or authors and costs $2.95 a month. (Commercial editions of Movable Type are also available at prices ranging up to $70 a month. Personal blogging does not require a commercial version.) The beginners' account is called Mini-Me, and is priced at $6.95 without the Movable Type add-on. So, to blog at Nexcess.net, count on paying a minimum of $9.90 a month; that account gives you 500 megabytes. The next plan leaps up to $25, so if you intend to blog voraciously, or with memory-hogging pictures, shop around.

Pair Networks

`www.pair.com`

Pair scares by listing high-priced plans first. Scroll down the Web Hosting page to see more reasonable prices. The Basic plan allows for 500 megabytes of space for $9.95; then add $5.95 for Movable Type. As with a few other companies, Pair allows you to host multiple domain names, so a great value can be had by squeezing a few modest blogs into the Basic plan.

2MHost

`www.2mhost.com`

The oddly named 2MHost started providing Movable Type in March 2005. They offer one of the best value deals around for preinstallation: $6.95 a month includes the blogging add-on and delivers 500 megabytes of storage. 2MHost gets into template design with several exclusive themes that are picturesque and idiosyncratic — less sedate and businesslike than the themes designed by LivingDot. (See Figure 12-2.)

WordPress Hosts

WordPress installation is not as daunting as Movable Type, but why do it if you don't have to? If you're starting a new domain, and would just as soon avoid server installations, each of the hosts profiled here offers good values compared to traditional, nonblog Web hosting. In fact, you could make a good case for these hosts even without the WordPress feature. Because WordPress is free software, hosts have less justification for charging additionally for it than with Movable Type.

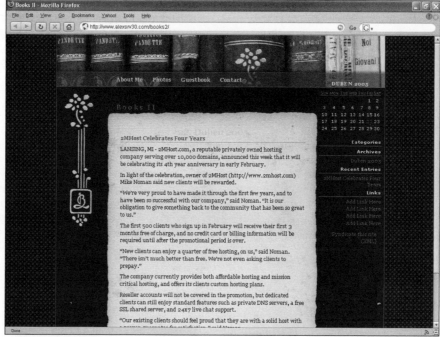

Figure 12-2:
2MHost
furnishes
uniquely
designed
Movable
Type
templates
for its
hosting
customers.

BlueHost

www.bluehost.com

If you already own and host a domain name on another server, BlueHost stands ready to provide whatever customer service is necessary to easily transfer your business to its WordPress-enabled plan. The basic account shows excellent value: For $6.95, you get 4 gigabytes (4000 megabytes) of storage, and you can divide it among six domain names (six separate Web sites or blogs).

PowWeb

www.powweb.com

At the time of this writing, PowWeb was offering various incentives: two free months with a one-year sign-up or six free months with a two-year sign-up. In a basic $7.77 per month account, 5 gigabytes (5000 megabytes) of storage are included — the best storage value of the hosts in this section. (That rate was based on annual payments.) There was no mention of multiple domain names being allowed; without that feature, the 5 gigs is probably a waste of space.

DreamHost

www.dreamhost.com

Another outstanding package of values, DreamHost prices monthly plans at $9.95 with WordPress included, or $7.95 per month when paid two years in advance. You get a whopping 4.8 gigabytes (4800 megabytes), and you can host an unlimited number of domains (each representing a different blog) in that space. This value is better than the TypePad Plus or Pro account.

Laughing Squid

www.laughingsquid.net

Laughing Squid prides itself on community feeling and great customer service. Interestingly and uniquely among the services in this chapter, the company discounts prices upon perceived need in some cases (the "starving artist discount"). Published rates range from $7 to $12 per month for — this is a disappointment — only 100 megabytes. WordPress is included.

Part IV
Total Blog Immersion

The 5th Wave   By Rich Tennant

"Tell the boss you-know-who is talking smack in his blog again."

In this part . . .

*T*his part has fun ideas and information. It also contains a crucial, no-nonsense chapter on RSS feeds (Chapter 13). They are the growing distribution mechanism of blogs, and every blogger must have a handle on using them. Chapter 14 is an intriguing revelation of blogging customs. The blog universe is like a distinct nation, complete with unwritten but compelling rules of behavior. This chapter spells out the do's and don'ts, so you can avoid embarrassment and, in some cases, more serious repercussions.

Have you wondered about making a little money from blogging? Perhaps you've read articles profiling a new breed of professional blogger. Chapter 15 charts a path to a bit of revenue from your blog. You probably shouldn't count on becoming rich and retiring early. But income opportunities are quickly becoming more available even to modest blogs with small audiences.

Chapters 16 and 17 explore the audio and video realms of blogging. The first of these chapters covers podcasting, the relatively new phenomenon of audio blogging that has taken off tremendously. Chapter 17 investigates the role of photos, videos, and music in blog content.

Chapter 13

Hooking into RSS Feeds

*S*yndication might not be a word you were hoping to grapple with on this day, or on any other day. "Blogging is supposed to be easy," you're thinking. (Yes, I can hear your thoughts. Deal with it.) Does *really simple syndication* sound friendlier? Because that's what RSS stands for, and honestly, I kid you not, RSS is simple and friendly for both bloggers and readers. Relatively painless as it is to bring into your Internet life, RSS is hugely important. Predictions about the Internet are risky, but I'm not going too far out on a limb to predict that RSS will get much bigger than it is today, quickly. I expect nearly every online citizen to be using RSS eventually, even though many people will be unaware that they are using it.

As a blogger, you should have some awareness of RSS; it should not be a completely invisible feature for you. The truth is that some blog services, platforms, and programs make RSS so easy that it does become invisible. But knowing the basics opens the door to better use of RSS in your blog (if you use a service that allows variable RSS settings). Furthermore, active participants in the blogosphere benefit from knowing about the opposite side of RSS: As readers of other blogs and many information sources, they use RSS to gather their favorite content into one window — doing so saves a ton of time.

 In this chapter and throughout the book, when I refer to RSS, I usually mean all types of syndication feeds, of which RSS is the foremost. Several versions of RSS exist, as well as one main competing feed format called Atom. Atom feeds are used by Blogger.com, a service profiled in Chapter 6. The competing feed types and different versions of those types make little difference to most users. Most programs that translate feeds to actual readable stuff understand all the variations. For all intents and purposes, a feed is a feed. Many big publishers that provide feeds, such as Yahoo!, Microsoft, and Google, make up a new name to erase the differences and to avoid calling them RSS, Atom, or any other tech buzzword.

This chapter gives you a basic understanding of what feeds are, how they can give your blog more exposure, and how they bring you deeper into the blogosphere.

Understanding the Greatness of RSS

RSS feeds make the Internet easier to use, and they save time. They bring more content to your screen and distribute your blogging work beyond the boundaries of your site. Your first leg up in understanding RSS is a return to the word *syndication*. Syndication means distributing a piece of work (such as writing, photos, a TV show) to multiple places beyond the original outlet for that work. TV shows go into syndication when local network affiliates purchase the right to rerun episodes. Newspaper columns and comic strips are syndicated by agencies to newspapers all over the world.

On the Web, any content on a Web site can be syndicated to another site or to a program that understands syndication formats. The mechanism that you, as a blogger, are mostly concerned with is blog entries being syndicated to newsreaders. *Newsreaders* are Web sites or desktop programs that display the contents of syndication feeds — RSS feeds in most cases, but also other formats such as Atom. Even if you're not a blogger, RSS represents a huge advance in Internet usability.

The value of syndication feeds might seem technical and unimportant. Untrue. To "get it" about RSS, look at the information sites you visit regularly — all of them, including these likely candidates:

- Online versions of traditional news organizations such as CNN, TV network news, and MSNBC
- Online-only news establishments like CNET, Topix.net, Slate Magazine, and financial news sites
- Online editions of big-brand newspapers and magazines such as *The New York Times, Business Week, Wired,* and *Scientific American*
- Online editions of local newspapers
- Nearly every Weblog in the world, from those written by Hillary Clinton and Donald Trump to individuals writing primarily for themselves
- Information tracking sites such as a real-estate listing service or a shopping portal for digital cameras
- News portals with search engines, such as Google News and Yahoo! News

I could continue, but that's enough to start. Every example just cited offers RSS (or some kind of equally easy feed). The value of RSS is as great as your appetite for online information of nearly every type. Perhaps you bookmark your favorite sites in your browser. Look at the bookmark list and imagine that, instead of visiting each site individually in your daily circuit of information grazing, you could pull all those sites into one window. In that window, you could organize the information streams in several ways, looking at each source separately or mixing them up in certain groupings. That's what feeds allow you to do.

The demand for RSS has reached a point at which blogs and information sites *must* syndicate their content or risk being left behind as irrelevant dinosaurs. Bloggers have furthered this revolution, because many thousands of topical bloggers use the link-and-comment format in their blog entries. These active bloggers feed their voracious appetites for information by using newsreaders — believe it or not, no serious topical blogger surfs Web sites anymore to read headlines or glean articles. There is simply no time for individual site visits, with their graphic-loading delays. Therefore, if an information site does not offer an RSS feed, it will never get cited by the most important bloggers, and it won't receive traffic referred to it by those bloggers.

The upshot of the RSS/newsreader revolution catalyzed by bloggers is that nearly everywhere you go to read articles or get information, you see buttons and links offering syndication feeds. Later in this chapter, I explain how those buttons and links work with newsreaders. The result for savvy information consumers is a universe of information from almost every major provider and millions of small publishers and bloggers, all swiftly streamed to a single window — the newsreader of your choice.

Spreading Your Word

As a blogger, you are an information provider. This is true in a literal sense even if you write a highly personal, diary-style blog. If you want to be a relevant, up-to-date information provider, you must offer an RSS feed. Most services at least allow you to turn the feed on or off, and others also allow a setting with which you choose whether to syndicate full entries or partial entries. Offering a feed plugs you into the blogosphere more completely than if you operated a feedless site. Remember that the demand for feeds is growing. With every passing month, blogs that *don't* provide syndication increasingly risk being avoided as too much trouble to read.

But what about my site?

All this focus on RSS and reading blog entries in newsreaders makes it sound as if Web sites are becoming irrelevant. What is the fate of a lovingly designed blog with a beautiful, colorful atmosphere and careful navigational design? What about the hundreds of design templates offered by blog services and the hours you spent combing through them to find the perfect layout and color scheme for your blog? If everyone is going to end up reading your blog off-site, in a cold, black-and-white newsreader, what's the point of creating good pages?

Frankly, this gloomy perspective has some truth. But not total truth. My newsreaders contain hundreds of feeds, and I spend all day reading and writing. It's important to me to avoid visiting sites as much as possible. But newsreaders do let you click through to the page on which any entry resides, and there are good reasons to do so. First, you cannot write a comment on somebody's blog in a newsreader; you must go to the blog. Likewise to just read comments. Second, you cannot see all the typical blog elements that surround each entry, such as the blogroll, the archive directory, and entry categories. Third, some bloggers and other information providers put partial entries in the feed, so you must click through to the entry page to read the full entry.

It is too soon to predict that RSS will completely obliterate Web sites or just blog sites. It is possible, and if that day comes, perhaps RSS will be far more dressed up than it is today, with graphics and other elements that currently are not syndicated with the feeds. Communication elements, such as comments, would certainly have to be included. (I have seen one experimental version of a feed in which you could enter a comment and send it back to the site.) The days of templates and colorful navigation sidebars might be numbered, but we are far from that reality now.

Assuming you have the RSS feed of your blog turned on (or are using a service in which it is always turned on), the software usually puts a link or button on your index page. (Blogger.com is a notable exception.) Most programs and blog services create just one feed for your entire blog. Advanced blog services and programs allow multiple feeds; each subject category of the blog might have a separate feed or there might even be a distinct feed for comments. Feeds for entries carry each posted entry (or an excerpt of the entry, in some cases) to the newsreader of anyone who has *subscribed* to your feed. Subscribing is free — it's not like a magazine subscription. The next section explains how to subscribe a feed to a newsreader.

So for most bloggers, RSS really is easy: You sign up with a blog provider and start writing entries, and the software creates your feed and places a subscription link on your pages. Figure 13-1 shows the subscription button (labeled RSS 2.0) on one of my blogs. Most services have the RSS option turned on by default. If it is not activated, the hardest thing you have to do is turn it on.

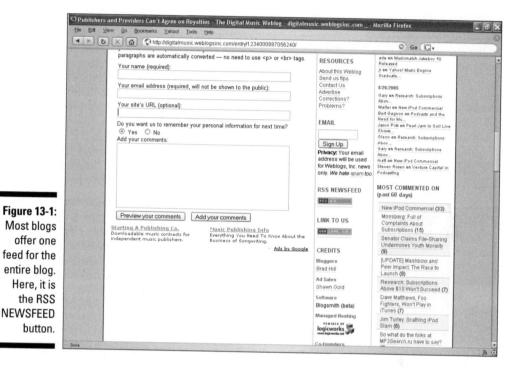

Figure 13-1: Most blogs offer one feed for the entire blog. Here, it is the RSS NEWSFEED button.

Feeding on Feeds

Bloggers tend to be feed consumers as well as feed providers; the two sides of RSS syndication thrive on each other. (I was going to say "feed" on each other, but I was afraid my dazzling wit would actually injure people with laughter.) The busiest bloggers tend to be the most dedicated newsreader users. But RSS is an Internet tool for the masses — or it will be soon — so you should probably try a newsreader whether you're a light or heavy blogger.

Choosing a newsreader

Newsreaders come in four basic types:

- **Web newsreaders:** These newsreaders are Web sites whose purpose is to offer newsreading functions. I recommend Web newsreaders for two reasons. First, they require no installation. Second, because your subscriptions reside on the Web and not on your computer, you can access your feeds from any Internet-connected computer. Most Web newsreaders offer free service.

✔ **Desktop newsreaders:** These newsreaders are stand-alone programs installed in your computer. Some people like the power of these dedicated programs. Your feeds are not portable if they are tied to the computer in which the program is installed (unless the computer is a laptop, which can be carried around). Even if you install the program on all your computers, each copy cannot track your reading in the other copies. This is important because most newsreaders do not show you the same entries more than once unless you deliberately backtrack to previously viewed entries. (Or, if the newsreader shows you entries that you've already seen, those entries are marked as having been read.) Some desktop newsreaders are commercial programs; others are shareware programs that you can try for free; still others are completely free.

✔ **Portal newsreaders:** Giant information platforms are building feed subscription and reading into their home pages and other products. Yahoo! is a good example; that popular online service allows users of the My Yahoo! personalized home page feature to easily subscribe to feeds without leaving Yahoo! Google also has a home page customization feature that allows unlimited feed subscriptions; likewise, Google has put feed-reading into the Google Sidebar (which is part of Google Desktop). Use of these services is free.

✔ **Browser and e-mail add-ons:** RSS is worming its way into application programs such as e-mail and Web browsers. NewsGator runs within Microsoft's Outlook e-mail program. The Firefox browser and its companion e-mail reader, Thunderbird, both support RSS reading. Firefox recognizes the presence of an RSS feed anywhere on a Web page and displays a small icon inviting you to subscribe. Clicking that icon creates a "live bookmark" in the bookmark list; running the mouse over that live bookmark expands it to reveal links to the current entries embedded in the feed. (See Figure 13-2.) The "live bookmark" turns the Bookmarks menu in Firefox into a small, yet functional, newsreader. Clicking an entry takes you to the entry page. Firefox and Thunderbird are free; NewsGator is shareware.

Newsreading within the browser (the last choice in the list) is regarded by some as the future of RSS. Meanwhile, Yahoo! has quietly become one of the foremost providers of newsreading services, thanks to its enormous customer base of My Yahoo! users subscribing like crazy to feeds. The future will unfold in its usual surprising manner, but for the present I am sticking primarily with Web newsreaders, which give me plenty of power and flexibility, while keeping my hunger for information satisfied on any connected computer.

Figure 13-2:
In Firefox,
live
bookmarks
show RSS
feed entries
in the
bookmarks
list.

The selection of a newsreader is getting both easier and harder as the choices proliferate. On one hand, making the right choice requires an understanding of the alternatives. On the other hand, RSS feeds are becoming so seamlessly integrated into familiar services that eventually everyone will use them without even knowing it. As a generality, the more you know about newsreaders, the more your choice is likely to incline toward powerful Web or desktop newsreaders. Of course, power comes with a learning curve, but newsreaders are inherently easy to use.

Newsreaders and newsreaders

The term *newsreader* is a slippery one. Before RSS became popular, newsreaders were (and still are) programs or Web sites that facilitated the access of Usenet newsgroups — the Internet's ancient bulletin board system. Newsreader in that application was always a bit of a misnomer, based on the name newsgroups, which also doesn't really describe the discussion groups of Usenet. RSS newsreaders really *are* newsreaders — and were even before blogs became popular and widespread. Because of this confusion of meanings, RSS newsreaders are sometimes called *RSS aggregators*, *feed aggregators*, or *RSS readers*.

TIP

The more feeds you subscribe to, the more you should gravitate toward a Web reader or desktop reader. The portal newsreaders and browser-feed bookmarking features do not place limits on the number of feeds you're allowed, but long lists of feeds don't work as well in those environments as they do in windows dedicated to feeds. Most Web and desktop readers allow feed-handling conveniences such as folders and keyword searching. Figure 13-3 shows Bloglines, the most popular Web newsreader.

When it comes to choosing between a Web service and a stand-alone program on your desktop, portability is a big issue. If you use more than one computer, choose a Web newsreader. The Web services are also free, whereas desktop products are often shareware, requiring a payment for continued use beyond a trial period. But if you want all the power and flexibility you can get in a program that acts as a surrogate browser, try a desktop program. Figure 13-4 illustrates a shareware program, Headline Viewer, in action.

If your RSS use will be of modest scale, you might prefer to integrate your feeds into a broader service such as My Yahoo! or Google's personalized home page. My Yahoo! (see Figure 13-5) is one of the friendliest RSS environments; the service treats RSS feeds no differently than the news headline service it has offered for years. Millions of people who have used My Yahoo! as their home page now add RSS feeds to their pages with the same ease that they add non-RSS news sources. Even though My Yahoo! does not use *RSS* as a term, it has quickly become one of the most-used RSS services.

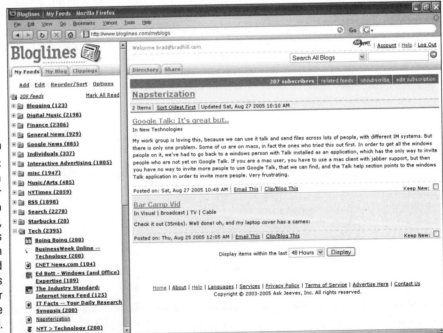

Figure 13-3: Bloglines, a popular Web newsreader, arranges feeds in folders and displays entries for any single feed.

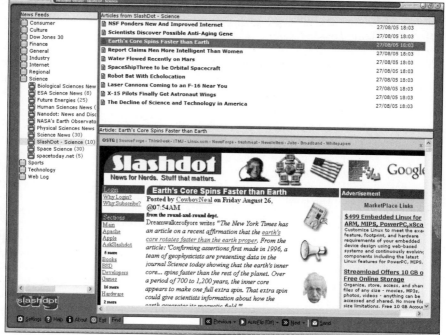

Figure 13-4:
Headline
Viewer is a
desktop
newsreader
that displays
the site
page below
the feed
headline.

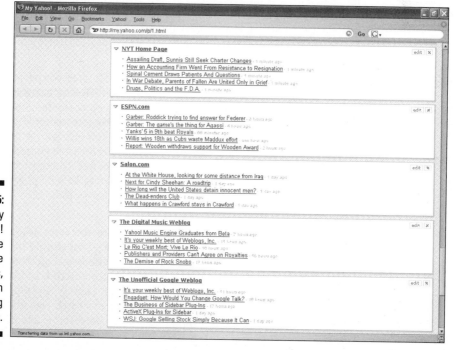

Figure 13-5:
This is a My
Yahoo!
home page
showing five
RSS feeds,
each
displaying
five entries.

Google's home page personalization is much younger and less evolved than My Yahoo!, but offers an uncluttered page upon which to display feeds. (See Figure 13-6.)

Whichever newsreader you use, there are important features to keep in mind:

- **Folders:** It is important to organize your feeds, and folders help keep your topics straight.

- **Tags:** Tags are an alternative organizing feature. Tags and folders tend to exclude each other; a service that uses one probably doesn't use the other. Tags are arguably more flexible because one feed can be assigned more than one tag. So, a feed from your sister's blog that contains many pictures of dogs might be tagged *family, pictures,* and *dogs.* Those tags put the feed in three virtual folders simultaneously.

- **Search:** Being allowed to perform keyword searches of your feeds is essential. Along with that function, the search box should be able to also prowl through the blogosphere for content that matches your keywords. I prefer to find new feeds by searching the Web (in a general search engine, or in a blog search engine, or by surfing around), not in the newsreader. Still, the newsreader should supply a method of searching for feeds from the information universe and even a directory of popular feeds in which to browse.

- **Tracking and backtracking:** A good newsreader keeps track of which items in a feed you have looked at and doesn't show them to you twice — or marks them as having been read. And if you want to see hidden, already read entries, the newsreader should have a way to show them to you. Bloglines, for example, lets you look back in time by increments of a day or a week.

- **Feed display options:** Feed providers (the Web sites whose feeds you subscribe to) sometimes shorten their feed entries by allowing only excerpted entries into the feed; readers must click the feed headline to see the entire entry on its Web page. Most blogs furnish full entries in the feed, so you don't have to click through. Full entries are more convenient than partial entries, but many people prefer to scan headlines only, clicking through to see entries of interest. The newsreader should offer this compression from full entry to headline only as a display option. Ideally, it should be easy to switch back and forth. Ideal also is the ability to set this choice separately for each feed.

- **Resorting and retagging:** Whether the newsreader uses folders or tags (don't choose a newsreader that uses neither), you should be able to revise your initial sorting choices. Moving feeds from folder to folder is generally more cumbersome than retagging but worth it to users who prefer the folder method of organizing (which closely resembles how files are organized in the Windows operating system). Tagging systems should allow you to add multiple tags at one time and erase previously set tags.

Figure 13-6:
Google allows you to personalize the home page with RSS feeds and other information not shown here.

Subscribing to feeds

You've decided to try a newsreader for some (or all) of your blog and news reading. It will revolutionize your online lifestyle. Now you need to load it up with feeds. The presence of an RSS feed on any page of any Web site is usually announced in some combination of four ways:

- ✔ XML chicklets on the page
- ✔ Subscription buttons on the page
- ✔ Subscription links on the page
- ✔ A bookmarklet on your browser

XML chicklets

I realize you think I've made a ridiculous typo, but it really is *XML chicklet*. The name derives from the candy-coated appearance of a bright orange button labeled XML. (See Figure 13-7.) Sometimes the button is labeled RSS. Either way, this button contains a link to the RSS feed.

XML (extensible markup language) is the computer language in which RSS is written. Therefore, the XML initials on the chicklet button announce the presence of an RSS feed. If you look at the address to which these buttons link, you'll see that the file extension is *.xml*. But I don't recommend looking at that address or paying much attention to this entire technical explanation.

Here is what you must know about XML and RSS chicklets: Clicking them will give you no joy. Clicking them might make you weep. Don't click them. Figure 13-8 illustrates the sort of gibberish you see if you do click one; it is raw XML code that needs to be cooked by an RSS reader (a newsreader) before it is useful to you.

Therefore, follow these steps to grab an XML/RSS chicklet and add its feed to your newsreader:

1. **Right-click the chicklet.**

   When I was a little boy, I never dreamed I would type that sentence. Anyway, a context menu drops down when you right-click.

2. **Select Copy Link Location (or Copy Shortcut in Internet Explorer) from the drop-down menu.**

3. **In your newsreader, click the Add (or Add a Feed) selection.**

Your selected newsreader might word this feature a little differently. You might not be using a newsreader yet, and I describe how they work and how to get them later in this chapter. For now, imagine you have one.

4. **In your newsreader, click Finish or OK to add the feed to your collection.**

The newsreader might give you the opportunity to put the feed into a folder if you divide your feeds into folders, or to tag the feed by keyword if your newsreader uses tags.

The important point is to right-click that XML chicklet and copy and paste the link into your newsreader.

Subscription buttons for specific newsreaders

In their eagerness to promote their feeds, some bloggers and other publishers put newsreader-specific feed buttons on their pages. Contrary to XML/RSS chicklets, these buttons *want* to be clicked — left-clicked in the normal fashion. Doing so brings up the Web newsreader represented by the button and starts the subscription process unique to that newsreader. In cases where the subscription process is quite simple, the feed might simply be added with no more action on your part. In newsreaders that always allow you to choose which folder a new feed is placed in, or which tags are assigned to it, that assignment page is displayed with the correct feed address already plugged in.

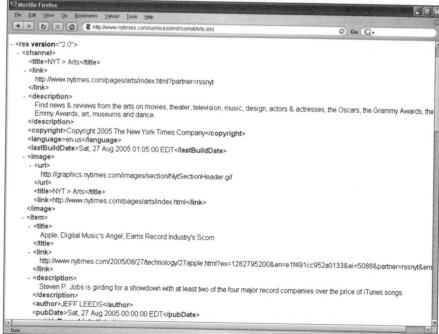

Figure 13-8:
This is what you see if you click an XML chicklet in the normal fashion. Right-click and copy, instead.

When you click a newsreader-specific subscription button, the newsreader's Add page displays in the same browser window or tab, wiping out the blog or news page you were reading. Perhaps you were finished with that page anyway. But if you want to keep that page in view, simply right-click the subscription button and choose to open the link in a new window (Internet Explorer, Firefox, or Netscape) or in a new tab (Firefox or Netscape). Complete your subscription process, and then close that window or tab and return to the original page.

When bloggers use newsreader-specific subscription buttons on their pages, they generally choose buttons of the newsreaders they use and recommend, plus whatever the currently popular newsreaders happen to be. (See Figure 13-9 to see a blog that offers several buttons.) The button is provided by the newsreader, so any newsreader that doesn't offer a subscription button to information publishers is not going to appear on their pages. That doesn't mean you can't add that publisher's feeds to your newsreader, but you have to do it manually as described in the series of steps in the preceding section. One reason to use an RSS service such as My Yahoo! is that subscription buttons for widely used services appear fairly frequently on blogs and news sites. Those service-specific buttons make subscribing to the site's feed a breeze.

Figure 13-9:
This blog offers several subscription buttons grouped together on the right side.

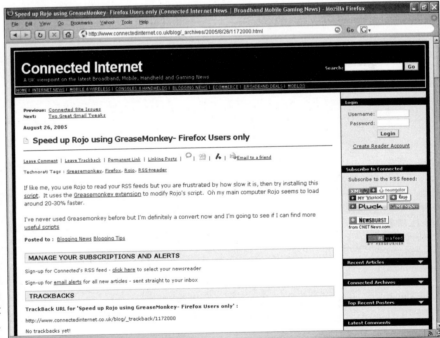

Subscription links

Some blogs (and a few news sites) use plain links instead of XML chicklets or subscription buttons. These links don't stand out on the page (see Figure 13-10), so you have to look for them. In fact, the difficulty of finding subscription links (and even buttons on busy pages) is one good argument in favor of RSS bookmarking in browsers such as Firefox. Firefox instantly identifies any feed links on a page and displays the live bookmark icon on its status bar; if you glance down to the lower-right corner, you know immediately whether a page's content is subscribable. (What you don't know is whether *subscribable* is a word.)

However, assuming that argument isn't good enough to make you abandon your full-featured newsreader, you must look for those text links and treat them just the same as XML chicklets. Do not click the subscription links in the normal fashion. Instead, right-click them, copy the link location, and paste it into your newsreader's Add function. (See the series of steps presented earlier.) Text subscription links usually say something like "XML feed," "Subscribe to this blog," or "RSS feed for this page."

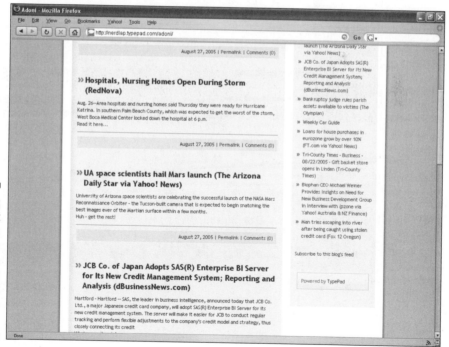

Figure 13-10: Text subscription links, such as the one in the right column, are far from obvious.

Subscription bookmarklets

One final method of subscribing to an RSS feed is to use your newsreader's bookmarklet. Not all newsreaders provide these handy tools. A *bookmarklet* is a small button that attaches to your browser's toolbar — usually the Bookmark toolbar if your browser has one. (See Figure 13-11.)

If your Web newsreader supplies a bookmarklet, it will provide instructions for placing it on the toolbar. In nearly all cases, doing so is easy: You just use your mouse to drag a link from the newsreader site up onto the browser toolbar. When you do that, the button miraculously appears on the toolbar and stays there while your roam the Web. On any page that contains a feed that you want to add, click the bookmarklet; your newsreader's Add page appears with the feed address plugged in.

Figure 13-11:
A Bloglines bookmarklet makes it easy to subscribe to an RSS feed on any Web page.

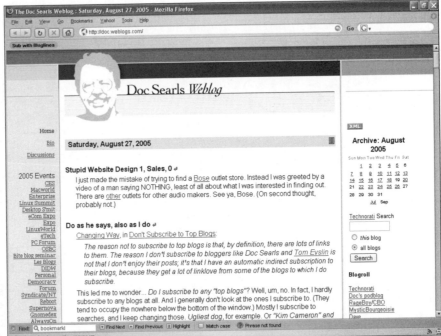

Chapter 14

Rules of Blogosphere Citizenship

In This Chapter

▶ Correcting mistakes in your blog entries

▶ Finding a balance of competition and cooperation

▶ Showing the big picture by embedding links in your entries

▶ Making prudent decisions in workplace blogging

▶ Using RSS to your advantage while keeping readers happy

In Chapter 1, I talked a lot about how a blog could be anything you wanted it to be. Now, in this chapter, I'm laying down a bunch of rules. Well, call them customs. The blogosphere is relatively new and even newer as a large enough category of Web site to be considered a publishing genre. The customs that govern its expression as a publishing genre are still forming and evolving. This chapter considers several items of accepted behavior that you should know about, even if you decide to bend these nascent rules.

Some blogosphere "don'ts" have legal implications and can lead to serious liability. People have lost their jobs by blogging with poor judgment. But most of this chapter's advice is intended to spare you from the angry repercussions of other bloggers, and readers, that can befall the careless or unaware blogger.

There is more to responsible blogging than just virtual safety. The blogosphere is, at the core, a cooperative network, if an informally connected one. The most important customs regulating behavior in the blogosphere are designed to honor the whole over the parts, diminishing competition in favor of cooperation. It is the fastidiously responsible and somewhat selfless blogs that (when they present great content) gain prominence and even fame.

There is also the future of blogging to consider. Nobody really knows what will become of this new genre and what role it will eventually play in the growing infrastructure of digital culture. It is up to individual bloggers to maintain high standards of honesty, truth, credit, originality, and opinion. Like most new technologies, blogging has a mixed reputation. Standards of citizenship, whether they are called rules or customs, aim to further legitimize blogging as it matures.

The Truth about Truth

The words *honesty* and *authenticity* are often applied to Weblogs — by bloggers. Honest blog writing is universally cited as a requirement of the genre. This ideal appears on nearly all how-to lists compiled by bloggers. I doubt that the public at large considers blogs any more or less honest than other types of Web sites. But because so many prominent blogs straddle the line between objective news and personal opinion, all bloggers demand attempted truthfulness at all times.

Speed and accuracy: A difficult match

The emphasis on truth applies mainly to topical blogs, of course, not the personal diaries. If you post about what you had for breakfast, chances are good nobody will care if you lie about your cereal. Topical blogs typically follow a link-and-comment format in which a news story (or other blog entry) is cited with commentary. The commentary, or a summary of the linked article, might introduce facts to the reader, and that is where mistakes can happen. Naturally, mistakes *do* happen and are perfectly well accepted as long as they are acknowledged.

The lightning reaction speed of the blogosphere creates errors. Topical blogs are often on the cutting edge of news discovery, reporting, and commentary. The quest for recognition and status can lead to carelessness — a fact known all too well by the mainstream media, especially on election night. In fact, acknowledging the inevitability of errors is a distinction of the blogosphere, which has evolved customs and standards for dealing with mistakes.

Rules of correction

Along with truth, transparency is held in high regard by bloggers. That means not only correcting mistakes but acknowledging them and, ideally, making the correction in a way that reveals a before-and-after trail. This style, in which an error is corrected but not eliminated from view, is considered far preferable to simply rewriting the post. You leave yourself open to special criticism if you receive a comment pointing out a mistake, and then erase the mistake with no acknowledgment. And if you also fail to respond to the comment, look out.

So, what's the best way to recover from a mistake? Two primary rules hold forth:

- ✔ Correct it quickly.
- ✔ Leave a trail.

Two methods exist for publicly and transparently correcting mistakes in posted entries. Both involve using the Edit function in your blog software.

✔ Use the strikethrough. The *strikethrough* is a simple HTML tag. Some blog programs give you one-click formatting of strikethroughs (no more difficult than making a word bold or italicizing it). In other cases, you need to put the tag in by hand, on an HTML screen. The opening and closing strikethrough tags are: <s> and </s>, respectively. Good blogging protocol would be striking through a mistake and typing the correction immediately afterward. (See Figure 14-1.)

✔ Correct the mistake and write out an explanation for your changed entry. It's perfectly fine to avoid strikethroughs if you divulge the error and simply correct it.

In both cases, you might consider *resurfacing* the entry to the current date and time, if your software allows time-shifting an entry. Doing so puts the entry back on your index page, if it had fallen off over time, and back into the RSS feed. Visitors and feed subscribers will see the entry again, with your corrections. Resurfacing isn't always necessary; I do it when I've made a whopping blunder and I want to conspicuously correct myself. Of course, that happens only once a year. Once a month. Every couple of days. Never mind how often it happens.

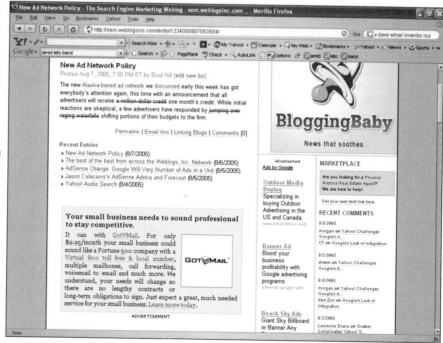

Figure 14-1: Strike-throughs correct mistakes without erasing them, in the proper blogging manner.

With the exception of resurfacing an entry to correct an error, it's best not to alter your archives. That means you should not change the date and time, not alter the permalink (remember, some readers might have bookmarked the permalink, so don't move the page around), and not delete past entries. That last bit of advice — don't delete — can present tough decisions. If you really get in a jam, perhaps by offending somebody, you might want to (or promise to) eliminate the offending post. Do what you must, but remember that blog archives are regarded as inviolable historical records of the blog. Leaving them untouched is part of the ethos of transparency that governs blog culture.

On Competition and Cooperation

Competition and cooperation present a push-pull dynamic in the blogosphere. If you're a beginner, you might not feel competitive in the slightest. And if you write an online-diary type of blog, you might never feel the quivers of competitive blogging vibrating through the Web. But topical bloggers do compete — for attention, traffic, influence, TrackBacks, prestigious citations in other blogs, and scoops. At the same time, the Blogosphere organism has an underlying cooperative spirit. Competition is not particularly frowned upon, but violation of basic cooperative rules is.

Transgressions of the line dividing competition from cooperation can brand a blog as inauthentic — perhaps the most damaging reputation. In theory, blogs are authentic above all else, aspiring to an editorial purity that honors strict topicality, careful crediting of sources, and avoidance of gratuitous commercialism. In this context, commercialism refers to self-promotion, especially by using other blogs to drive traffic to your blog. This cultural breach can be committed in subtle or obvious ways; they are all scorned. The following sections explore problems and solutions.

You didn't do it alone

In a topical blog, few entries exist in isolation, unsupported by the work of others. It does happen; if you write an essay on your topic containing original thoughts (they needn't be unique thoughts), there might be no need for attributions. If an entry contains no links to outside sources (articles or blog entries), it means you are not crediting any influences upon your thinking. As a matter of style, topical blog entries are enhanced by links, but style is up to you. As a matter of fairness, attributions for links *and ideas* are a blogosphere mandate.

Attribution negligence usually occurs with bloggers who read many other blogs. Most topical bloggers do, in fact, stay up to speed with other blogs in their field, usually using a newsreader to check feeds. As part of the daily survey of what's being written where, bloggers link to news stories being discussed and cited in other blogs. Then, wishing to join the discussion with some original commentary, a blogger might also link to the same news source and build an entry around it. The proper attribution in that case is to give credit to the blog in which you saw the linked article. You didn't find the article on your own, and failing to attribute credit makes it seem as if you did. In the blogosphere, this is a big deal.

Naturally, as a topical blogger, you do find some articles on your own, because you probably read feeds from online newspapers in addition to blog feeds. But when one blogger takes the lead in linking to an article and developing blog commentary around it, that blogger deserves credit for influencing other bloggers in his or her readership. An attribution typically is located at the bottom of the blog entry with a quick *[via XYZblog]* or *[Thanks XYZblog]*. (See Figure 14-2.)

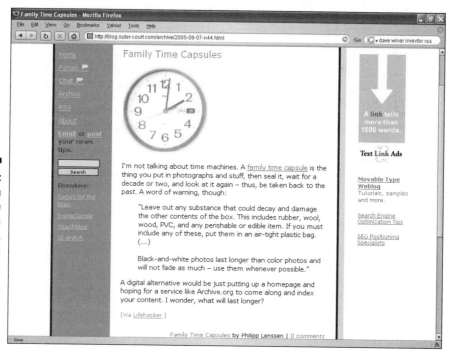

Figure 14-2: Credit given to the source of a blog entry, using the standard "via" attribution below the entry.

Blog spam

You're probably familiar with spam; most people think of it as junk e-mail. Actually, spam has a broader definition and refers to any unwanted, irrelevant, or inappropriately placed promotion. In the blogosphere, spam is not quite as pestilent as in e-mail, but it is a major problem in high-profile blogs. At Weblogs Inc., the blog publisher I work for, various technologies in the background thwart the placement of commercial junk messages in our comment fields. It doesn't always work. Like e-mail spam, blog spam is persistent, sometimes delivered by automated software *bots* that rip through blogs depositing junk comments.

Most blogs present a smaller spam target than a big blog network. Even so, spam can be an issue. Individuals with something to sell (often affiliate marketers who receive commissions for driving traffic to commercial sites) visit blogs of all sizes to leave semirelevant or completely irrelevant comments that include links to their affiliate sites.

I won't insult any reader by saying "Don't do that" about these flagrant forms of comment spam. The point of this chapter is to warn you away from inadvertently crossing a line in your eagerness to be seen and heard in the blogosphere. The mistake some people make is to overparticipate in the comment sections of other blogs, sprinkling comments around indiscriminately. Many blogs offer commenters the chance to embed a Web site (such as their own blog) into the comment; the commenter's name becomes the link to that person's blog. If you make too many lightweight comments with that link in place, it conveys the impression that you're more interested in promoting your site than in contributing meaningfully to the blog discussion.

The same danger holds true for barely relevant comments, even if they are few in number. Some of these are flagrantly promotional. It's common to see this type of comment: "I agree completely. See my write-up on this subject at www.MyBlog.com." Such a comment leaves a poor impression, and although I cannot cite statistics, I believe that self-promotions like this do not attract many clicks. Granted, sometimes the write-up being advertised is a fabulous entry that should be read by everyone. In that case, a better tactic is to summarize the entry as a comment in the other blog, and over the course of many meaningful comments build your name's reputation for high-quality discussion.

As a rule, never spell out a link to your own blog in a comment. If you build a reputation for good blogging, readers in your topic will recognize you by name, and you'll get your traffic that way.

Another point to remember: Bloggers are a self-adoring bunch who relentlessly track down every reference made about them on other blogs, using search engines described in Chapter 3. If you merely say something complimentary (but keep it authentic) about another blogger, chances are good that person will see it and put a link to you somewhere, perhaps in the blogroll. (See Chapter 1 for more about blogrolls. They are not breakfast items.) A blogroll link is arguably worth more than an isolated entry link, because the blogroll remains on the index page even as the entries on that page change. It fact, putting sites you admire in your blogroll is a *de facto* invitation to be reciprocally linked. The recipient of your blogroll link will eventually discover you if your blogroll sends a little traffic to the other blog.

Link, don't quote

The flip side of spamming a blog with links to your site is reproducing another blog's content without linking to it. Any use of another site's material, even if you just paraphrase a single idea found on another blog, should be accompanied by a link to the source. Two major errors to avoid:

- ✔ **Excessive quoting:** Wholesale lifting of another person's content, even if done with respect, is generally done with permission only. Some judgment is required. If you are writing a long entry whose multiple points key off another blogger's entry, lots of quoting might be called for (accompanied by a link). When a long quote makes up most of an entry, whose only point is to quote someone else's entry, you are basically stealing that person's traffic. That might seem like a harsh judgment, but a more appropriate entry would offer a small quote and a link, so readers can get the goods at the source, not from your blog.

- ✔ **Mirroring:** Some blogs are pure mirror sites that employ automated software to crawl other blogs and reproduce entries. Then they compete with their source blogs for traffic, while contributing nothing original to the blogosphere. These sites might link back to their sources, but that doesn't make it any better; they are stealing traffic. To top it off, mirror sites sometimes run ads, making money on the work of other bloggers. Needless to say, don't run a mirror blog.

Mastering the Link

You don't have to use lots of links, but blog entries characteristically are riddled with them. Good blog entries have a selfless quality that encourages readers to click off the page to see source articles and other blogs.

Blogs use embedded links freely. An *embedded link* turns a word or phrase in the entry text into a link. All blog software and every blog service provides easy, click-and-type creation of embedded links. Used liberally, a heavily linked blog entry is bristling with opportunities to put the entry into wider context by reading source and supporting material. As noted earlier in this chapter, linking is *de rigueur* for tracing the blogger's influences in writing the entry and crediting its sources. Figure 14-3 illustrates a link-infused entry at Techdirt, a blog that is consistently generous with providing credit to other sources.

Choosing words to carry the links is a personal matter. Naturally, you should choose a word or phrase that directly relates to the material you are sourcing. Some people like to select long phrases to conspicuously carry the link; some prefer to assign the link to single words. I like to choose verbs, because the action of clicking somehow matches the action of the verb in my mind. But it's most important to choose a word that most directly tells the reader what will be found at the other end of the link. Look at this example text from a fictional blog entry:

> *Fredericks might have been speaking prematurely when he was quoted in The Wall Street Journal saying that he guaranteed a five percent growth in revenue next quarter. Sounds like 2003 all over again.*

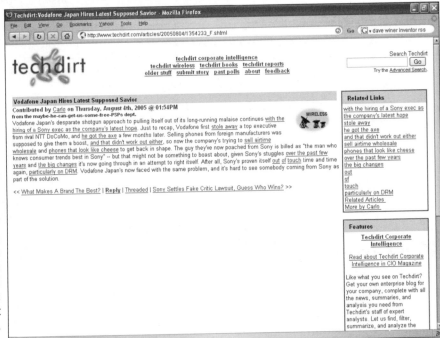

Figure 14-3: Links are embedded in blog entries to provide background information and credit sources.

At the very least, the article in which Fredericks is quoted must be credited and linked, which I would do like this:

> *Fredericks might have been speaking prematurely when he was <u>quoted</u> in The Wall Street Journal saying that he guaranteed a five percent growth in revenue next quarter. Sounds like 2003 all over again.*

The underlined word contains an embedded link. (Metaphorically speaking. Stop clicking the book.) A more conspicuous attribution would be:

> *Fredericks <u>might have been speaking prematurely when he was quoted</u> in The Wall Street Journal saying that he guaranteed a five percent growth in revenue next quarter. Sounds like 2003 all over again.*

Here is how a liberally linked entry might read:

> *<u>Fredericks</u> might have been speaking prematurely when he was <u>quoted</u> in <u>The Wall Street Journal</u> saying that he guaranteed a five percent growth in <u>revenue</u> next quarter. Sounds like <u>2003</u> all over again.*

Those five links could lead to the following sources:

- ✔ <u>Fredericks</u> links to a short executive bio of Fredericks.
- ✔ <u>quoted</u> links to the article containing the quote.
- ✔ <u>The Wall Street Journal</u> links to the home page of The Wall Street Journal site.
- ✔ <u>revenue</u> links to a revenue chart for Fredericks's company.
- ✔ <u>2003</u> links to an old article in which Fredericks made an unrealistic promise.

Linking to your own entries is considered perfectly acceptable. It's a good way to promote your work and keep visitors in your site. Deceptive? Not at all — just make sure the link is relevant and provides useful background. On most computers, rolling the mouse cursor over a link displays the destination in the browser's status bar, so anyone curious enough to look realizes it's an in-house link.

You can never link too much. Infesting your entry with links is a sign of hard work on your part and gives your readers many choices. I have never heard anyone complain that a blog linked too much, but I have heard complaints of too few links.

Avoiding the "Blog Firing"

Believe it or not, unwise blogging has derailed lives. At some point, the prevalence of blogging hit a tipping point and started a rash of job firings because of employee blogs. It's not that blogging, per se, is illegal, but blogging is legally regarded as a public utterance. Therefore, saying the wrong things in a blog carries the same consequences as saying the wrong things in public or broadcasting the wrong things on a radio wave.

Many companies have implicit or explicit agreements with their employees that regulate how employees may talk publicly about the workplace. Company secrets, for example, generally cannot be divulged in any medium. Libelous or just offensive remarks about the boss or co-workers can be harshly punished. In fact, merely writing a blog could be against company policy, especially if the blog is about your job or your professional field.

For various combinations of the above offenses, several individuals have achieved blogging fame, or sorts, by getting fired. Ellen Simonetti was a flight attendant before getting sacked for writing behind-the-scenes blog entries (her blog continues at www.queenofthesky.com). Heather Armstrong's blog, Dooce.com, won Web site awards before her confidential workplace revelations earned her a pink slip (the blog lives on). Even Google, a technologically hip company that is also one of the most secretive corporations, fired a young engineer named Mark Jen, pronto, when Jen disclosed aspects of his stock compensation in a blog.

The lessons in all this are several, and the course of action for bloggers with day jobs is clear:

- ✔ If you plan to blog about anything remotely connected to your office or your profession, find out what company policy has to say about it.

- ✔ No matter what your blog is about, ask at work whether employees are permitted to have blogs. Few occupations actually forbid blogging, but ask anyway.

- ✔ Don't blog in secret. Tell your boss. Even a personal-diary blog, which might seem to be none of your boss's business, is bound to touch on work. And that is your boss's business.

- ✔ No matter how carefully you've prepared your supervisors and coworkers for your blog, do not amuse yourself by ratting them out in any way. Don't voice your frustrations and dislikes in the blog. Any number of legal angles can lead to an individual or the company shutting you down or throwing you out.

Combining soapbox and discussion forum

Comments on or comments off? That's a question that can inspire sputtering passion in bloggers who believe that a dated-entry site is not a blog (literally, *not a blog*) if readers cannot leave comments. Bloggers of this opinion believe that blogs are fundamentally community sites with discussion tools built in.

My view is more moderate; therefore this page (among others, no doubt) will get me flamed to a crisp when the book comes out. It is simply preposterous to state categorically that a blog without comments is not a blog. Beyond hyperbole, I believe it is important to keep the definition of Weblogs slim and sparse. Loading the definition with requirements restricts the unknown potential of a new genre. Who knows what imaginative forms future blogs will take? As I write in Chapter 1, a Weblog is a site run by software that makes frequent dated updates easy and organizes the management of those updates. That's *all* it is. The technical, unglamorous, unnuanced definition serves the blogging genre well because it doesn't put roadblocks in the path of its evolution.

Now let me equivocate. Also in Chapter 1 I emphasize the importance of the macrologue — the big conversation that flows continually across the blogosphere. Comments are a vital driver of the macrologue, which probably wouldn't exist without them. I believe in the vital role of comments in evolving blogs as we know them today.

The practical truth about comments is that most blogs use them but many high-profile blogs do not. The tremendous volume of comments in a blog trafficked by millions could stress the bandwidth limitations of the server, not to mention stressing the time and patience limitations of the blogger(s). It's ridiculous to say that *Boing Boing* (www.boingboing.net), by some measures the world's most successful and popular blog, isn't a blog. Yet you cannot leave a comment there. Alex Ross's *The Rest Is Noise* (www.therestisnoise.com) is a terrific work of blogging that fulfills every aspect of the blogosphere's cultural mandate. Except, no comments. On the other hand, political blog *The Daily Kos* (www.dailykos.com) so relies on its readers for content that the owner regularly posts blank entries just to provide more discussion space.

Most people want comments and hope readers will leave them. But the choice is yours. And if you turn off your comments (which you can do in self-installed programs and hybrid blog services, but not necessarily in social networks or hosted plans), you are still a blogger.

I expect this problem to get worse as blogging becomes more mainstream while its ramifications remain murky. Remember that no matter how cozy you feel with your regular readers, a blog is a publication with worldwide distribution. Don't say anything in a blog entry that you wouldn't say in a TV interview that you knew would be seen by everyone you work with.

RSS Strategies

Using RSS (or an alternate feed technology such as Atom) comes close to being an etched-in-stone requirement of blogging. In fact, by 2004, even nonblog news organizations felt pressure to package their stories in a feed format or risk irrelevance. It is a rare blog indeed that doesn't offer a feed.

The truth is, use of newsreaders is still not mainstream — but it is getting there fast and I'm comfortable predicting that eventually the newsreader will be as popular and necessary as the Web browser. (In fact, the two functions — browsing Web sites and browsing RSS feeds — are merging in programs such as Firefox.) My newsreader has almost completely replaced my customized page at My Yahoo!, which used to be my first stop every morning. Now I go straight to the newsreader.

Note: Chapter 13 contains a detailed introduction of RSS and newsreaders. Some chapters of this book are less important to every reader than others; Chapter 13 is essential. For the remainder of this section, and in the book generally, when I say "RSS" I mean all feed technologies. The two main ones — RSS and Atom — are indistinguishable to most feed consumers. RSS itself is offered in three main versions, the differences between which are invisible to most people.

At the more sophisticated end of blogging options (self-installed programs, hybrid services, and some hosted blog platforms), you have control over how much content goes into the RSS feed. Three choices are generally available:

- ✔ Headlines and entire entries
- ✔ Headlines and partial entries
- ✔ Headlines only

You might think it's frustrating to read a feed containing only partial entries or just headlines. Indeed, it can be frustrating. On the other hand, blog sites and news sites that typically run long entries or articles do their feed subscribers a favor by not stretching the feed to accommodate entire entries. In this light, a feed is like the crawl that cable news networks put on the bottom of the TV screen; it covers the highlights briefly. Readers of partial-entry feeds can click through any headline to the source site, where they can read the whole entry or article. (See Figure 14-4.)

Clicking through, in fact, is usually the strategy of incomplete feeds. Blogs and online newspapers that withhold content are often trying to lure the reader to the site. Imagine how RSS is affecting the online businesses of publishers that have spent years building their online editions into ad-supported ventures. Suddenly RSS splashes on the scene, and readers start bundling all their news into a single newsreader window, with all ads, promotions, registrations pages, graphics, and other revenue generators stripped out. At the time of this writing, advertising is starting to appear in RSS feeds (we use RSS ads at Weblogs Inc.), and that trend will grow. But RSS readership is growing much faster than RSS revenue. To combat this trend, publications such as *The New York Times* use partial feeds and hope their headlines will bring readers back to the site; *The New York Times* feeds contain headlines plus the first sentence of its articles. (See Figure 14-5.)

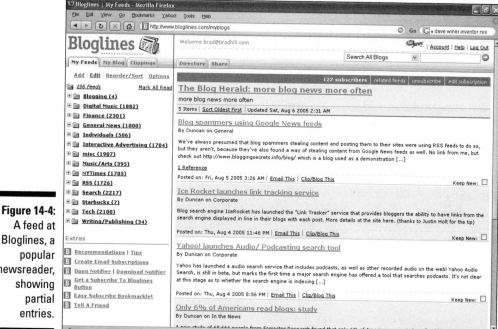

Figure 14-4:
A feed at Bloglines, a popular newsreader, showing partial entries.

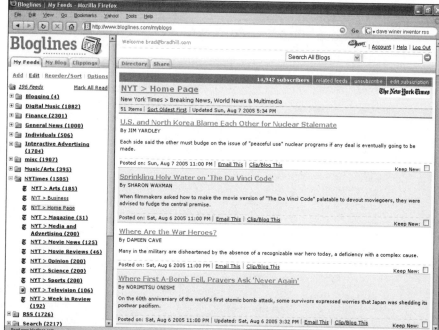

Figure 14-5:
A feed of the front page of *The New York Times,* containing headlines and first sentences of articles.

The inevitability of ads in RSS

Like the question of allowing comments (see the preceding sidebar), the subject of advertisements in RSS feeds catalyzes extreme passion and scalding opinion. RSS, a free technology, is regarded as a pure information medium that (according to purists) should never be polluted with commercial intrusions. Think what they may, the commercialization of RSS is coming. By the time you read these words, it will have become somewhat more accepted and more common. As I write these words, RSS is still overwhelmingly noncommercial, and resistance to ads remains high in many quarters. A personage no other than Dave Winer, who developed the original RSS standard, has loudly opposed running ads in feeds. But what do inventors know about how to use their inventions?

I say that tongue-in-cheek, but in all seriousness, RSS purists suffer the same short-sightedness as purists in the early days of other new media. The World Wide Web, also a free technology, was absent of ads in its earliest period. We all know how *that* turned out. Television's ad-based business model has changed over the decades. Movies in theaters didn't have ads for a long time. Each of these examples — the Web, RSS, television, movie theaters — represents a content channel, and all content channels are subject to commercialization. Bloggers should be glad if their content is worthy of commercialization. The association of advertising with RSS, insofar as blogging is concerned, helps legitimize the genre.

Purists of all degrees of clout will take me apart for printing this. But to pretend that RSS is different from other public media is foolish, forest-for-the-trees thinking. Bloggers who want to experiment with blogging revenue (see Chapter 15) should feel free to try RSS ads. We run ads in our Weblogs Inc. feeds, as you can see in the figure, which shows my Digital Music Weblog RSS feed.

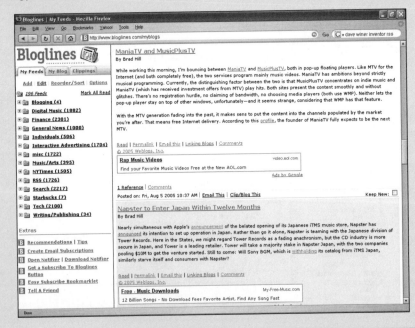

So, a full-fledged RSS strategy embodies two decisions:

- ✔ How much content to put in the feed
- ✔ Whether or not to run ads in the feed

The two decisions are synergistic; they depend on each other. If you make money at your blog through advertising, or hope to, you probably want to either withhold some of each entry from RSS or put ads in the feed. Putting ads in partial feeds will likely get you torched and blacklisted. As it is, you'll likely get some angry response simply by introducing ads in a full feed; that's because some RSS purists (like some early adopters of any technology that started out commercial-free) believe that RSS should forever remain unsullied by advertising. (See the sidebar titled "The inevitability of ads in RSS.")

If you are not out to make any bucks from your blog, there is no reason to withhold content from the feed unless all your entries are very long. (If you specialize in long-windedness, you limit your readership by that fact alone.) If your site contains no ads, putting partial entries in the feed — thereby unnecessarily tormenting your readers — will bring a blogosphere thrashing down upon you. And you'll lose a lot of silent readers who won't bother to complain.

Chapter 15

Blogging for Bucks (or Pennies)

*T*his chapter is for the most ambitious bloggers who believe that their entries are worth money. Well, why shouldn't they be? Your blog is Internet content, and Internet content has a value. How much value you realize from your blog depends on several variables, the most important of which is traffic. The more traffic there is passing through your site, the more chance you have to turn those eyeballs into money.

Does this all sound too mercenary? That's fine, too. Many people who write personal blogs have less interest in making money from their online diaries than they do in selling stale bread. I don't mean to compare your blog entries to stale bread. Perhaps that wasn't the best analogy. My point is that blogging started as a *giving* activity, and it still is for most individual bloggers. For most people, trying to generate a revenue stream (as they say in the business world) from their hobby blog is not worth the trouble.

But an equally valid point is that any site with even a handful of readers can serve as a modest home business. Making money can be a hobby, too, even if your ultimate goal is just to cover blogging expenses. In the case of a basic TypePad account, as an example, that means earning a few dollars a month from your blog. I know people who never imagined they would turn a blog into money, tried it, and did indeed recoup those few bucks every month.

Chances are good that a few dollars per month is the high end of a blog's earning potential — let's be realistic. But the attempt has the side benefits of making the blog a little more professional in appearance and making the blogger a little more professional, too. If you're making 50 cents a month to start, you might be motivated to reach one dollar, and move forward from there. In the effort, you're likely to make your site look better and explore the marketing tricks that bring more traffic. With more traffic comes more influence in the blogosphere, and suddenly you're on your way to the next level in the blogging lifestyle.

So, again — this chapter isn't for everyone. Skip it if the subject doesn't attract you. Or stick with the first two sections, which deal with the theory of blog income and tips for making your blog more attractive and more visible. The information in those sections is valuable even if money is of no interest.

Frontiers in the Business of Blogging

Now that blogging is famous, it has become commercial. Those of us who were online when the World Wide Web was introduced saw the same transformation. The Web started as a free, unexplored medium populated by the primitive sites of early adopters. For the most part, those sites were lists of links to other sites, with a bit of commentary — sound familiar? The first Web sites were similar in spirit (if not in design) to today's casual blogs. It didn't take long for the commercial potential of the new medium to explode into reality. Likewise with blogs.

You can make money on the Internet in four basic ways:

- ✔ Sell a product (like Amazon)
- ✔ Provide a service (like Expedia)
- ✔ Sign up subscriptions to content (like the *Wall Street Journal*)
- ✔ Run ads (like millions of sites)

Some sites, such as eBay and Yahoo!, manage to conduct online business in more than one of the four basic ways. Currently, commercial blogs are ad-supported, for the most part. Just as many thousands of small Webmasters have earned online income from running ads on their nonblog sites, bloggers are doing the same thing. And with the emergence of some high-profile blogs attracting millions of readers, a few bloggers are making very good money.

Blogging is a legitimate and maturing genre of publishing. Some companies hire professional bloggers (or pro writers who have never blogged and learn on the job) to produce corporate blogs in the same way that these companies hire copywriters to produce marketing brochures. That is one path for writers who want to ply the blogging trade.

Then there are the blog networks, which are pushing the envelope of the blogosphere as a publishing force. I write for Weblogs Inc. (`www.weblogsinc.com`), by most measurements the most extensive blog network. The company is somewhat like a large magazine, with a masthead of editors, writers, and management. Just as independent magazines are sometimes acquired by larger media companies, Weblogs Inc. was purchased by AOL in the fall of

2005. The entire venture (again, like a magazine) is supported by advertising. Magazines also sell subscriptions; blogs don't do that yet, but it's not beyond the imagination.

So, advertising is the business format of necessity if you are to make any money from your blog. But before discussion of advertising options, you need to know the other half of the blog marketing equation. Like two sides of a coin, earning money from a blog requires two considerations:

- ✔ **Visibility:** Ad revenue depends on site traffic (lots of readers), and site traffic depends on making the blog visible. Several skills and tools go into site visibility, and having a general understanding of them can help your site even if you never run a single ad.

- ✔ **Monetization:** I have a friend who laughs every time I utter the word *monetize*. I don't blame him for getting the chuckles over such a geek-speak term, but that's what everyone calls it when a site earns money. Something that previously generated no income has been monetized.

Raising the Visibility of Your Blog

When you first put up a Web site of any kind — blog or nonblog — it's like putting up a billboard in the desert. A new site is invisible until somebody links to it and looks at it. (Does an unvisited blog really exist? That's the question Einstein worked on at the Institute for Advanced Blogging at Princeton.)

I should note that new blogs in hosted services such as MSN Spaces, Yahoo! 360, Blogger.com, and TypePad suffer through shorter periods of invisibility than blogs hosted on independent servers (WordPress and Movable Type blogs). Hosted blogs get a push toward visibility by the host services, which spotlight new sites and new entries and also by circles of friends that often surround new blogs in Yahoo! 360. In these cases, a new blog can get an instant toehold in the blogosphere. Even so, the principles of visibility described in this section apply to, and can be practiced by, any blogger on any platform.

The quest for links

The key to visibility is links. People find online destinations through links. Traffic is driven by links. Every ambitious blogger wants links leading to the blog's home page or its individual entries. In the quest for linkage, two important arenas exist:

- ✔ Links on other blogs
- ✔ Links in search engines

Links on other blogs are powerful, and there are two kinds. First, gaining a link in another blogger's blogroll (the list of favorite sites in that blog's side-bar) means continuous promotions for your blog, in some cases repeated on every page of the other blog. Blogroll links usually lead to a blog's home page (the index page). Second, getting linked in another blogger's entry as a cita-tion for that entry promotes something you said. These links are extremely targeted and can bring bursts of traffic. Such a link can be an endorsement or an argument against something you posted in your blog; either way, you gain some degree of notoriety and visibility. Citation links usually go to one of your entry pages.

You can gain visibility in the blogosphere and start getting linked on other blogs in two ways:

- ✔ Ask for links.
- ✔ Write a good blog that naturally draws attention.

Sometimes those two tactics go together. If you know other bloggers writing in your subject, it doesn't hurt to ask for a place on their blogroll. Just ask in private e-mail, not in a comment on their blog, and back up your request with some good content on your blog. Wait until you've been blogging for a month or so and can display at least a small archive of entries. *Never* place a link to your site in another blog's comment section, unless it's part of a substantial comment. Even then, you probably shouldn't do it.

Practicing optimization habits

For several years, an Internet marketing field called *search engine optimiza-tion* has been growing in influence. Abbreviated as SEO, search engine opti-mization involves writing and design skills that make a Web site (blog or nonblog) higher in search results listings than a nonoptimized site. Search engines (such as Google, Yahoo!, or MSN Search) look for certain qualities and site characteristics, and use these cues to determine how good a site is, how closely it matches a searcher's keywords, and how it should appear on a result page for those keywords. Savvy Webmasters improve their search-engine visibility by optimizing their pages according to principles that tend to improve search ranking. There is no reason why bloggers should not do the same thing.

Keep your pages short

Because blogs tend to feature short bursts of content, with each entry on its own page, they are optimized for optimization, so to speak. Blogs are perfect for SEO because one of the most important optimization principles is to keep your pages short and highly topical. So, if you write a blog about folk music, you might post an entry about the Celtic band Filska; as long as that entry doesn't veer off-topic, you end up with a naturally optimized Web page.

Keep your pages on-topic

It is important to stay on-topic with each entry. Posting a long entry about Filska that also discusses other Celtic bands broadens the page's focus and dulls its optimization. Naturally, you want to feel free to write naturally in your blog. Optimization principles shouldn't inhibit your style. But for the most part, good optimization is good for your visitors, not just good for your traffic. People don't have a lot of time, and they like to land on Web pages that are clearly about one thing. That goes for blog entry pages as much as for any other type of page.

Be mindful of keywords

Search engines match Web pages to keywords people search for. If you want better visibility in search engines, use the keywords you think your readers would be searching with. Don't use them arbitrarily or indiscriminately; doing so is called *keyword stuffing* or *keyword spam* and is easily detected by search engines. Sites are penalized in search listings for trying to game the system. The trick here is to write your entries to the point, so that they are clearly topical to your readers and to the search engines.

Make your entry titles count

It is amazing how many entry titles have nothing to do with the entry. This point is an optimization downfall for many bloggers. A scathing criticism of a public figure might be titled "It's an outrage!" and never mention the public figure's name. An entry about that Celtic band Filska might be titled "The most beautiful fiddle music I ever heard," without relating the band's name. Blogs are famously informal and personal, but you miss an important chance to optimize your entry pages by not putting key topical words in your titles. And your readers might thank you for being clearer in your headings, too.

Feed the nets

The page optimization tips of the preceding section are important. But it's likewise important to remember that many people — and the most influential ones — read their blogs in newsreaders. Your most loyal and voracious readers might never visit your site after their first visit, when they find and subscribe to your RSS feed. (See Chapter 13 for everything you need to know about RSS, subscription feeds, and newsreaders. Plus a delightful recipe for peach cobbler.)

Because of the increasing importance of a blog's feed in promoting and delivering a blog's content, a relatively new set of practices that could be called feed optimization has developed alongside search engine optimization. Feed optimization is closely related to search engine optimization, thanks to the presence and popularity of blog search engines (see Chapter 18), which get their listings primarily from RSS feeds. Just as general Web search engines crawl Web pages to build their searchable indexes, blog search engines crawl RSS feeds (and sometimes pages also) to build their indexes.

Make your feed visible and easy to grab. Some blog services and programs bury the feed link, making it hard for a visitor to find. In those cases, it's difficult to copy the link into a newsreader, which is how many people subscribe to blog feeds. Some WordPress templates bury the feed link in miniscule letters at the bottom of the page. Blogger.com does not put the feed link on the page at all, as a default page design.

Ideally, the feed link is positioned up on the page, in a sidebar, with letters or an icon big enough to find easily. Chicklets and newsreader-specific subscription buttons (see Chapter 13 for explanations of all this) make life easy for your visitors. It might seem counterproductive to make it easy for your readers to leave the site and never return, but obscuring your RSS feed is the truly unproductive tactic, and a good way to lose readers forever.

Using FeedBurner

Bloggers who are serious about their feeds know about FeedBurner. A free service (with an upgraded paid version) designed to optimize and monetize content feeds, FeedBurner works with just about any blog program or service. Almost every blog service generates a feed for your blog entries, but FeedBurner doesn't care about these native feeds. FeedBurner creates a new feed for your blog, shows you how to put a new link on your blog, assists in feed promotion, pings blog directories and newsreaders when you add an entry, measures the readership of your feed, and can help make a little money by putting ads in the feed if you want. That's a lot of work for a feed optimizer, and FeedBurner is deservedly popular.

I should mention that a bit of technical fluency is required to use FeedBurner. The main requirement is a willingness to place new code in your blog's template. This is an issue that comes up in some of this book's chapters, especially when working with WordPress, Movable Type, Blogger, and TypePad. FeedBurner works only if you replace your blog's native feed with a FeedBurner feed, and to do that you must remove your old feed from your pages and plug in the FeedBurner feed. Making that substitution requires mucking around with your blog's underlying code. FeedBurner provides the new code, but only you can insert it into your blog template. FeedBurner helps by providing instructions for each of the major blog platforms, but some trial and error can be expected.

You can get started with FeedBurner without making any commitment and without changing your blog in any way. Simply go to the FeedBurner home page (www.feedburner.com) and enter your blog address. You don't need your RSS feed address; the URL of your blog's home page works fine. Here's how it works:

1. FeedBurner finds your original feed from your blog's URL.

2. You plant the new FeedBurner feed address in your blog's template code.

After you create a username and password for FeedBurner, you can start managing that feed. Figure 15-1 shows a FeedBurner account page. You can set up multiple feeds in FeedBurner and manage them independently.

One of the most excellent changes FeedBurner makes to your feed can really help your visitors who are unfamiliar with RSS get a handle on it. With normal feeds, clicking the feed link displays a page of gibberish code. Feeds work beautifully in newsreaders but are not meant to be displayed in browsers. FeedBurner feeds, however, are designed to display in the browser and convey a good deal of information about the selected feeds and about feeds generally. When a visitor clicks a FeedBurner link that you've put on your blog page, something like Figure 15-2 is displayed. Any visitor who clicks unknowingly on your feed link is invited graciously into the world of feed subscriptions.

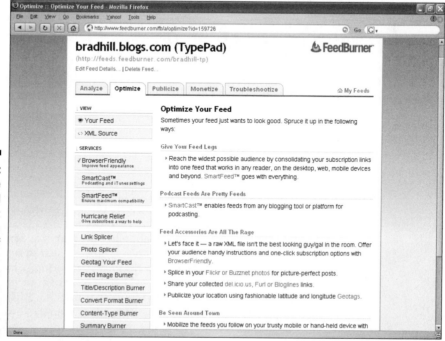

Figure 15-1: Optimize and monetize: That is the mission of FeedBurner. Thousands of serious bloggers use it.

Experimenting with Ads

If you get truly ambitious about commercializing your blog, the final step is putting advertisements on it. The three possible scenarios are

- Banner ads on your site
- Relevant text ads on your site
- Relevant text ads in your RSS feed

A banner ad is a picture ad of any size. (See Figure 15-3.) A relevant text ad is a different sort of widget altogether. Supplied by Google, Yahoo!, or another company that specializes in *contextual ads,* these no-picture ads are relevant to the topic of the page upon which they appear. This feat is accomplished using the same basic technology that produces relevant search results to your keyword queries in Google or Yahoo! Nobody is entering keywords on your blog page, but Google and Yahoo! crawl every page of your blog, determine the topicality of the pages, and deliver ads that match up. The theory is that relevant ads are more interesting to your readers than irrelevant ads, and therefore less disruptive of your blog's mission.

Any blog service or program that allows the user access to its template code can run ads. Of the platforms covered in this book, that would include Blogger, TypePad (Plus and Pro accounts), WordPress, Movable Type, and Radio UserLand. The two social networks — Yahoo! 360 and MSN Spaces — do not support the placement of ads.

Three types of payout are associated with blog ads; they do not necessarily correspond with the three types of ads just listed:

- ✔ **Time:** An ad placement is sold for a week or a month, and the blogger is paid a flat fee. The price is based on the blog's traffic; the greater the number of readers, the more the ad placement is worth. The BlogAds service (`www.blogads.com`) is a pioneer and leading advertising broker for bloggers, and sells ad placements by the day, week, and month. (Participation in BlogAds requires the sponsorship of a blogger already in the system.)

- ✔ **Impressions:** On the Internet, an impression is one display of an advertisement. Some ads are sold on this basis, with the cost usually measured by every thousand impressions. This method (among others) is used by the CrispAds service (`www.crispads.com`) to help bloggers monetize their sites.

✔ **Clickthroughs:** Contextual ads placed by Google and Yahoo! are paid for every time a visitor clicks one. Every month, Google and Yahoo! add up all the clicks, collect the money from the advertisers, and divide it among the bloggers on whose sites the ads appeared. See the next section for a more detailed account of Google's and Yahoo!'s services.

To top off the blog-ad landscape, you can also place ads in your RSS feed. In the preceding section, I advise marketing and promoting your RSS feed with as much care and enthusiasm as you promote your site. If you succeed, your readers will leave your site behind and follow your blog work in a newsreader, where your on-site ads do not appear. That's a bummer. More than that, the migration of the blog audience to newsreaders is a crisis for professional bloggers. You can handle this crisis in two ways:

✔ Provide partial-entry feeds, forcing readers to click onto your site to finish reading the entries of interest

✔ Migrate your ads to the RSS feed

That second solution is controversial, with some influential voices speaking out loudly against it. No matter; commercialization of feeds will happen as surely as did the commercialization of the Web.

Self-Serve Ads from Google and Yahoo!

Google AdSense is a self-serve advertising syndication partnership. What? Let me break that down. Google allows Webmasters and bloggers to run Google ads on their sites. Google ads are contextual, which means that Google crawls and indexes the pages on which the ads appear, determines the subject matter of each page, and puts relevant ads on those pages. The Webmaster (blogger) chooses from many layout and ad-design options and can tweak the colors to make the ads stand out or blend in. (See Figures 15-4 and 15-5.)

Yahoo! is getting into the game of distributing its ads on blogs, following Google's lead, but at the time this book was completed, the Yahoo! Publisher Network was in a beta testing phase and was not open to all bloggers. By the time this book is published, the service might be more open. Go here to check:

```
publisher.yahoo.com
```

Google AdSense is for placing ads on Web pages. Google AdSense for Feeds is for placing ads in RSS feeds. (Figure 15-6 shows an example of Google ads in an RSS feed.) Both programs are self-service, meaning you open an account and step through the process of placing the ads.

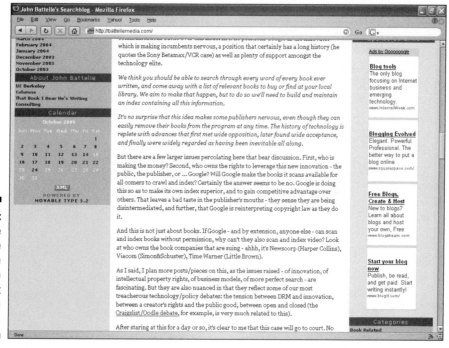

Figure 15-4:
These Google ads are designed to stand out from the page.

Figure 15-5:
These Google ads, positioned between two blog entries, are designed to blend into the page.

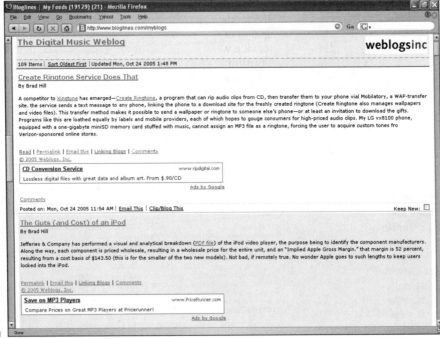

Here is how it works:

1. You open a Google AdSense account here:

   `www.google.com/adsense`

2. You choose your ad design from a selection of horizontal and vertical templates.

3. Google provides a snippet of HTML code.

4. You paste that code into your site page or blog template.

5. Google crawls your site to determine the subject of each page.

6. When a visitor hits your page, the code activates and retrieves relevant ads from Google.

7. Google keeps track of visitors clicking through your ads, and pays you a portion (an undisclosed percentage) of the resulting revenue each month.

This type of Internet earning is called *passive revenue* because once the system is in place, you don't do anything but collect the paychecks. In most cases, those paychecks are too small to send every month. But for a blog with some traffic, recouping hosting expenses is not out of the question.

In this chapter, I mention both Google and Yahoo! as suppliers of contextual ads embedded in RSS feeds. Advertising in RSS is new stuff; both companies are in the early stages of coming to grips with it. Google's service is up and running. Yahoo!'s service was in the planning stage as of October, 2005. Google is a definite option for you, and other options will no doubt multiply over the months and years.

A much more complete account of Google AdSense is in my book *Building Your Business with Google For Dummies.*

Chapter 16

Using Your Real Voice: Podcasting

*I*f Weblogs are a little tricky for many people to understand, podcasts are absolutely indecipherable. I have been approached by experienced Internet marketers, long-time radio broadcasters, and all manner of other folks begging me for an explanation. Podcasting has received a lot of press, and the word is definitely getting around. But what the heck is it? And what does the strange name mean?

This chapter answers those questions and points the interested reader toward a couple of programs and services that help make personal podcasting happen. Podcasting is closely linked to blogging, for reasons that I explain here, but it is also very different from blogging. Despite its raging growth, podcasting is not a requirement for bloggers. Creating a podcast involves entirely different motivations, skills, and equipment than creating a blog. It is more difficult than blogging and will remain so until the nascent services mature.

Stepping through the details of making and distributing a podcast would take space that this book doesn't have. But it is important to understand the general steps, if not all the variations and details. Then you can know whether podcasting is for you. That's what this chapter is about.

Tuning In to the New Radio

Podcasts are audio programs distributed in RSS feeds. There. All your questions answered in eight words! It's been a pleasure talking to you. Good night!

But seriously, those eight words do indeed define podcasts. Now let's expand them into a full understanding of why podcasting is a big deal.

In one sense, podcasts are not new at all. Podcasts are not a new technology; they represent a new way of using existing technology. Podcasts are MP3 files that can be downloaded and listened to on the computer or a portable MP3 player. MP3 is the same file type that helped turn the music industry on its ear, made the original Napster possible, and continues to provide relatively small audio files that can be uploaded and downloaded to and from the Internet over high-speed connections.

So a podcast is just an MP3 file. What makes it special? Two things:

- **Podcasts are repeating programs.** Produced daily, weekly, or according to some other schedule, podcasts resemble scheduled radio shows.

- **Podcasts are distributed in RSS feeds.** This fact connects them to blogging, which is also widely spread in feeds. The standard for enclosing podcasts in RSS feeds also makes it possible to organize podcast content into directories for easy browsing and listening. The programs that do that organizing are like blog newsreaders but are dedicated to podcasts.

My podcast adoption curve

I didn't get podcasting at first, possibly because I have a lot of experience with online music and audio. To me, podcasting seemed like just more MP3 files, and rather large, cumbersome ones at that. Much of the podcasting I first encountered was little more than a reading of blog content — or if not literally a reading of blog entries, an attempt to transfer the blogging impulse into an audio format. I prefer to read information, not hear it, so I remained unimpressed.

Then I listened to *The Dawn and Drew Show,* one of the first podcast success stories and still one of the most popular podcasts. *The Dawn and Drew Show* is 30 minutes long and consists solely of a rambling conversation of a young married couple living in a Wisconsin farmhouse. They are the sort of people you want to hang out with just for the great conversation and laughter.

Doesn't sound like much of a show? Well, remember that *Seinfeld* was called "the show about nothing." As I listened to my first *Dawn and Drew Show,* doubled over with laughter and exhilarated by their soaring freedom from broadcast decency standards, it hit me: This thing could replace radio. I didn't mean the *Dawn and Drew Show* specifically, but podcasting.

Podcasting might and might not actually replace radio. Working against podcasting is the difficulty of licensing music for podcasts, and the result of that difficulty is that most podcasts are talk shows, not music shows. Podcasting certainly won't replace music radio unless and until the licensing roadblock is eased.

But podcasting has already shaken up radio. Like newspapers that were forced by the popularity of the Web to publish online editions, radio stations are finding themselves under a growing popular mandate to put their shows in podcast format for downloading. I now listen to some of my favorite NPR programs whenever I want instead of when they are broadcast. And I still listen to Dawn and Drew when I want to hang out.

That's really it — the combination of factors that make podcasts what they are. Are you not sparkling yet with excitement over podcasts? I understand. It takes some experience to "get it," and some observers of the podcast scene have never warmed up to the format. Falling in love with the promise and reality of podcasting depends partly on taste and partly on diving in and experiencing the growing scene.

Podcasts are called podcasts because of the Apple iPod portable music player. Some confusion surrounds this curious naming. The iPod is very popular and by far the most prevalent MP3 player on the streets. But *any* MP3 player can play podcasts. Podcasts were so named because most people put them in iPods and carry the shows around — it's portable broadcasting through iPods. Podcasting.

If you're reading along, you probably still have loads of questions about how podcasting works, on both the creative side and the receiving end. I'll get to all that. First, I suggest immersing yourself in some browsing and listening, to awaken some of the joy of the genre.

Getting a First Taste

This section is a lot easier to write now than it was, say, at the start of 2005. Before user-friendly podcast directories came on the scene, podcasts were distributed mainly in RSS displays in newsreaders. That environment made podcasts a little geeky. You can still receive your podcasts in that manner, by subscribing directly to their RSS feeds and putting those feeds in your text-based newsreader. (See Chapter 13 for everything important about RSS and newsreaders.)

The directories that are now bringing millions of new listeners to podcasts are colorful, cheerful, ungeeky, and easy to use. These browsing environments resemble online music stores such as the iTunes Music Store. Hey, one of them *is* the iTunes Music Store! When Apple released version 4.9 of the iTunes Music Store (which I sometimes abbreviate as iTMS), it incorporated a full-fledged podcast directory and download page. In one stroke, podcasts were introduced to an entirely new market. (I say "market" as if podcasts were commercial products, but they are universally — as of this writing — free of charge.)

The iTunes software encompasses both the music store and the podcast directory; you can browse, audition, and download podcasts to your heart's content without buying any music in the store. iTunes presents podcasts as a whole new world. Submerge yourself by following these steps:

1. **Go to the iTunes download site at** www.itunes.com.

2. **Download and install the iTunes program.**

3. With iTunes open on your screen, click Music Store in the left sidebar.

4. Pull down the menu labeled Choose Genre, and select Podcasts.

Podcasts, though mostly talk, are a genre within the iTunes Music Store. Figure 16-1 shows part of the podcast directory page in iTunes.

5. Click any podcast.

iTunes displays recent episodes and a Subscribe button. You are always free to listen to a single podcast without subscribing to the series. When you do subscribe, iTunes downloads new episodes every time you open the program, and keeps track of what you've listened to so that activating a partially heard episode starts it up from where you left off. You can also easily transfer the downloaded episodes to an iPod.

As you can see from the podcast main directory page in iTunes (refer to Figure 16-1), podcasts have gone prime-time, with content from Major League Baseball, the producers of the movie *Serenity,* the Discovery Channel, ABC News, Disney Online, and other recognized brands. So what's all this about podcasting providing a voice to the common person and replacing Big Media? Well, you know how it goes. In podcasting, as on the Web, big media has a louder voice and flashier brand than the small players. Nevertheless, podcasting — like blogging — *does* provide an outlet for self-expression and the chance for wide recognition.

Figure 16-1:
The iTunes podcast directory.

If downloading and installing software isn't to your liking, you can try a Web-based podcast directory. One relatively new one is produced by Yahoo! and is aptly named Yahoo! Podcasts. Try it here:

```
podcasts.yahoo.com
```

Yahoo! Podcasts presents excellent explanations of podcasting, in addition to a tagging environment that allows users to label podcasts with tags that everyone can see and use to find shows. Tagging a podcast is a simple matter of typing keywords that you think are descriptive of the podcast in a special tag box (see Figure 16-2). When other users click your tag, they see that podcast, along with other podcasts to which the same tag has been assigned by other users.

Yahoo! Podcasts is best when integrated with Yahoo! Music Engine, a program similar to iTunes that works with non-iPod MP3 players. But the directory functions fine as an auditioning medium on the Web, without any downloading.

Figure 16-2: Yahoo! encourages users to tag podcasts with keywords.

Two other podcast directories you should know about:

- **Odeo:** Odeo promises to be a full-fledged podcast studio, where you can create your own podcasts, in addition to providing a directory. As of this writing, the studio part was not yet open, but the directory part was. Go to www.odeo.com.

- **Loomia:** A nicely designed podcast directory on the Web (no program installation required), Loomia allows users to assign tags to podcasts and browse each other's tags. Go to www.loomia.com.

Creating and Distributing Podcasts

This section covers *general* steps in creating a podcast and pushing it out into the world. The specifics would warrant their own book. I point you in a few productive directions and convey, I trust, a fairly detailed understanding of how it all works.

The basic outline of podcasting can be boiled down to two steps:

1. Record an audio file.

2. Distribute the audio file in an RSS feed.

Let's expand each part separately.

Recording a podcast

Podcasts can be as high-tech or as low-tech as your ambitions and standards demand. If you have something important to say, it doesn't matter whether you say it in high-fidelity or low-fidelity. Some of the best podcasts are recorded over cell phones, and you can imagine the sound quality. Three basic production levels are used in podcasts:

- Recording over the phone using a Web-based service such as Audioblog.com

- Recording into your own computer using a headset microphone and recording software

- Producing high-quality audio either in your computer or in a studio, and adding music or effects to the show

Audioblog is an audio- and video-uploading service that I discuss in Chapter 17. You can use Audioblog for posting voice clips in blog entries, but that is not the same as podcasting. (Remember, a podcast by definition presents regular episodes and is enclosed in RSS feeds.) Audioblog also offers podcast recording over the phone; once you have an account (which, at this writing, cost $4.95 a month), you just pick up the phone, dial a special number, and talk up to 60 minutes. Please, for everyone's sake, if you're going to hold down a 60-minute podcast by yourself, solve the basic riddles of the universe. Anything less probably won't fill up the entire hour.

You can record into your computer by connecting a headset microphone to your MIC input jack of you computer's sound card; that jack is usually located on the back panel of the computer (or the front panel of a laptop computer). One good and much-used program for recording podcasts is called Audacity (see Figure 16-3). Audacity is a free download available here:

```
audacity.sourceforge.net
```

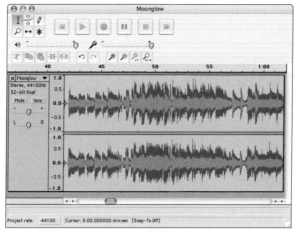

Figure 16-3:
The free
Audacity
recording
program is
popular for
creating
podcasts.

Distributing a podcast

Podcasts go into RSS feeds in a special way. A standard podcast delivery mechanism in RSS is called an *enclosure.* The podcast must get into that enclosure to be recognized by podcast directories such as iTunes, Yahoo! Podcasts, Odeo, and Loomia. Those directories pluck the podcasts out of the RSS stream, leaving behind any text that accompanies the podcast. So, a podcast is very much like a blog entry and can even be bundled with a blog entry on the blog site. But the podcast must be distinctly identified as an enclosure in the RSS feed.

Some blog programs are better than others at recognizing podcasts and creating the necessary enclosure. TypePad and WordPress are two of the best; both programs recognize podcasts when they are uploaded and linked to in the blog entry. After the podcast is recognized, the RSS enclosure is created without effort on your part. That level of automation makes life easy for bloggers. They simply create, upload, and link the podcast (not unlike uploading a photo and putting it in an entry). The blog program does the rest, and the RSS feed is updated with the necessary enclosure for the podcast.

A Web service called FeedBurner (see Chapter 15) easily creates podcast enclosures. FeedBurner is a full-service RSS enhancer that helps bloggers promote their feeds. Basic accounts at FeedBurner are free (upgraded service is also available for a monthly subscription), and many podcasters on various blog platforms use FeedBurner to effectively distribute their episodes. For more information about creating an RSS feed with podcast enclosures, go to FeedBurner:

```
www.feedburner.com
```

Chapter 17

Photoblogging and Audioblogging

. . . .

In This Chapter

▶ Knowing what you need to photoblog

▶ Posting photos to your blog from anywhere

▶ Voice blogging with Audioblog

. . . .

*N*o typing is required in this chapter. Here, we discuss photoblogging and audioblogging. If you are reading straight through the book and have managed to retain your sanity, this is not your first encounter with either concept. I touch on audioblogging in Chapter 6, because Blogger has a built-in tool for putting audio in a blog entry. Photoblogging has come up again and again during the reviews of blogging services and programs in Parts II and III.

Photoblogging is more common than audioblogging for several reasons, not least among them the fact that more people own digital cameras, and know how to use them, than own and use computer microphones. But audioblogging is easier than you might think, and this chapter illuminates its mysteries.

In case you're wondering, this chapter is not concerned with podcasting, which is a specific type of audioblogging and is covered in Chapter 16. In this chapter, I examine how to put a short audio clip in a blog entry. Podcasts are related to RSS feeds and are usually produced on a regular schedule. Audioblogging is more informal and not necessarily tied into the RSS feed. (See Chapter 13 for more about RSS and feeds.)

Information in this chapter might influence your choice of blogging service; some platforms are much more photo-friendly than others. If you're already blogging in a program or hosted service that makes working with photos difficult, consider starting another blog that is dedicated to photos, on a more supportive platform.

Preparing to Photoblog

It's easy for you to say "I want to photoblog." And it's easy for me to respond, "Anyone can photoblog." It's a different matter to know exactly what is required. Let's start from scratch.

Going digital

Photoblogging nearly requires a digital camera. I say "nearly" because you could conceivably photoblog with a film camera and digitizing service provided by a developer, or a camera/scanner combination. But using film doesn't lead to a happy photoblogging life. The path from film to blog is too slow, too expensive, and too complicated.

A digital camera stores photos on a memory card, from which they can be uploaded to your computer. Many digital cameras are marketed with printers, promoting how easy it is to put the memory card into the printer and print photos — without putting the pictures in the computer at all. Indeed, bypassing the computer is convenient when the goal is a collection of printed snapshots. But in photoblogging, the goal is a photo posted on your site, so it's the printer you want to bypass. That's not to say you shouldn't own a printer, of course. But the printer is irrelevant to blogging.

Other camera considerations:

✔ Picture quality in a digital camera is most commonly measured in *megapixels* (millions of pixels). A higher number of megapixels yields more detailed pictures, especially when the photos are enlarged. Blogging and photoblogging are not known for high-quality photos, where the size is often constrained to fit into an entry or a sidebar. (Some professional photographers do use photoblogs to showcase their work, and they display their albums using thumbnails that expand when clicked.) You don't need a great, expensive camera to photoblog. Even a 1-megapixel camera delivers photos that are just fine for a blog.

✔ More important than picture quality might be the size of the memory card. One of the joys of digital photography is its freedom from film's cost-per-exposure expense. After you buy the camera, digital photography doesn't cost anything per photo, and most people quickly get in the habit of snapping the shutter freely and sorting it all out later. High-quality cameras (5 megapixels and above) need large memory cards because their photos result in large file sizes.

✔ Most cameras use a USB connector to upload pictures to the computer. USB 2.0 is much faster than USB 1.0; you'll be glad you have it. Many computers are equipped with memory card slots, enabling you to remove the card from the camera and stick it in the computer, uploading the pictures without a cable.

✔ Camera-equipped cell phones (camera phones) represent another possibility. A camera phone, when combined with a blogging service that supports remote hosting, makes it possible to send a photo to a blog immediately after taking it, without removing the picture from the camera.

Photoblogging, just like written blog entries, can be as profound or superficial and as objective or personal as you like. Serious photobloggers are like amateur photojournalists, covering current events with a camera. Casual photobloggers document their lives with photos like a picture diary.

Choosing a photo-friendly blog service

Strictly speaking, a photoblog is a Weblog whose primary content is photographic. But there is no harm in taking a broader and more relaxed view. In this chapter, I use the term *photoblogging* to mean any use of photographs in a blog. So in these pages, you are photoblogging if you include a single photo in your blog, in any fashion, for any purpose.

Photos can be featured in a blog in three ways:

✔ Embedded in an entry

✔ Displayed in a sidebar and often linked to a larger pop-up photo

✔ Collected in photo albums integrated with the blog

The blog services and programs profiled in this book vary alarmingly in their ability to handle those three display possibilities. You would be justified in supposing that putting a photo in a blog entry is a piece of cake for any blog program, as it generally is in an e-mail program. Not so.

Table 17-1 compares how the seven blog platforms in this book handle the three photo-display options in blogs. Evaluating the programs is a little tricky because many offer compromised methods rather than built-in tools to do the job. That is the criterion for this table — the presence of a native ability to include photos in a blog. When no native ability exists to put photos in, for example, the sidebar (unless you use another service linking into the blog), the verdict is "No" with an explanation in parentheses. In cases where there is a built-in tool but it's not as user-friendly as it could be; the verdict is "Yes" with an explanation.

Table 17-1	Using Photos in the Blog Services		
	Photo in Entry	*Photos in Sidebar*	*Photo Albums*
Blogger.com	Yes	No (must alter template code or stream photos from Flickr)	No
Movable Type	Yes	Yes (requires entering URL)	No
MSN Spaces	Yes	Yes	Yes
Radio UserLand	Yes (requires entering URL)	No (must alter template code)	No
TypePad	Yes	Yes	Yes
WordPress	Yes (requires entering URL)	Yes (requires entering URL)	No
Yahoo! 360	Yes (cannot position or resize photo)	No (must use Yahoo! Photos or Flickr)	No (must use Yahoo! Photo or Flickr albums)

A few notes about this table:

- ✔ MSN Spaces and TypePad provide the most complete built-in tools for photoblogging among the services in this book. MSN Spaces displays ads in your site. TypePad is a subscription service and has no ads. See Chapters 4 and 7, respectively, for details.

- ✔ Plugins for Movable Type and WordPress are available that provide photo functions, including the creation of albums.

- ✔ Manually entering the URL of a photo location is not necessarily difficult, but a more automated uploading system that places the photo in an entry or in a sidebar is preferable.

Moblogging with Photos

Moblogging is mobile blogging — posting entries to your blog from a remote location. Remote-control blogging takes two forms:

✔ **E-mail blogging:** You use any connected computer to e-mail an entry to your blog. This method might or might not allow photos to be sent, depending on the blog service. Also, you might be required to use a certain e-mail account that you specify with the service — again, depending on the service.

✔ **Cell-phone blogging:** Mostly used with camera phones, this method involves sending a picture from an Internet-connected, camera-equipped cell phone to an e-mail address that is set up to post the photo to your blog.

Photo moblogging has gained fame through bad times — notably, in the aftermath of storms and bombing during which citizens with blogs posted photos faster, in greater volume, and from closer to the events than the mainstream media. People escaping the London subways after the 2005 bombings took out their camera phones and streamed photos of that terrible day to their blogs. Happier moments are just as susceptible to moblogging, and after your system is in place, sending a photo remotely to your blog can be easier than posting a regular entry.

The Flickr solution

Blog programs installed on your server, such as Movable Type and WordPress, do not come with built-in moblogging tools. This is where Flickr comes in. Flickr is a photo-sharing service that, among many great features, can accept moblogged photos and pass them on to many of the blogs described in this book. Specifically, Flickr works with Blogger, TypePad, Movable Type, and WordPress.

Flickr accounts are free, though you can upgrade to a paid account that has no storage limits. For our basic moblogging purposes, the free account works fine. Go to the Flickr home page to get started:

www.flickr.com

After you have a Flickr page of your own, find the Your blogs link and click it to get started setting up your moblogging system. Flickr allows you to set up multiple blogs, if you have them. But Flickr provides just one e-mail address for remote entries, so you must choose which blog you want to use before hitting the road with your camera phone.

After you're set up, add that e-mail address to your cell phone's address book. Send your photos to it. Watch them appear in your blog. It's that simple, that fun, and definitely worth the effort of setting it all up in Flickr.

As with all photo work, some blog services make moblogging easier than others. Of the platforms covered in this book, Blogger and TypePad lead the way with built-in moblogging tools:

- ✔ Blogger.com provides two remote services, one e-mail and one phone. The e-mail service (called Mail-to-Blogger) does not accept photos, so that's off the radar in this chapter. The phone service (called Blogger Mobile) works beautifully and gives you the option of moblogging to your already existing Blogger blog (if you have one) or creating a new blog just for your remotely posted pictures. See Chapter 6 for the details.

- ✔ TypePad merges e-mail blogging with cell-phone blogging by allowing you to list several e-mail addresses from which your messages will come. You can assign one slot to your regular e-mail address and another slot to your phone's address. (You might have to contact your cell-phone provider to obtain the address.) Then you assign blogs for text entries and photo entries. In TypePad Plus and Pro, where you can operate more than one blog in the account, you can assign one blog to receive text entries and another blog to receive any pictures you beam over. The final piece of the puzzle is a special e-mail address assigned to your TypePad account to receive all remote entries. See Chapter 7 for the details.

Audioblogging with Audioblog

I mention aubdioblogging in Chapter 6 because Blogger.com has a built-in service that lets you create talking blog entries. Here, I want to highlight a different service that works with many blogging platforms: Audioblog.

Audioblog is a subscription service that lets you phone in a blog entry or upload a recorded audio file from your computer. Either way, the near-instant result is a blog entry with a Play button in it. That Play button works in nearly any browser on any computer, without opening another program. It just . . . plays. This system is an advantage over Blogger's audioblogging service, which connects the audio to the blog but opens a program such as Windows Media Player or iTunes to play the audio. Audioblog is not free, but it works with many blog programs and provides a better experience for your visitors.

 Audioblog is not the place to start a blog. The service places audio content on a blog you already operate. If you are blogging with WordPress, TypePad, LiveJournal, or Movable Type, follow these steps to get started:

1. **Go to Audioblog at www.audioblog.com.**

2. **Click the Sign Up Now! button.**

These sign-up buttons are always so jubilant, as if they were suggesting you pop open a bottle of champagne.

3. **Fill in your billing information, and then click the Go to Confirmation button.**

4. **Click the Yes, Submit button.**

   That is, after you confirm that your information is correct.

5. **On the next page, click the Go to Log In Page button.**

6. **Log in with your username and password.**

7. **On the My Blogs page, click the <u>Add Blog</u> link.**

8. **On the next page, name your blog and enter the details of your blog.**

   The blog name you enter here identifies the blog within Audioblog; it does not change the name of the blog *on* the blog. Use the drop-down menu to select your blog program or service.

9. **Click the Save and Update Blog List button.**

   You can register multiple blogs with Audioblog.

10. **On your account page, click the Audio tab.**

11. **Click the <u>My Moblog</u> link.**

12. **Write down your phone number and PIN number.**

    You need these numbers to record a voice entry over the phone. You might want to print this page. I also have the phone number in my cell phone's address book, so I can post an audio blog entry anytime, anywhere.

After you reach this stage, you're ready to audioblog. Follow the instructions on the page displaying your personal numbers. You need the four-digit number that identifies your blog; it appears next to your blog's name on that page.

So now you can unfold your phone at any time and post a voice entry that just about any visitor can effortlessly hear. If you did the Flickr routine described earlier in this chapter, you can also post photos remotely, perhaps using the same cell phone. How cool is all this? I'll answer that; on a scale of one to ten it maxes out at ten. This is great stuff. The step-throughs in this chapter might seem long and complicated, but they are worth it. Set aside some time and take them slowly. When you're all set up, the actual photoblogging, moblogging, and audioblogging become as easy as making a phone call.

Part V
The Part of Tens

The 5th Wave   By Rich Tennant

"He should be all right now. I made him spend two and a half hours reading prisoner blogs on the state penitentiary web site."

In this part . . .

This part is about blog resources. Chapter 18 zeroes in on blog search engines and directories which, taken as a group, represent the most-used resources by bloggers. Chapter 19 spreads out to resources of many kinds. There are some real gems in both these chapters — sites that I and many other bloggers find indispensable every day.

Chapter 18

Ten Blog Engines and Directories

Millions of blogs. Multiple millions of blog entries. Many of those blog entries contain links to other Web content, and bloggers like to know who is linking to whom. How does one keep track of it all? Google? Yahoo!? Sure, those generic search engines do index blog entries and mix them into Web results along with nonblog pages when you run a keyword search. But the blogosphere has grown so rapidly, and is so rich in content, that an urgent need exists for dedicated blog search engines. That need has been met by several engines that collect only blog content. In addition to traditional keyword-entry search engines, directories and useful lists have sprung up to help you navigate the oceanic blogosphere and find the writers you want to read.

This chapter deals exclusively with written blogs, not podcasts. Specific podcast-finding services are described in Chapter 16. Also, see Chapter 3 for a quick rundown of four blog search engines and how bloggers use them. Those four engines are

✔ Technorati (`www.technorati.com`)

✔ Feedster (`www.feedster.com`)

✔ BlogPulse (`www.blogpulse.com`)

✔ Bloglines (`www.bloglines.com`)

I did not want to duplicate mentions of those engines here, but any one of them could have been selected for this chapter. Each is worth investigating. BlogPulse is currently my favorite blog engine; Technorati is a grandfather of blog searching still loyally used by many; Feedster likewise has a strong reputation; and Bloglines is one of the most popular RSS newsreaders that also includes a blog search engine.

PubSub

`www.pubsub.com`

The credibility of blog engines ebbs and flows quickly, driven by the voracious and demanding nature of the blogosphere. At the time of this writing, PubSub was riding high thanks to the quality of its search results and the ease with which it can be personalized. PubSub gets part of its name from the fact that you can "subscribe" to searches. This tracking feature is not a subscription in any traditional sense; it is free, and you don't even have to register at the site to use it. That last fact is remarkable in this era of ubiquitous site registrations and contributes to the site's wildfire popularity. You can just go there and start using it. Here's how:

1. **On the PubSub home page (see Figure 18-1), click the mouse inside the keyword entry box labeled 1.**

   Doing so clears the welcome message in that box and readies it to accept your keyword(s).

2. **Type a single word or a phrase.**

3. **Click the Start Matching Now! button.**

   The page reloads, and your keyword string is added to the My Subscription Stack on the left side of the page.

4. **Click any subscription in your Subscription Stack to launch a search for that keyword string.**

   The results page displays full blog entries (and articles) for the 32 most recent matches to your keyword(s). Figure 18-2 shows PubSub search results for the keyword RIAA. You might have to wait a few minutes to see results. Try adding another keyword or phrase, and then click the first subscription — you should see results by then.

Figure 18-1:
The PubSub home page. Type keywords, click the button, and you have subscribed to a search.

Figure 18-2:
PubSub shows 32 search results, representing the most recent blog matches to your keywords.

PubSub claims to work in reverse of typical search engines, which build data-bases based on periodically crawling the Web. Contrary to such *retrospective* indexing, PubSub keeps a database of search queries (Subscription Stacks) and matches that database to blog entries as they are published; PubSub calls this *prospective* searching, and the results are amazingly current.

PubSub automatically identifies your computer and recognizes you when you return to the site on that computer. This invisible and effortless tracking of your Subscription Stack makes PubSub a breeze to use, though some people don't like Web sites leaving cookies (identifying bits of information) in their computers, especially without asking. I find PubSub's method a refreshing change from the hassle of registration and logging into a site every time I use it — plus, I know PubSub isn't going to sell my e-mail address because it doesn't have it.

Actually, PubSub does accept registrations (click the <u>Login</u> link), the main benefit of which is use of the PubSub Sidebar. The Sidebar attaches to your browser (there is an Internet Explorer version and a Firefox version) and deliv-ers continually updating results to your Subscription Stack, so you don't have to visit the site and initiate a search. (Figure 18-3 shows the PubSub Sidebar in action.) With a PubSub account, you can also add an RSS feed for each of your search subscriptions to a newsreader and check ongoing search results there. (See Chapter 13 for the complete story of RSS and newsreaders.)

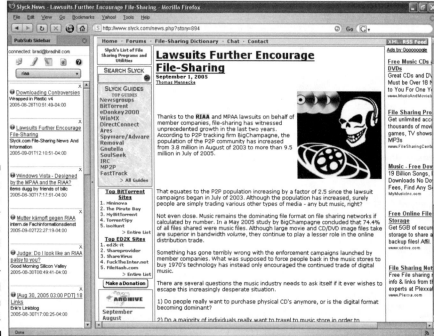

Figure 18-3: The PubSub Sidebar delivers continual updates to your subscribed search results.

PubSub offers another valuable feature to bloggers who want to track how many (and which) sites are linking to their entries. Try this:

1. **On the PubSub home page, click the <u>PubStats</u> navigation link.**

2. **On the PubStats page, click SiteStats.**

3. **On the SiteStats page, enter your blog's URL.**

The resulting page, shown in Figure 18-4, crunches all kinds of numbers related to your blog and its incoming links (that is to say, links from other blogs to your site). If you click the InLinks column of the main table, PubSub shows you which specific sites linked to you on that day.

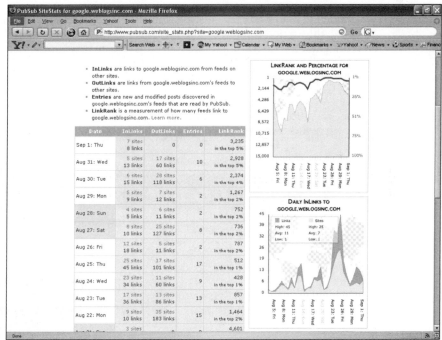

Figure 18-4:
PubSub
SiteStats
show how
many sites
link to your
blog, and
can even
tell you
which sites.

Blogdex

www.blogdex.net

A product of the MIT Media Laboratory, Blogdex calls itself "The Weblog Diffusion Index," and it tracks the most-linked pieces of Web content at any given moment. Most of those content pieces are articles, because bloggers so often link to articles and comment on them. So, Blogdex is an ever-changing directory of the most important daily topics of conversation in the blogos-phere. Unlike traditional online directories, though, there is no division into topics and no drilling down into subtopics. Blogdex simply presents a list of articles (and whatever else is being linked to), and notes how many links cur-rently exist to each page. (See Figure 18-5.) Click the track this site link below any item to see which blogs have linked to that page.

Blogdex is not used popularly as a search engine, but it does have a search function. Click the Search link on the home page. Two modes of searching are available:

- ✔ **URLs:** Your keywords are matched against Web addresses.
- ✔ **Text:** Your keywords are matched against page titles.

The page title of any Web page appears in the top bar of your Web browser. The page title is determined by the page creator or site administrator; some creators and administrators take more care to title their pages accurately than others. As a result, the Text type of search can return uneven results. However, I find it more valuable than the URL search, the results of which tend to be predictable.

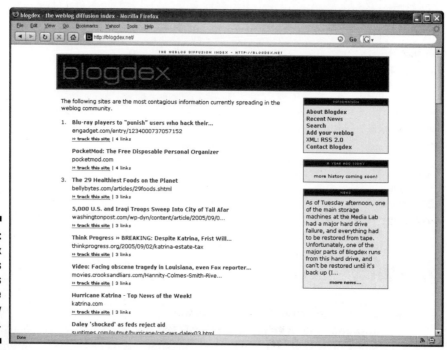

Figure 18-5:
Blogdex identifies Web pages that are popularly linked to.

To be sure your blog is represented in the Blogdex index, use the <u>Add your weblog</u> link and fill out the short form.

If you want to keep up-to-date with Blogdex listing results but don't want to be bothered visiting the site repeatedly, use RSS in your newsreader (see Chapter 13). Copy and paste the <u>RSS 2.0</u> link destination into your newsreader.

Clusty

`www.clusty.com`

If you have never used a *clustering* search engine, Clusty might be a revelation. One of the problems with a generic Web search (at Google, Yahoo!, or MSN Search, for example) is that the search engine does not divide your results by topic. You, the searcher, determine the topic by typing keywords. That's fine and gives you a lot of power to find things, but most keywords and key phrases are rather general. People don't usually make the effort to craft long key phrases that narrow a topic with great precision. And because most people don't have much patience at sifting through unsorted search results, the "top-ten phenomenon" holds sway: People look at the first ten search results, and then move on to another search or settle for a top-ten result that might not be ideal.

Here's an example in a general search engine. Imagine you're searching for information about lawsuits brought by the music record companies against individuals for trading music online illegally. You might be vaguely aware of the facts, and your search might be determined by this key phrase:

music lawsuits individuals

A more sophisticated and targeted search string is

file sharing lawsuits +(riaa OR mpaa) -site:riaa.org -site:riaa.com

If you're interested in unlocking the power of generic search engines, get your hands on a copy of *Google Search and Rescue For Dummies*. I understand the author needs money to fund his espresso addiction. But to get back to our example, the second search string delivers a more finely targeted set of search results, and an accomplished keyword jockey could slant the search in many other directions. But that second search string requires more knowledge than the average person would have before starting to learn about music lawsuits.

This is where clustered searching comes in. Using the first search string in a clustering engine delivers results packed into folders, each of which targets a subtopic of the general search. Look at Figure 18-6, and notice the folders in the left sidebar. Two folders contain keywords that might be new to beginners in this topic; both keywords appear in the second search string above (*riaa* and *sharing*). So, right away, you get a better overview of the subject than you would in Google. Click any folder to see that folder's search results or, as in Figure 18-6, more subcategories of results.

Clusty is not the only clustering search engine, but it enjoys a lot of buzz for its speed and quality of results. Its buzz factor only increased when it added the Blogs tab to its selection of engines. Click that tab on the Clusty home page to start searching for clustered blog results. You can transfer a Web search to a blog search by clicking the Blogs tab after getting your Web search results.

Clusty doesn't do any of the recursive, who's-linking-to-whom link analysis typical of other engines in this chapter. It's just straight text searching of blog entries.

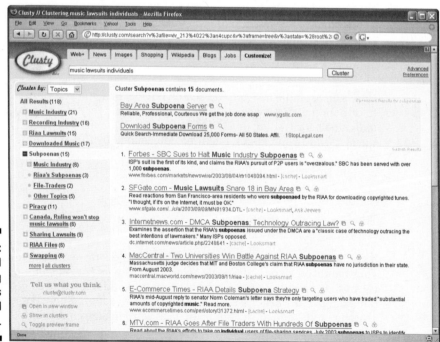

Figure 18-6:
Clustered
searching
sorts results
into topical
folders.

Blog of the Day

If you were online in 1995, you probably remember all the fuss over Cool Site of the Day, an early Web site whose only purpose was to run a daily "best of" feature spotlighting one site. The chosen site was given a ticket to instant fame and readership. It's only natural that the same treatment would be given to blogs. The best one-blog-a-day site is Blog of the Day, located here:

```
http://www.shrednow.com/botd/
    index.html
```
The selections at this site key off current events; during the aftermath of hurricane Katrina, several daily picks highlighted blog coverage of the disaster. Many choices during less momentous times feature lightweight personal blogs that offer stylish writing or fun photos.

Blogwise

`www.blogwise.com`

Blogwise is a blog directory and search engine whose top priority is immediacy. The home page displays a frequently updated list of blogs that have updated entries; the top items on the list are usually fresh by just a couple of minutes.

You can search by keyword at Blogwise (click the Search link in the left sidebar), but the site is not known as a great searching resource. My experience is that you need to enter very general search queries to get any results at all. Carrying forward the example I used in the preceding Clusty section, a search for *music lawsuits individuals* returned no results. Simplifying the search string to *music lawsuits* likewise delivered no joy. Trying *riaa* (the name of a music organization that initiates lawsuits) does bring home some results, but that is an extremely broad search query by any standards.

Search results are distinguished, as on the home page, by immediacy. The results are sorted by keyword match, and then sorted again by freshness. The blog with the most recent entry is placed atop the list, even if that recent entry does not exactly match your search terms.

Blogwise offers a Blogs by Country directory that is fun to explore, especially if you can read non-English languages. Look for it on the home page and click a country. As always, results are sorted by freshness.

TIP

What I really want to talk about is Blogwise's coolest feature: Blog Maps. Blogwise uses open development tools at Google Maps to display the geographical location of blogs. You don't search by blog; you search by location. The database at Blogwise is gradually growing, and not all map locations are ready for prime time as of this writing. Figure 18-7 shows the Blog Maps display of London. Try out Blog Maps here:

```
www.blogwise.com/blogmaps
```

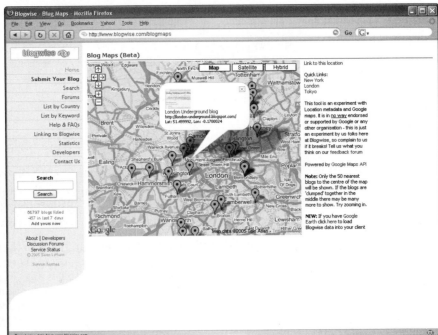

Figure 18-7: Blog Maps, at the Blogwise site, reveals the geography of blogs. Bloggers submit their blogs for inclusion.

Blogdigger

```
www.blogdigger.com
```

Your first impression of Blogdigger will probably be along the lines of: "Oh, another blog search engine." Indeed, its Search portion operates as a standard text-crawling engine that returns blog entries to keyword queries. You have two sorting options: Date and Relevance. Sorting by date doesn't ignore relevance, but it lists broadly relevant matches in reverse chronological order according to posting date. The Relevance option exactly matches your keywords first and foremost, when possible, disregarding the date.

Note the five tabs on Blogdigger's pages (see Figure 18-8):

- **Search:** This is where you conduct standard blog searches. Blogdigger crawls the text content of blog entries.

- **Links:** Here, you enter a site URL (blog or nonblog) to find out which blogs link to that page.

- **Media:** Under this tab, you can search for audio, video, images, and Bit Torrent downloads. (Bit Torrent is a file-sharing network often, but not necessarily, associated with unauthorized music and movie downloads.) The audio part is somewhat useful when searching for podcasts (see Chapter 16) but not as useful as other options I explain in Chapter 16.

  Local: Clicking this tab brings up a search engine that finds keyword-matched pages written by bloggers in certain geographic areas that you specify. You can use a city or zip code.

  Groups: This is the juicy one. Keep reading to know more.

Figure 18-8: Search results at Blogdigger. Note the Groups tag, which leads to a blog-merging feature.

The Groups function at Blogdigger allows you to combine the output of multiple blogs. This type of mashup is called *blog merging* or *blog aggregation,* though the latter term is used also to describe simple newsreaders (see Chapter 13). Merging two blogs is more useful and less chaotic than you might imagine. Most people mash blogs that are about the same topic — for example, several blogs about dogs, or baking, or Google, or some other subject. Some newsreaders allow merging of RSS feeds that you've subscribed to. Blogdigger provides an effective public interface for creating and sharing merged blog groups.

Follow these steps to create a Blogdigger group:

1. **On the Blogdigger home page, click the Groups tab.**

2. **On the Groups page, click the <u>create a new group</u> link.**

3. **On the next page, fill in the information fields.**

   These fields ask for a group name, your name and e-mail address, and a group description.

4. **Scroll down the page to choose your accessibility features.**

   Your group can be public (seen by everyone who views the Blogdigger Groups list) or private (seen just by you). Also, you can choose whether anyone or only you can add new blogs to your group. Think twice on this page because, as of this writing, you can't alter these accessibility choices later.

5. **Click the Create Group button to reach the next step.**

6. **On the next page, enter the addresses of feeds you want included in your group. Click the Submit button after pasting each feed address.**

   Be clear on an important point: On this page, you must add the addresses of RSS or Atom feeds, *not* the URLs of blogs. Do not take the Web addresses from blog sites and try to plug them in here. Instead, go to blogs you want to add, find the feed addresses of those blogs (see Chapter 13 for more about this), and then copy and paste those addresses into this Blogdigger page. It's not difficult; just be sure you get the feed address, not the blog's site address. If you use a newsreader, you can get feed addresses there for blogs you subscribe to.

After adding your last feed (last for now; you can add more later, or delete feeds), your group is finished. You don't need to click a Save button. If your group is public, it is immediately added to the Blogdigger Groups list. Click the <u>Back to the Group Page</u> link to see your group in action — that is, to see the latest entries from your combined blogs, listed in reverse chronological order. Use the <u>See list of public groups</u> link to view all available groups. There is good reading ahead, thanks to other users' resourceful and sometimes imaginative merging of blogs. If you'd like to see a merged output of the blogs I write at Weblogs Inc., look for Brad's WeblogsInc Blogs.

The mashup-sharing aspect of Blogdigger Groups is the best part. Browsing other people's merged collections is almost too much fun. Not to sound like a Boy Scout leader, but remember to tread responsibly when editing publicly accessible groups. Don't add your blog willy-nilly to several groups. It will only get pulled out eventually. Add relevant blogs that add substance to the group feed.

Daypop

`www.daypop.com`

Daypop is an iconic blog engine and ranking site that a lot of people have been using for a lot of years. The basic search engine mixes traditional news sources with blogs — or keeps them separate if you prefer. Use the drop-down menu next to the keyword box to select News, Weblogs, or News & Weblogs. (You can conduct searches of RSS feeds also by using the drop-down menu, but I find the two RSS-search options to be relatively unproductive.)

For me, Daypop distinguishes itself in the features surrounding the basic search engine. Check these links at the top of the Daypop home page:

- **Top 40:** Bloggers link to these top-40 pages in greater volume than other pages at the time of your search.

- **Top News:** Similar to the Top 40, this attractive and useful page is presented differently, like a front page of a news site. Click the <u>Citations</u> link to see which blogs are linking to that story.

- **Top Posts:** This page displays a list of most-linked blog posts — that is, blog entries most linked to by other bloggers.

- **Word Bursts:** This extraordinary feature measures increases in word usage from day to day in blog entries. These suddenly popular words and phrases indicate emerging topics of discussion in the blogosphere.

- **News Bursts:** Like Word Bursts (see the preceding bullet), News Bursts result from scanning news pages instead of blog entries.

- **Top Wishlist:** This interesting but peculiar feature lists the most popular wish-list items at Amazon.com and has nothing to do with blogging or blog sites.

- **Top Weblogs:** This list is derived from citations. That is, the blogs on this list are linked to most often in Daypop's blog database.

Three Directories

```
www.getblogs.com
www.bloguniverse.com
www.postami.com
```

I'd like to point out three blog directories that always yield interesting finds and sometimes produce valuable hidden gems when I visit them. Yet, I find that I don't include these sites in my regular content trolling. Every once in a while I remember one of them, go to it, am pleased with the visit, and then forget about it again.

✔ **Getblogs:** The most typical directory category lineup of the three, Getblogs divides into topics such as Health, Science, and Sports. Each category displays an alphabetical presentation of blogs. No ranking or link-worthiness is presented.

✔ **Blog Universe:** An adventurous directory, Blog Universe includes International Blogs and Sex Blogs categories. At the time of this writing, a Business Blogs section and a Spirituality Blogs section were recently added.

Postami: Gossip? US Presidential? Unusual topics and eye-burning page layout make this directory a challenging visit but not without interest. You might not be surprised to learn of 1216 blogs devoted to President Bush, but would you guess that 91 people write blogs about Dennis Kucinich?

Top 100 Lists

Every blogger wants to be on a top-100 list, or even a top-100,000 list. The following sites keep the dream alive, in different ways:

✔ **Technorati Top 100:** Probably the most-watched "top list" in the blog universe, the Technorati Top 100 derives its results by counting links to blogs. The most-linked blogs get on the list, which is located here:

```
www.technorati.com/pop/blogs/
```

✔ **BlogStreet Top 100:** BlogStreet takes a different approach from Technorati. Rather than count links to popular blogs, BlogStreet examines blogrolls — the lists of blogs, with links to those blogs, that most bloggers put on their sites. The result is sharply different from Technorati's list and arguably less useful. At the same time, the list is arguably more fun to browse than

Technorati's, which predictably features the same top-ranked blogs over and over. Find the BlogStreet list here:

```
www.blogstreet.com/top100.html
```

IceRocket

```
www.icerocket.com
```

Founded by Internet entrepreneur Marc Cuban, IceRocket is, at its core, a standard blog search engine. But wait — one important feature makes IceRocket a standout. That feature is a customizable date filter to search for blog entries. You can restrict the search to entries posted on the current day or during the last week, the last month, or (and this is best) any period of time you set. (See Figure 18-9.)

The options to filter by time period appear below the keyword box on any search result page. Click one of the presets or use the <u>Custom</u> link to set a date range.

Figure 18-9: IceRocket's customizable date range shows blog entries posted between April and June of 2004.

Diarist.net

`www.diarist.net`

Diarist.net is a source for journaling bloggers and those who like to read online personal journals. Click the <u>Diary Registry</u> link on the home page to see the directory of personal blogs. You are presented with a long list of countries. If you select United States, you then get a list of states. This geographic sorting is somewhat interesting, especially when browsing in other countries, though it doesn't make much sense in the U.S. No matter. Personal diaries rarely have a topical focus, so who cares how they are sorted? This site is a treasure trove of chatty and informal writing.

Chapter 19

Ten Resources for the Power Blogger

This chapter features miscellaneous blogging resources that didn't find a home elsewhere in the book. If you browse through this chapter and wonder why I don't highlight important blogging tools such as FeedBurner or Audioblog, the answer is that they are profiled elsewhere (FeedBurner in Chapter 15 and Audioblog in Chapter 17). The items in this chapter were chosen to fill those spare moments when you might want to read a blog about blogging (The Blog Herald or Blogging Pro), try an interactive tool that could enhance your blogging (The Wizbang Standalone TrackBack Pinger), or consume other blogs in a new way (Blogarithm). Have fun!

Blogging Pro

www.bloggingpro.com

Blogging Pro is a blog about blogging resources. A recent collection of entries on the index page features new releases of blog template themes for WordPress (see Chapter 10), how to increase AdSense earnings (see Chapter 15), and a notice of Weblogs seeking to hire a blogger. Living up to its name, the site inclines toward issues of interest to professional (and semiprofessional) bloggers.

Categories include News, Tools, and How-to, with strong coverage of the Movable Type and WordPress blog programs. (The site is written in WordPress.) Blogging Pro is managed by one person who also owns other blogs, so the posting isn't as frequent as would be ideal.

Wizbang Standalone TrackBack Pinger

`www.aylwardfamily.com/content/tbping.asp`

Some people think TrackBacks are dying — they have not been universally adopted by blog programs, and many bloggers don't understand them. That last point is true, but if you read my lengthy (and, I hope, clarifying) explanation of TrackBacks in Chapter 3, you might take a liking to the principle of tracking back from one site to another. TrackBacks are a method of remote commenting, by which one blogger can write an entry commenting on a post by another blogger, and leave a notice linking to the entry on that other blogger's page.

TrackBacks were invented by the blogging company SixApart, which gave away the tool to any other company that wanted to implement it. Some did; some didn't. The Wizbang Standalone TrackBack Pinger gives TrackBack power to anyone using a blog service or program that doesn't have TrackBacks built in. This means that even if you blog with the simple tools of a social network (see Chapter 5), for example, you can still use the sophisticated TrackBack tool.

Next, I briefly step through how to use Wizbang. This description makes little sense, most likely, unless you have read the TrackBack sections of Chapter 3. Figure 19-1 illustrates the following steps:

1. **On the Wizbang page, copy the TrackBack URL into the top field.**

   The TrackBack URL is published below the entry on the blog where you want to plant your TrackBack. Do not confuse the TrackBack URL with the permalink; they are different. Use Ctrl+C to copy it from the entry page, and then Ctrl+V to paste it into the top field.

2. **In the second field, paste your permalink URL.**

   This URL is the Web address of the entry you have just written. The entry should be relevant to the entry you are commenting on, which resides on the other blog.

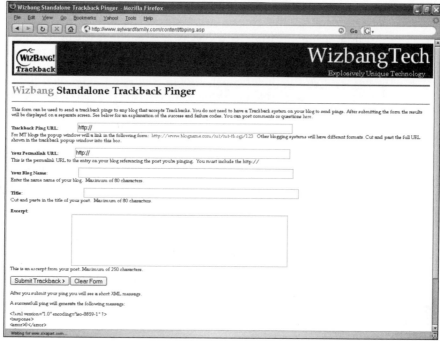

Figure 19-1:
The
Wizbang
Standalone
TrackBack
Pinger
allows
anyone to
plant
TrackBacks
on blogs
that enable
them.

3. **In the third field, paste your blog name.**

4. **In the fourth field, paste the title of your entry.**

5. **In the large field, type or paste an excerpt of your entry.**

   By blogging standards, this excerpt should not be very long; Wizbang limits you to 250 characters.

6. **Click the Submit TrackBack button.**

Remember that the receiving blog (the blog upon which your TrackBack is planted) must have TrackBacks enabled. Both sites in a TrackBack must be running TrackBacks. Wizbang solves the TrackBack deficit on your blog but not the other blog. You can tell that a blog accepts TrackBacks by the <u>TrackBacks</u> link next to the <u>Comments</u> link below each entry on the index page.

Bloglet

    www.bloglet.com

Bloglet is a Web service that allows you to collect subscriptions to e-mail updates of your site. It's hard to predict whether demand will continue for this service as RSS feeds and newsreaders become more popular. (See

Chapter 13 for everything you need to know about RSS feeds.) The purpose of RSS syndication is to give your readers an easy way to check for updates without taking the trouble to visit your site. That's the purpose of e-mailed updates, too, but an e-mail gets into your readers' faces more than an RSS feed does. Bloglet is a pushy reminder that you've added content to your site. Many people still prefer e-mail, though, on both the sending and receiving ends. Certainly, nothing is wrong with offering this service on your pages and seeing what happens.

The Bloglet service is highly automated. You just sign up and place the Bloglet subscription form on your site. (Some knowledge of HTML is required to place the form.) Bloglet does the rest: It monitors your posting, keeps track of the e-mail addresses of subscribers, and sends a daily notice informing them of your new blog entries.

Note: Bloglet works with specified blog programs and services, and not with others. Of the services covered in this book, Bloglet works with Blogger.com, Movable Type, and Radio Userland.

Blogjet

`www.blogjet.com`

Blogjet is a posting screen on steroids. And even that description understates the power of this program. Blogjet is not free (the program costs 40 bucks as of this writing), but its features are worth the price to many power bloggers.

Blogjet is a downloadable program that resides on your computer desktop like any other application. It enables you to post a blog entry without using your browser. Furthermore, Blogjet solves some of the inadequacies of blog services. For example, if you run a WordPress blog, inserting a photo in a blog entry is more difficult than it should be. Blogjet's posting interface (which works with most major blog platforms) makes posting photos a point-and-click affair, as it should be (and is in some services, such as MSN Spaces and TypePad). Blogjet even includes a voice recorder for creating audio entries. Overall, Blogjet provides the ideal posting interface, and applies it to whatever platform or service you are using.

How to Write a Better Weblog

`www.alistapart.com/articles/writebetter/`

How to Write a Better Weblog, a style guide written in 2002, applies to all bloggers no matter when they read it. Good blog writing shares some points with good general writing, and this resource advises concision, humor, simplicity, and descriptiveness of style. When it comes to selecting content, *How to Write a Better Weblog* advises making the effort to find original source material instead of commenting on the same items everyone else is commenting on. The piece is encouraging and inspirational: "No matter what your audience size, you ought to write as if your readership consisted of paid subscribers whose subscriptions were perpetually about to expire. There's no need to pander. Compel them to resubscribe."

The article is part of a larger site for Webmasters that includes resources on coding, page design, and other issues that might not be of interest. I would normally hesitate to include a single article — just one page of prose — in this chapter, but this one is a winner that could improve anyone's blog presentation.

Blogarithm

`www.blogarithm.com`

Blogarithm delivers blog entries to your e-mail box. You choose the blogs, naturally. Why use Blogarithm when you can stock your favorite newsreader with RSS feeds from every blog you care about? That's a good question, and I asked it myself when I first tried Blogarithm. Then I got hooked on Blogarithm's efficient means of displaying blog entry titles (using a drop-down menu, as shown in Figure 19-2). I find that I use Blogarithm to remind me of certain blogs that tend to get buried in my RSS pile in the newsreader. When that e-mail comes in, I remember that those blogs are worth checking every day, and I get right to it. Blogarithm is one of several delivery mechanisms I use.

Another service that delivers blog entries by e-mail is R|Mail. I use Blogarithm, myself, but both are worth checking out. R|Mail is located here:

`www.r-mail.org`

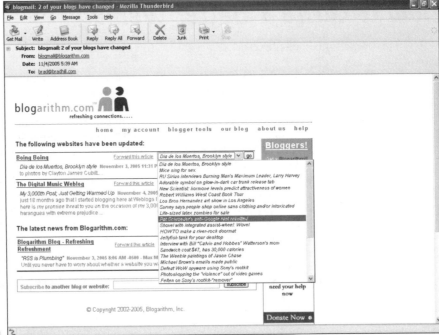

Figure 19-2:
Blogarithm
delivers
blog entries
through
daily e-mails
and displays
new entry
titles in a
drop-down
list.

Google Directory of Weblog Templates

```
directory.google.com/Top/Computers/Internet/On_the_Web/Web
logs/Templates/
```

Blog services such as Blogger.com and programs such as WordPress offer a range of design templates to personalize your blog. The problem is that these big blog providers have so many millions of users that any personalization statement you make with one of their preset templates is the same statement made by countless other bloggers. As a result, an underground network of template designers exists, offering fresh alternatives.

This page of Google's directory contains a healthy selection of template providers and template directories. Templates are often free of charge, though some designers require payment.

BlogRunner

www.blogrunner.com

This intriguing and addictive site tracks articles and spin-off blog conversations on the most important and most discussed issues of the day. Each topical header is followed by a few choice excerpts from traditional media outlets, followed by a few choice excerpts of blogger commentary. All this is fully linked, of course. Click the <u>Related</u> link to see hundreds (in some cases) of excerpted sources — it's an amazing overview of published reporting and opinion on high-profile current events.

Figure 19-3 shows the BlogRunner home page. The blending of traditional reporting with blog reporting captures the essence of topical blogging. A good read in and of itself, BlogRunner is also a powerful source of entry ideas for topical bloggers and a necessary update of the current state of conversation.

Figure 19-3: BlogRunner captures traditional reporting and mixes it with blogger commentary.

BlogPatrol

www.blogpatrol.com

BlogPatrol offers traffic statistics for blogs, at a level of sophistication that falls between a basic hit counter and detailed traffic logs. BlogPatrol makes it easy to generate a bar chart of traffic results. Here's how you get going:

1. **On the BlogPatrol page, click the <u>Signup</u> link.**

2. **On the Signup page (see Figure 19-4), fill in a username, an e-mail address, and a blogger address.**

   Leave the counter value set at 0.

3. **Choose a counter style.**

   The counter is really a logo for the benefit of BlogPatrol, but it also displays total hits at your site.

4. **Click the Signup button.**

   Leave the remaining check boxes blank.

5. **On the next page, click your mouse within the text box showing your BlogPatrol code. Press Ctrl+A to select the entire block of code, and then press Ctrl+C to copy the block of code.**

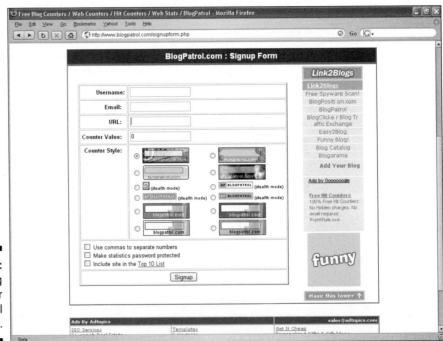

Figure 19-4:
Signing up for BlogPatrol is simple.

6. **Paste the code (using Ctrl+V) into your Web page where you want the BlogPatrol logo to appear.**

BlogPatrol handles everything, if you know enough HTML to place the code in your blog. You also need access to your blog's HTML to do so; that leaves out the social networks.

The code communicates site visits to BlogPatrol, which keeps track of them. When you want to see your statistics, go to BlogPatrol, click the <u>MyStats</u> link, and log in with your username and password.

The Blog Herald

www.blogherald.com

The Blog Herald (see Figure 19-5) affects a newspaperish theme for its blog. In an era in which *metablogs* (blogs about blogs) are on the decline, Blog Herald upholds the genre with pride and increasing dominance.

Frequent posts every day keep the site fresh and interesting. One of six blogs in a small company called Weblog Empire, Blog Herald covers software, RSS, professional blogging, blog politics, and the comings and goings of blogs everywhere.

Figure 19-5:
The Blog Herald, the preeminent blog about blogs.

Glossary

• •

AdSense: AdSense is an advertising publishing program offered by Google that enables participating bloggers to make some money on their Weblogs. (See Chapter 15.) After signing up for AdSense, eligible blogs can run Google text (and sometimes banner) ads on the blogs' pages; the advertisers pay Google when blog visitors click those ads, and Google shares the money with bloggers.

AdSense for Feeds: A variation on Google AdSense, the AdSense for Feeds program places small text ads in RSS feeds when they are displayed in news-readers. (See Chapter 15.) This program enables bloggers to make money even if most of their readership occurs off-site. Placing ads in RSS feeds is somewhat controversial but is becoming less so.

AdWords: Google AdWords is an advertising program in which advertisers place context-sensitive ads on Google search result pages and, if the advertiser opts to, on other Web sites participating in Google AdSense. (See Chapter 15.)

anchor link: Anchor links exist in blog entries to cite relevant Web pages that the reader might want to look at. See *embedded link.*

archives: Archives are the historical record of a blog. Blog programs and services keep track of every entry posted by the blogger; nothing is discarded unless the blogger intentionally deletes an entry. Most bloggers do not delete entries except under exceptional circumstances; blog culture requires keeping even regrettable entries available. Links to archived posts are sometimes provided on each page's sidebar, organized as a list or as a monthly calendar.

Atom: One of two major syndication *feed* formats (the other being *RSS*), Atom is used by Blogger.com.

audioblogging: Audioblogging refers to creating a spoken-word entry. Some blog services (Blogger is one) provide tools for recording audio entries. Other general services (such as Audioblog.com) allow posting audio entries to blogs on other services. Audioblogging is not the same as podcasting.

blawg: A blawg is a blog about law and legal issues.

blink: This slangy term is a nickname for Web link, especially a link to a cited Web page in a blog entry. "He blogged about that article in yesterday's *Times* but forgot the blink, so nobody could read the article."

blog: A contraction for *Weblog,* a blog is a Web site powered by software that makes frequent updates easy. New content is usually presented as a dated *entry,* with the entries displayed in reverse chronological order. Because of the organizational scheme, blogs are often used as personal and public diaries, but a blog can be about anything at all, and some blogs are professional publishing ventures.

blog digest: A blog digest provides no original material but quotes and points to entries from many other blogs. Taking its model from the *Readers Digest* magazine, blog digests reprint other people's work, but the most ethical of them do not quote entire entries.

blog search engine: A blog search engine specializes in finding blog entries that match keywords and blog entries that link to URLs entered by the searcher.

blogathy: Blogathy occurs when you become apathetic about posting in your blog. One always hopes that blogathy is temporary.

blogerati: A vaguely defined and sometimes sarcastically employed term, blogerati refers to the aristocracy of the *blogosphere.*

blogger: A blogger writes a blog.

bloggerel: This derogatory term refers to blog entries of little merit, often because they repeat widespread discussion points without adding original thinking or because they represent debunked viewpoints.

blogging: Blogging is the act of writing and posting blog entries.

Blogistan: Similar to *blogosphere,* the term Blogistan represents the blogging nation. *Blogosphere* carries a more amorphous and nebulous feeling than Blogistan, but they mean essentially the same thing.

blognoscenti: As with *blogerati,* this term is vaguely defined and generally refers to the most knowledgeable inner circle of bloggers.

blogorrhea: Not to be gross, but blogorrhea is too much insubstantial blogging. I didn't invent the term; I'm just reporting it.

blogosphere: The entire global networked universe of bloggers and blogs is called the blogosphere. Often called a community, even though millions of bloggers cannot realistically get to know each other, portions of the blogosphere are woven together by connected strands of discourse. The mechanics of this connection include comments, TrackBacks, and embedded links in blog entries.

blogroach: This derogatory term denotes a blog reader who crawls through comment sections leaving many unnecessary comments.

blogroll: The blogroll is the list of favored sites displayed in a blog's sidebar. Attaining a spot on the blogroll of a popular and influential blog is a sign of success and usually results in more visitors to the blogrolled site.

blogstipation: Blogstipation is writer's block for bloggers. The condition might be due to a lack of inspiration, as with traditional writer's block, or it might result from exhaustion after blogging too much.

business blog: A business blog, quite simply and obviously, is a blog about business.

comment: Most blogs allow readers to write and post responses to blog entries; these responses are in public view and are called comments. Some blog experts believe that when comments are disabled, preventing readers from discussing entries, a blog ceases to be a blog. The viewpoint of this book, however, is that deciding whether to accept comments is the universal prerogative of bloggers.

comment spam: A pestilent fact of blogging life, comment spam is unsolicited, irrelevant, inappropriate, and usually commercial messages deposited in the comments section of a blog. Comment spam is widespread, particularly afflicting blogs with high readership. Spammers use automated programs called spambots to crawl through the *blogosphere,* leaving junk comments.

commentariat: Meant as a term of respect, the commentariat is the global community of people who write comments in blogs. The term can also be used in a local sense. One might say, "His blog entries are a little boring, but his commentariat turns out interesting conversations despite that."

commenter: Someone who writes and posts a comment in a blog.

embedded link: Blogs characteristically provide many context links in their entries, so readers can see the source material (articles, other blog entries, and so on) that inspired the blog entry. Rather than extensively quoting source material, bloggers cite it by linking to it directly from the blog entry. These links, also called *anchor links,* are embedded in the entry using a simple linking function in blog software.

entry: The foundation of a blog, the entry is the piece of new content that keeps the blog updated. Each new entry written and posted by the blogger is placed at the top of the *index page* — the home page of the blog. Previous entries are pushed down the page until they eventually fall off the page, which has a preset entry limit. Entries are never lost, however, because each new entry is assigned a unique page in the blog and can always be read on that page.

entry page: The Web page permanently assigned to a blog entry is called the entry page. Blog entries are placed on the *index page* when first posted; simultaneously, each entry is placed on its own page, instantly created to hold it. Entry pages are cited by other blogs discussing the entry. The URL (Web address) of the entry page is called the *permalink*.

event blog: Event blogs are temporary sites set up to cover an event. Typical event blogs include concert blogs, Academy Award blogs, and professional trade conference blogs. Often, event blogs feature "live" reporting, by which a blogger attends the event with a connected laptop computer or other device, and posts frequent updates of the proceedings. Event blogs are sometimes left in place as archived histories, even after their events have concluded.

feed: A feed is a summary of blog entries, displayed in *newsreaders* using a format in which graphics and other page elements are stripped out. Feeds always contain the headline of the entry and usually contain some or all of the entry text. Depending on the blog program or service, the blogger has variable control over how the feed is presented. On the newsreader end, the reader also might have some control over how much of the entry is viewed. Feeds enable the blogger to *syndicate* blog entries globally, so that readers do not need to visit the blog. However, the feed always links back to the blog entry it is displaying, so readers can visit the blog to leave a comment or for another reason.

feed aggregator: A feed aggregator is another term for *newsreader.*

fisk: One of most peculiar blogging terms, to fisk is to deconstruct (usually with some viciousness) an article or blog post written by somebody else. Fisking involves quoting the target piece point by point and refuting each point. Dogmatic as it is, fisking is a common blogging style.

flame: Throughout the Internet, a flame is an argument that has turned personal. Flaming is intended to wound with words and can be found in Usenet newsgroups, Web-based message boards, and any other discussion environment (such as blog comments and TrackBacks).

group blog: Group blogs are written by teams of bloggers. Some of the most influential blogs are team efforts.

hit: When a piece of Web content is viewed, that instance is called a hit. Any sort of Web page can be hit, including a blog *index page* or *entry page.* Likewise, an RSS feed is hit when it is accessed and viewed. Hits are measured by *traffic logs* to determine the size of a blog's readership.

hitnosis: The sad condition of obsessively monitoring one's *traffic logs* is called hitnosis. This entranced state often results from a spike in traffic coming from a citation in a popular blog or being added to a prominent *blogroll.*

HTML: An acronym for HyperText Markup Language, HTML is the computer code underlying all Web pages. It is necessary to know HTML for the self-installed blog programs discussed in this book and useful to know for some of the hosted options. Casual bloggers working in write-and-click blogging services can safely ignore HTML.

index page: The home page of a blog, the index page contains recently posted entries, with the most recent entry at the top of the page.

instalanche: An effect similar to being *slashdotted,* an instalanche occurs when a blog post is cited by Instapundit (www.instapundit.com), one of the most influential of blogs. The resulting tidal wave of traffic to the cited blog can sometimes overwhelm that site's server.

journal blog: A journal blog is a personal, diary-style blog.

link love: Link love is a friendly link from one blog to another. Links drive traffic, and most bloggers desire traffic, so incoming links are loved.

log: A measurement of a blog's readership. See *traffic log.*

macrologue: A term I coined for this book, the macrologue is the global conversation woven into the blogosphere through comments, TrackBacks, and links embedded into entries. Primarily a feature of topical discussion blogs, the macrologue furthers discourse spread out over many blogs around the world.

meme: A somewhat overused term that causes some bloggers to roll their eyes, a meme is an idea or a set of arguments that has attained a life of its own through widespread discussion.

metablogging: This term sounds like a gigantic blog, but its meaning is different and self-referring. A metablog is simply a blog about blogs and blogging.

moblog: A blog run by mobs? Nope; it's a mobile blog. Moblogs contain content sent from remote locations using portable computing devices such as Internet-enabled cell phones.

MSM: This acronym stands for mainstream media, and is often used scornfully by bloggers who regard blogging as superior to traditional journalism publishing. This attitude regards mainstream media as slow and insular compared to the quick and disclosing culture of blogging.

news blog: A news blog is a general term for a blog that revolves, in some way, around news stories. General news blogs cover current events broadly, but more commonly a news blog focuses on some aspect of daily events such as politics.

newsreader: In a generic sense, newsreaders are programs that display news articles in original or summary form. In the context of blogging, a newsreader is a specialized site or desktop program that lists and displays syndication *feeds* chosen by the user. Most blogs offer their content outside the Web site by means of a feed, the most common format for which is *RSS*. Newsreaders are sometimes called RSS aggregators. (See Chapter 13.)

old media: A somewhat (but not necessarily) disrespectful term, old media refers to newspapers, magazines, and other printed media that make up the *MSM* (mainstream media). More generally, an old medium is any genre of culture that has been supplanted, or will soon be supplanted, by a new format.

partial entry: On a blog index page, partial entries can be used to save space. Readers can click through to an archived page that contains the full entry. In an RSS feed, a partial entry likewise saves space and encourages readers to click through to the site, where they can read the full entry.

permalink: A blog entry's permalink is the *index page* link to its permanent page in the blog. Putting the permalink below each blog entry on the index page makes it easy for visitors to copy the permalink's URL and cite the entry in another blog.

photoblogging: Photoblogging refers to posting a digital photo in a blog. Serious photobloggers operate blogs with no text entries — just pictures. Casual photoblogging produces a mix of written and photo entries and often includes photo displays in the sidebar. Photo albums are often attached to photoblogs.

ping: When two Internet locations communicate with each other, they are said to ping each other. The word is especially used in the context of *TrackBacks,* which use pings to complete the two-way link. (See Chapter 3.)

podcast: A podcast is simply a series of audio programs recorded in the MP3 file format and distributed in a blog and an *RSS* feed. Their name derives from the iPod, the most popular MP3 player, but they can be heard through any portable player and through any desktop audio program that plays MP3s. There is nothing new about MP3 programs. Podcasts have become so popular due to their distribution mechanism that they are really more part of the RSS revolution than the blogging revolution. That said, it's worth noting that the RSS revolution is dependent on the blog revolution. Anyway, podcasts and blogs are closely related.

post: Both a verb and a noun, a blogger can actually post a post. As a verb, bloggers post entries. As a noun, bloggers put their posts in their blogs.

reciprocal link: When two bloggers agree to add each other's blogs to their *blogrolls,* the links are called reciprocal links.

referral log: Part of a site's *traffic log,* the referral log shows where a site's visitors came from. The referral log, when available, is useful to bloggers who want to know which sites are linking to them most effectively. If, for example, a blog's traffic leaped upward, the referral log could show that an influential site linked to a blog entry, giving it an unusual amount of visibility and sending lots of traffic.

RSS: An acronym that stands for both Really Simple Syndication and Rich Site Summary, RSS is a type of syndication feed. As a generic term, RSS represents all feed formats.

RSS aggregator: Another name for a *newsreader.*

sidebar: Located on the left or right side of a blog's index page (and sometimes replicated on every page in the blog), the sidebar can contain links to archived entries, a blogroll, photos, lists of many kinds, and other content that relates to and enhances the blog.

slashdotted: In an effect similar to an *instalanche,* a citation from the hugely influential site Slashdot (`www.slashdot.com`) sends so much traffic to the cited blog that its server can become disabled. This phenomenon is also known as the slashdot effect.

spam: Generally, spam is advertising deposited inappropriately and unwantedly. In a blog, spam can be found in *comments* and *TrackBacks.* Spam is increasingly a problem for bloggers, causing some popular blogs to remove their comment and TrackBack sections.

spamblog: A scourge of the *blogosphere,* spamblogs are generated automatically, contain no useful or hand-written content, contain mostly (or exclusively) links, and are intended to manipulate search results at major search engines. These engines rank Web sites partly by the number of incoming links, so shady Web marketers set up spamblogs containing hundreds of links to their sites. In theory, the search engines count all those links and rank the target sites higher in search results. In fact, search engines are more sophisticated than that, and spamblogs are of questionable value.

splog: Another word for *Spamblog.*

syndication: Syndication is a method of distributing blog entries beyond the blog site, primarily to *newsreaders.* Crucial to the syndication mechanism are *RSS* and *Atom,* two syndication formats. Both these formats create *feeds,* which are text-only displays of blog entries. *Newsreaders* organize these feeds and display them, allowing their users to gather their favorite blog content in one window.

template: A template is a set of design elements replicated throughout a blog. Templates can determine the blog's appearance (the color scheme) and layout (number and placement of sidebars).

theme: In some blog services, themes are identical to templates. More specifically (in TypePad, for example), a blog theme can refer only to the site's color scheme and does not affect page layout.

thread: A thread is an online discussion. In the context of blogging, a thread is a series of comments on an entry page.

TrackBack: A remote-comment system used by some blogging programs and services, TrackBack enables one blogger to deposit a link to his or her blog on another blogger's entry page. (See Chapter 3 for a detailed clarification.) TrackBacks represent an important part of the conversational aspect of the *blogosphere,* but their use is hampered by blog services that don't support TrackBacks and also by widespread confusion about how they work.

TrackBack spam: Irrelevant and commercial messages deposited on blogs as *TrackBacks.*

traffic: Blog traffic is blog readership. Every visitor to a blog is counted by that site's measuring tools as a *hit,* the smallest increment of Web traffic. *RSS* feed readers also count in a blog's traffic.

traffic log: In any Web site, blogs included, the traffic log measures how many people visit the site and where they came from (the site from which they linked to the blog). Many other measurements can be included in a traffic log, such as the type of browser used by the visitor, how long that person stayed in the site, and which pages were viewed. These statistics are typically aggregated and displayed in graph or chart format.

vlog: A vlog is a video blog. At this writing, the vlogosphere (to coin a term) is small but growing, with some observers claiming that vlogs will overtake podcasts.

Weblog: The formal name of which *blog* is a contraction.

XML: An acronym for eXtensible Markup Language, XML is the underlying language of *RSS,* a standard *syndication* format.

Index

• *D* •

• **Q** •